Giving and Taking Help

Giving and Taking Help

by
Alan Keith-Lucas

Revised Edition

**The North American Association
of Christians in Social Work
St. Davids, Pennsylvania**

Manufactured in the United States of America

Library of Congress Cataloging-in-Publication Data

ISBN 9780-9623634-5-0

Contents

PREFACE

Alan Keith-Lucas' *Giving and Taking Help*, first published in 1972, has become a classic in the social work literature on relationship. It has been used by several generations of social work students, social work practitioners, and other helpers to gain a balanced, wise, and humane perspective on the helping process. It continues to be cited by authors of major texts in social work practice methods. Since Keith deals with perennial issues in a way that is both practical and principled, the book has aged gracefully.

However, in his retirement, Keith has had the opportunity to continue his involvement in the human helping process through continued writing on the themes developed in *Giving and Taking Help*, extensive consultation, especially with children's homes, speaking, visiting professorships, planning conferences, and serving on professional boards and editorial boards. I have had the pleasure of being an occasional colleague and collaborator with him in some of these endeavors, primarily through our mutual service on the board of the North American Association of Christians in Social Work and my work as editor of *Social Work and Christianity*, for which Keith serves as book review editor. It has been my privilege to serve as the editor of several of his publications, including *The Poor You Have With You Always: Concepts of aid to the poor in the Western World from Biblical Times to the Present* (1989), *So You Want To Be A Social Worker: Primer for the Christian Student* (1985), and *Encounters With Children: Stories that Help Us Understand and help them* (1991).

So I was particularly pleased when I had the opportunity to serve as editor for the revised edition of *Giving and Taking Help*. This revision has given Keith the opportunity to reflect on the original (much has been left virtually unchanged), to deepen it with refined discussion and further practice examples (there are many), and to rework some material (sometimes adding new, sometimes eliminating, and re-writing entirely). If you are wise (which Keith is) you don't tamper too much with a classic and he has not. Reader of the first edition will find themselves in comfortably familiar territory in this one, but with some of the Landscape more clearly defined and developed. As a concession to our increasingly short attention span and contemporary custom, Keith has suffered the addition of sub-heads and other textual guides, but he still like to write a long, complex and well balanced sentence.

Readers who liked the first edition will find even more to like in this one (as, I suppose those who hated the first may hate this even more). First-time readers will find the book (as it always been) a uniquely clear, Straightforward, sensible, and wise examination of what is involved in the helping process— giving and taking help. It reflects on perennial issues and themes yet is grounded in highly practice—based and pragmatic realities. It respects both the potential and limitations of social science in understanding the nature of persons and the helping process. It does not shy away from confronting issues of values, ethics, and world views. It is at the same time profoundly personal and yet reaching for the theoretical and generalizable. It has a point of view.

When you read *Giving and Taking Help* you get the sense that you are hearing a real person who has really cared about helping others and who has spent rich hours both in trying to help and reflecting on that attempt. May this revised edition continue the legacy of *Giving and Taking Help* in guiding our effort to be better helpers of one another.

May we understand the difference between helping and controlling. May we recognize the role of choice and responsibility and that helping is not preventing choice or shielding from the consequences of choices. May we be characterized by courage, humility and concern. And above all, may we be enabled to embody *reality* (this is what we're up against), *empathy* (an "act of the loving imagination"), and *support* ("I am here to help you if you want me and can use me").

David A. Sherwood
Director, Social Work Program
Gordon College
Wenham, Massachusetts
July 1994

Introduction to the Revised Edition

This book originated in a paper I was asked to give to the Mental Health Society of Florence-Darlington, South Carolina, in February 1958. Prior to that time I had not given much thought to what actually happens when one person sits down with another, or with a group of people, in order to help. I did my best to conceptualize this process, and to my surprise my lecture apparently encountered a thirst for knowledge on this subject among many kinds of helping people, lay and professional, secular and religious, who asked me to put my thoughts on paper. This request resulted in an article, "The Art and Science of Helping," which was first published in the *Christian Scholar* in 1960.

This article has had a strange career. It has been reprinted, under different titles and with a few modifications, some twenty-five times and has been mimeographed even more frequently by such organizations as Alcoholics Anonymous, the Federal Extension Service, and the London School of Economics. It has appeared as a chapter in books. It has been presented, by request, to groups as varied as college deans of students, home demonstration agents, VISTA volunteers, church social service committees, dental health educators, vocational guidance counselors for the retarded, rural missionaries, probation officers, welfare workers, child care workers in children's institutions, and social work students. In a slightly expanded form it became part of the Covenant Life Curriculum of three Protestant churches, where it was directed at teenagers. It has crossed both the Atlantic and the Pacific oceans. An American welfare department asked to reproduce it from a British paper, and only last month a professor of psychology wrote to say that he had found it among his papers and had I written anything since?

It was this paper that I expanded into *Giving and Taking Help,* which was first written in 1966, rewritten in 1969, and published in 1972.

At that time I was much concerned in trying to show that there were more or less universal principles that could be learned governing the giving of help. I do not believe that this needs arguing today. While there may be some people who believe, as the British sociologist Barbara Wooton said in 1959,[1] that all helping requires is good manners and a willingness to listen, and a few who would argue that since every individual is unique, no common principles are possible — one just does or gives what the other person needs – today there are dozens of popular models of how to give some kind of help, some with catchy or important-sounding names, such as Reality Therapy, Transactional Analysis, Behavior Modification, Cognitive Behavioral Group Therapy, and even acronyms such as AGAPE. There is even a scientific study which deals with many of the same principles that are discussed in this book, Robert R. Carkhuff's *Helping and Human Relations: A Primer for Lay and Professional Helpers.*[2]

Counseling, too, is much in vogue. Columnists such as Ann Landers advise almost everyone whose behavior is in any way unusual to seek counseling. Social work, once a profession practiced largely in governmental or charitable agencies, is now as often as not a private business. Undergraduate curricula in social work or counseling have multiplied, interestingly enough particularly in Christian colleges. And more and more courts mandate that offenders receive professional treatment or counseling.

Much, too, however, has happened since the first edition of this book was published that has affected both the public's and the professionals' concept of help. Social workers, psychologists, even pastoral counselors can be sued for malpractice. Certain groups, such as, in my home state, children prone to violence, have established a legal right to receive help. Groups such as the learning-disabled have received much more attention than heretofore, and at the same time two administrations have cut back on government aid to whole categories of people in need. The plight of families on welfare, for instance, has worsened considerably in terms of what their grants will buy, by as much as 35 percent in the 1980s, and more restrictions have been placed on the recipients. Some social workers have questioned whether the kind of help most of us were practicing in the 1960s is or was effective – although they don't say effective for what – and many correctional officers have purportedly abandoned the concept of rehabilitation as a goal for a prison sentence and are thinking more in terms of retribution and punishment.

We have lived through – some people think not entirely through – the "me" generation. The word "permissive" (wrongly used – "indulgence" would have been a more appropriate word) has become a pejorative, causing even Dr. Spock to revise some of his ideas. We now have a number of movements that suggest that we fooled ourselves when we thought that most people thought and felt in much the same way. *Giving and Taking Help* may well be criticized as the work of a white male. Is there a black, an Asian, or a feminist model of helping that I am too chauvinistic to see? A recent article on our foster-care system written from a feminist viewpoint recommended exactly those changes which I, a male, have always favored. While women and black people have had experiences that I can only imagine, so have many white males, such as the very poor. It would be a strange world if one could only help people exactly like oneself.

Then there have been new problems. In the 1960s we knew little of drug addiction, sexually active teenagers, or childhood sexual abuse. Although we had known individual cases, these problems were not yet endemic. We had not yet heard of AIDS. Does today's preoccupation with these alarming social problems require a rethinking of the principles of helping? I don't think knowing how to help will cure society of these ills, any more than it has abolished poverty, crime, or the divorce rate, but then neither has repression. Help will still be needed not only for the victims of these ills but also for some of the offenders as well as for the millions of people who are trying to cope with an increasingly complex and puzzling world. As one writer has put it, help may soon become "routine, necessary and universal."[3]

For this reason, and because I do believe that the principles of help, as far as we understand them, do have something universal about them — human nature does not change much in twenty years — I have made rather few changes in preparing this second edition. I have added a few more insights that have been granted me over the years, particularly in the chapter on helping and religious belief, which several reviewers of the first edition before it was published counseled me to omit altogether. I have removed some dated material. I have rewritten chapter 1, which I thought was rather weak in the original edition, and I have tried to explain more clearly what I consider helping to be. I have omitted the chapter on the history of helping, principally because I have dealt with this in greater detail in another book, *The Poor You Have with You Always*, published by the North American Association of Christians in Social Work in 1989, and because it dealt largely with only one group, the poor.

Some readers may complain that most of the references I have given date from the 1950s and 1960s. This is not entirely laziness on my part, or a clinging to the past. Most of the basic principles of help were established some years ago — the first book on helping that I know of being Karl de Schweinitz's *Art of Helping People in Trouble*,[4] published in 1924 — and most modern articles or books deal with the specifics of helping in particular situations rather than with help as a whole. The books and articles that I cite are indeed the seminal ones. They are often, too, forgotten. There is a tendency in the social sciences to consider anything written thirty or forty years ago to be no longer valid. I am indeed somewhat surprised that *Giving and Taking Help* in its first edition is still being used in many places. It is, after all, more than twenty years old. Yet we were not really such fools back then. We may have relied more on practice wisdom and experience than on statistics and computers. We may perhaps have generalized too much, may have been more philosophers than scientists, but we were not exactly primitives, and perhaps the beginning helper needs to understand where more modern ideas come from.

My thanks are still due to those who helped me with the first edition, to the faculties of the schools of social work of the University of North Carolina, the University of Pennsylvania, and the London School of Economics; to my students in classes, workshops, and tutorials; to many colleagues in Children's Homes, welfare departments, and the North American Association of Christians in Social Work; to supervisors such as Edith Ross of the Louisiana State Department of Public Welfare; to clients, including many children who have shared with me what help they found useful; to the secretaries I named then, whose patient work should not be forgotten, Pauline Seawell, Janice Ingles, and Emilie Broyles, to whom I would now add Faith O'Neal; and to my wife, whose criticism of the first draft enabled me to write the second. Less directly, but just as surely, I owe so much to those who helped me acquire what few skills and little wisdom I may possess. While this list could be endless, those who have had perhaps the greatest influence on my life and work have been my mother; A. S. Neill, the British educator; F. R. Leavis, the literary critic who taught me to watch what I was writing; John Hallowell of Duke University; and Robert B. McMullen, who first helped me to see that the Christian explanation of things makes sense.

But this is a book not only for those who claim a religious faith but for secular helpers as well. Nor is it a book for social workers alone — indeed there are aspects of social work with which it does not pretend to deal — but for anyone in any profession, or in no profession at all, who wants to help someone else.

Author's Note

Because of the clumsiness of "he or she," "her or himself," and more, the ugly "s/he," I have arbitrarily used "she for the helper and he for the person being helped, except in specific situations where the sex of these persons is clearly the opposite. There is no suggestion, however, that men cannot be helpers or that women do not need help.

xii

CHAPTER 1

What Do We Mean by Help?

Help, as the word is used in this book, occurs when one person offers another something in such a way that the latter can use it to do something about a problem that he is unable to do alone.

The "something" that is offered may be large or small. It may be as simple as helping a stranded motorist change a tire or as complex as a course of psychotherapy. It may involve something material, such as money or clothing, or as intangible as advice, encouragement, or simply being there in a time of trouble. It may last only a few seconds and never be repeated, or last for weeks or even years.

Help is something a helper does, but the use that is made of it is entirely up to the person being helped--hence my use above of the word "can" rather than "does" or "will." The helper offers her "something" in such a way that the helped person or group is most likely to be able to use it, but how it will be used the helping person cannot determine or, in many cases, predict.[1] The problem is the helped person's, not the helping person's. She may hope that the other gains a little more courage, some clarity, some ability to make a choice with which he can live, say, twenty years from now, even to modify his behavior or become more capable of those two ultimate human emotions, love and joy. But this must be an unspoken hope, and the helper should not be surprised if the helped person does something quite different with what she offers, nor should she be disappointed if this happens, provided that she has done everything she can to make a favorable outcome possible and he chooses not to use it. One can't live other peoples' lives for them. One cannot know what steps other people may have to take to live a more abundant life, what it will cost them, what mistakes they may have to make and learn from, but one can sometimes remove some of the stumbling blocks to this journey. In fact a good deal of helping consists in doing exactly that.

The helper treats the person being helped as someone who acts, rather than as someone who is acted upon. The relationship between helper and helped is what Martin Buber, a Jewish theologian, calls "I-thou" (or "I-you") rather than "I-it."[2] The helped person is valued, and when some-

[margin, handwritten:] We can always offer help, but it may not be used in the way we intended it to be

1

→ Liberate the "helpee" to act by showing them they are seen as valued and competent

one is genuinely valued and the help offered is really help, most of the helped person's decisions will be positive.

When Helping Goes Wrong

Most of us want to help, and presumably people reading this book particularly want to do so. But all of us have had some helping we offered and hoped to be successful go wrong somehow. The person we tried to help did not take our advice, or misused it, or seemed to resent what he saw as interference in his life.

When this happens our first reaction is usually to blame the person we were trying to help. He is stubborn, ungrateful, wishy-washy, stupid, selfish, unreasonable, or mentally ill. And to a small extent this may be true, although not nearly as often as we would sometimes like to think. There are people whom we don't yet know how to help or who need the services of a highly trained expert, who live perhaps in a fantasy world or have shut themselves off from any attempts to reach them. But we should be very cautious in making such an assessment. There are many examples of apparently unreachable people being reached, such as Helen Keller, or Laura in Richard D'Ambrosio's *No Language but a Cry*,[3] and some of the work being done with profoundly retarded children offers new hope. For example, in a recent book entitled *Normalisation in Practice* a ten-year-old, who is introduced as a "young man of tremendous determination and good humour,"[4] we learn later has developed in his motor coordination only as far as a normal four-month-old and can neither talk nor walk nor even sit up in his chair. We certainly should not put all the blame on the person we are trying to help when our well-intentioned helping proves not to have been helpful.

What, then, went wrong with our attempt to help? One possibility is that the help we tried to give was inappropriate. An extreme example might be to offer someone who has been poisoned either a lecture on pharmacology or a feast when what is needed is an emetic. A more subtle, but common one might be to offer someone false reassurance when their real need is to come to terms with reality. Conversely a person contemplating suicide does not need sympathy for the problems confronting him, but perhaps some reassurance.

Is Diagnosis Necessary?

Some people are so convinced of the difference between people, and the difference in their circumstances, that they hold that one cannot really help others unless one knows a great deal about them, their environment, and their culture. Certainly this knowledge is potentially helpful,

2

especially if the help one plans to give is long-lasting, such as in psychoanalysis or extended physiotherapy. Certainly such knowledge does no harm, as long as it is accurate. This does not mean, however, that one has to have this detailed knowledge before one can help at all. Help often has to be given, or at least to start, the moment two people meet. To spend time in gathering facts about someone may delay or even inhibit help. The person needing help wants it here and now. He is put off if we insist on asking him questions. He questions why we want to know. Are we there to help him, or to find out things about him? Linus, the Peanuts character, was praised by Charlie Brown for studying human nature in order to be of help to people. "No," said Linus, "I'm just nosy." We also know that one of the times people are most amenable to help, and use it best, is in a crisis situation when something has to be done at once.

Furthermore, what has been called "psychosocial diagnosis," really knowing about another person (if indeed it is possible—and I am far from sure that it is) requires an expertise and an amount of time that most of us do not have. It is certainly not for amateurs. Despite all we have learned and are still learning from the social sciences, what really causes human beings to think and act as they do is still largely unknown, or unknowable, and the world in which they live so incredibly complex that it would take a person versed in psychology, medicine, sociology, epidemiology, economics, and several other sciences to be in any way sure. There are so many different theories, some of which change from year to year, and those theories themselves are so dependent on the value system of those who hold them that I question whether most such assessments are much more than informed guesses, and rather crude ones at best. This is true even when they are made by so-called trained staff, and certainly when made by the average person who wants to help.

One is constantly being surprised by people. An apparently hopeless person whom one had thought of as wishy-washy and indecisive suddenly shows initiative and courage. A child abuser, freed from what occasioned the abuse, proves to be a most loving parent. It is one of the joys of helping. Sometimes, I think, only the Holy Spirit can be responsible, and His actions are rarely included in a social summary.

The Importance of How Help Is Given
We cannot then blame all failures to be helpful on an inappropriate choice of what to give or what to say, any more than we can blame them on the character of the recipient. In fact these two factors are probably minor ones in most unproductive efforts to help. Just as important as

3

what is given, or even offered, is *how* it is offered or given. That is why I used the phrase "in such a way that" in my attempt to define help. One can help someone change a tire in a helpful or an unhelpful way. One can leave a person more capable of changing his own tire next time, or feeling stupid and frustrated.

I did a bad bit of helping myself the other day. It seemed like a very simple business. My neighbor, who is ninety-five years old and has a very limited income, had been buying gas from full-service pumps. When I happened to be with her in my car, I thought I would show her how easy it was to fill up at a self-service pump and save twenty cents a gallon. "Look, Martha," I said, "it's very simple," and I showed her how to do it, carefully and in slow motion, making sure that she understood the process. Yet Martha still buys her gas at the more expensive pump.

In analyzing my mistake later, I realized that I hadn't really been thinking about Martha and her fear of making a fool of herself. I was thinking of myself and how helpful and considerate it was of me to be concerned about how she spent her money, and in the process I had made her feel even more of a fool. Our State Department gives away millions of dollars for purposes of its own, and as often as not it makes enemies of its beneficiaries.

Helping, in fact, takes place in a relationship between a helper and someone being helped. And what the helper puts into the relationship, what she hopes to get out of it, may affect the way that the help is used, just as much as what the helped person brings to it. Lord Beveridge, the designer of Britain's social security system, has stated that the purpose for which money is given will determine, to a large degree, how the recipient will spend it. If it is given with goodwill, to help a family rear a child, for instance, it will generally be spent for that purpose. But if it is given grudgingly, as a handout or a dole, with the implication that it is undeserved, it will more likely be squandered. The experience of those countries which do have a child allowance tends to support his thesis.

Motives for Helping

We come to helping with a great variety of motives, some of which we may recognize and some of which we may hide from ourselves. We may really want to help, feel deeply for a person in trouble, and at the same time want to be thanked, or feel good about ourselves because we have done something kind and unselfish, or something that our religion says we should do. In the Middle Ages, and for nearly a thousand years, giving alms to the poor was seen as one sure way to get to heaven—a sort of eternal "fire insurance"—and such a belief was not absent from the

4

thoughts of many of the robber barons of the nineteenth century who gave millions of dollars to charity. The effect on the poor, however, was that no one had any real feeling for them or tried to understand their problems. Indeed even Saint Chrysostom, the fourth-century "Apostle of Charity," who fought valiantly against those who would only help those they thought "deserving" and said that the poor "had only one recommendation--their need," still held that God permitted people to be poor in order for the rich to have someone to give to.[5]

Some of us get into helping, too, because we want to reform people or society. We may have very noble aims—the good of society, justice, fairness, or the spread of the gospel, if we are Christians. Included, of course, is the good of the person being helped. He, we believe, would be healthier, happier, as well as more useful to society if he could stop drinking, get a job, get on better with his spouse, eat more nutritious foods, get some more education, accept Christ, keep the house cleaner, or do whatever it is that we think would be good for him. To achieve this we will use every device we can think of—rewards, penalties, influence, persuasion, argument, praise, blame, sympathetic listening, encouragement, cajoling, manipulation, even possibly false reassurance and a certain amount of harmless trickery.

Being the "Good Parent"

Others sincerely want to make up for what someone else has missed in life. They react to those whose life experience, and in particular their experience of the parent-child relationship, has been so meager, or so twisted, that in the opinion of many who work with them the most helpful thing one can do is to try to give them a better, if belated, experience of being loved and cared for in a parental way. The helper becomes the "good parent," at least for a while, in the eventual hope, however, that the helped person will "grow up" and become able to conduct his own affairs.

The first group in our society to be recognized professionally as possibly needing this kind of parenting help was, in America at least, unmarried mothers.[6] Here the rationale was in keeping with current psychological theory. It had long been believed that unmarried motherhood had a close relationship to unsatisfactory mother-daughter relationships and, indeed, was much more common, apart from its occurrence in segments of society where it was culturally more or less acceptable, where this relationship had been confining, moralistic, rivalrous, or distant. Unmarried mothers, too, were often, although by no means always, youngsters, to whom it was natural to offer a quasi-parental relationship.

5

Professional thinking had also been swayed by a feeling of responsibility for the baby, which had made it important to some, at least, that the mother's decision should be a "right" one.

The same divided responsibility may have been in part the reason why many social workers turned next to the neglecting parent as the subject of parenting.[7] When a mother, for example, obviously does not know the first things about caring for children, when she is irresponsible, confused, and lacking in imagination, it is very easy to believe that the best possible thing to do is to take her under one's wing, to teach her, to set her a good example, to supervise her expenditures, and in fact to treat her as a child. It may be indeed that it is the lack of loving instruction from her own mother, the lack of someone with whom she could identify, that is the root cause of her present inability. And meanwhile there are children to consider. This line of thought has been carried out in a number of programs and social experiments, such as the use of homemaker service to teach parenting skills in the United States, and the hostels for inadequate families in Great Britain. It also appears in much of the literature on protective services, alongside literature on the same subject that emphasizes reality and choice.

This concept has been much enlarged, first to the so-called hard-core families on the relief rolls,[8] and then, by implication at least, to large segments of the poor, the "culturally deprived" or "socially disadvantaged." This has come, in America, with the rather alarming discovery that there is a "culture" of poverty quite different from that of the middle classes. It has become clear that many assumptions that have been made about people and their capabilities are illusory, that there are hundreds and thousands of people in the United States who have not acquired the simplest living skills and are, as well, almost incapable of communicating their wants. In particular help provided by Aid to Families with Dependent Children, which had been based on a belief that if the means were given to them, families would find a way to live in decency and health and become independent, was apparently resulting instead, in all too many cases, in successive generations of marginal, dependent living.

Various experiments seemingly have supported this thesis.[9] Where social workers have had much smaller caseloads, where many things have been done for people, where workers have taken more initiative in making decisions, families have got along better.

6

Two Kinds of People

One might well ask, isn't such work helpful? And in some ways it certainly is. But there are some dangers in it unless clear limits are set. Implied is that there are two kinds of people in the world, those who are maladjusted, sick, incapable of making good decisions (perhaps in religious terms, the sinful or the unregenerate) and those who are free from such ills, who are more reasonable, better educated, more in tune with the norms of society, who know what is good not only for themselves but also for other people. These people then feel that they have the right and even the duty to try to get the others to behave in more acceptable ways and to make decisions for those whom they believe to be incapable of making wise decisions on their own.

There are certainly some people for whom other people have to make decisions. These are the seriously retarded, the senile, criminals, some persons with mental illnesses, and to some extent children, although we are finding that even they can and need to make many of their own decisions. The law may declare a person incompetent and that children are "infants," literally those who cannot speak for themselves. The danger, it seems to me, comes when people out of a feeling of responsibility for those whom they see as either unfortunate or inferior take it upon themselves to judge others incompetent and so never allow them to grow up.

Traditionally, those who have considered themselves the elite, the "good" people, have thought of as "incompetent" people of color (the "white man's burden"), the poor (as late as fifty years ago paupers were barred from voting in fourteen of our states),[10] and to some extent women. We are not free yet from such prejudices. Belief that these people are inferior still persists in the minds of many.

In the late 1960s, welfare recipients, a group whom everyone seems to want to "rehabilitate," protested vigorously that the services that social workers provided were being used not to help them with their problems but to exercise control over their lives. Much of what they received was probably intended as advice; but advice is hard to reject when it is given by the person who determines the amount of one's monthly check. As Barbara Wooten, the British sociologist, once said, one should not have to accept advice simply because one is poor. Nor, she added, should one have to listen to it.[11]

The welfare recipients won a few concessions, notably the separation of services from assistance, but under the Reagan administration even this separation was no longer mandatory. It is therefore with some trepidation that I make the statement (more as an article of faith than as a provable fact, and with no desire to discredit those whose experience

7

has been different) that all too often this "parental" kind of help is given because the helper either does not know how or has not the courage or the humility to help in a more self-disciplined way. This is not to deny that such help may occasionally be necessary, although I would like more safeguards around the practice than presently exist. Nor is it to minimize the need of many people for instruction in what may seem to be the simplest skills. But it is to say that my experience has been that when a person is approached with genuine reality, empathy, and support, when he is truly treated as an adult with responsibility, the chances are good that he will respond favorably, and that this kind of response is typical of many people whom it is all too easy to see as in need of a parental kind of care.

The Elite

The problem is that it is all too easy to consider someone else incompetent. Certain people, the elite, could declare incapable of making one's own decisions anybody, or any group, of whom they disapproved. Indeed jokingly I once suggested that a Democratic Congress should declare all Republicans incompetent, since in their view Republican decisions were never wise.

Who are these "good," well-intentioned people? Traditionally they are the upper or middle classes, likely to be white and Eurocentric, representative of the majority culture, and in general self-appointed. The authority they assume is based on class, money, political strength, education, or membership in a profession that claims expertise. Occasionally they have statutory rights, generally, however, only to investigate. Of course certain persons in any community, men and women whom we call judges, do have the right to prescribe for other people, but only in accordance with law and in relation to those who have broken it. Most of us do not have this authority. Although there has been a recent move to license those who advertise themselves as professional helpers, most people who help others have little or no professional training.

Political Implications

The political and philosophical implications of a self-appointed elite and an underclass are, I think, rather alarming. It is not that much harm has yet been done. For centuries the well-to-do have felt it both their right and their duty to oversee the behavior of the poor. We certainly do not want to go back to the days of paternalism or colonialism or to indulge in brainwashing, yet when we claim the right to change other people's behavior on alledgedly scientific grounds, or moral ones, we

8

may not realize that these forms of oppression can be the end product of what is at this time only a trend. It cannot be denied that during the past thirty years, social work, to take one example, has become more prescriptive. Most of the newer models of helping are somewhat manipulative, Behavior Modification explicitly so. And when Joel Fischer tells us that most of our efforts to help have been ineffective, what he means is that they have failed to alter human behavior in desirable ways.[12]

To try to alter someone else's behavior is not help as we have defined it. It might more properly be called "control." The two processes are entirely different. I do not plan in this book to discuss the methods, processes, or techniques of controlling other people, subtly or overtly. They are too varied and can be learned elsewhere. There may be—there probably is--a need for some profession or organization other than the law to be assigned to altering certain people's behavior. There are people who cannot, perhaps, be allowed to make their own decisions, who are a threat to others, to themselves, and to society, although I think rather fewer of them than many of us imagine. Maybe the profession to work with or on these people should be social work, but if so it would seem to be important that this function be limited and perhaps even monitored by the courts. Indeed such monitoring may be beginning to happen in the more obvious cases, such as in suits against social workers for malpractice.

Distinguishing Functions → *Need for control creates dependency*

I also believe that this control function of altering someone's behavior should be clearly distinguished from the function of offering help. Yet this distinction can be very difficult to make. It is hard to tell sometimes what a would-be helper is really doing. She may be allowing the person she claims to be helping quite a lot of freedom, but only in minor matters or in things she approves of. She may even hold that freedom of choice is one of her principal values yet have her own hidden agenda which she is subtly but relentlessly pursuing.

The situation is further complicated by the very fact that, as we shall see, a measure of temporary dependence, trust in the helper, even submission, is a necessary part of the helping process. A skilled helper will not prolong this phase, but a helper who feels more at ease with controlling rather than with helping not only may not know where to stop but may prolong this dependency stage under the impression that this is what is needed in a particular case.

Many persons who practice control techniques avoid the question of freedom of choice by having the client contract to receive them, in the same way that patients in a hospital may give "informed" consent to an operation. Such a contract may be unexceptional if control is really what the person needs and if his consent is really freely given or, as is happening more often today, he has been ordered by a court to agree to a service, perhaps in lieu of going to jail. But there is a real danger in such a situation of denying the person the chance to find his own way to wholeness. To use help is actually more difficult than to let oneself be controlled, but it is more likely to have long-lasting results. And more people than we used to believe are capable of taking part in a true helping process. I would instance, in particular, children. When I first got into child welfare some fifty years ago, children were not seen as capable of making decisions on their own. Their needs were carefully assessed and plans were made for them. Yet studies such as John Powell's *Whose Child Am I?*[13] show how utterly frustrating this can be to a child.

Authority and Help

It also should not be thought that a helping process is impossible in situations involving authority, such as child protection, probation, or prison work. Some of the very finest helping can be done in such situations. It is true that a person's freedom of choice is limited in such instances. A man cannot continue to abuse his children and at the same time avoid facing the issue in court. A probationer cannot violate his probation and not expect to be sent to jail. But the authority is not that of the social worker or probation officer. It is that of the law. The helping person can help the offender decide what he wants to do about the law, but she neither has nor should have personal authority over him.

Nor is help impossible when there are certain conditions or requirements placed on receiving help, appointments to be kept, for instance, or agency policy to be followed. In fact sometimes these conditions or requirements are a useful part of the helping process and serve to keep it on track.

Helping is not a free ride, nor is a belief in a person's right to make his own decisions a matter of indulging him or of protecting him from the consequences of his actions. A good helper is not a "bleeding heart" who makes excuses for people and condones bad behavior. She is a realist helping people with a struggle that is too big for them. A good helper may be permissive in that she does not take on herself the role of one who forbids—rarely a useful tool--but she is never indulgent.

The Therapeutic Approach

One way of looking at how one wants to be involved with another's problem is to consider two contrasting approaches to helping, or views about what needs to be done if people are to be more content, more productive, and generally better off. The one most in vogue today, although perhaps not so strongly as heretofore, might be called the therapeutic approach. It is basically a medical model. One looks to see what is wrong in the person or his situation and plans to put it right.

The helper in this situation becomes the dominant person in the relationship. It is she who, with the cooperation of the person being helped, decides what to do, much as a doctor does with a patient. Health consists largely in having one's problems solved and in attaining or resuming normal activities, although there is often the belief that if a person's problems are solved, he can express himself fully, develop his talents, and live a more abundant life.

In this approach the concept of a norm is important. So is adapting to the current culture. Those people who in general accept this culture are most favored by it. Also important is the notion of deviance, of things being "out of line" or "dysfunctional." The helper in this process may be compassionate. She may want the very best for everyone. But her compassion is largely pity. She finds it hard really to value those she is trying to help. While she may see that in many cases the environment rather than the person is at fault, so to speak, and needs to be changed, there is a big temptation to see the person in trouble as inadequate or sick. Science, on which this approach largely relies, when applied to human beings, tends to concentrate on deviance from the norm.

One social worker, in an article in which she pleads for social agencies to make themselves more available to people in trouble, yet has this to say about her clients: "Sharper social science brings us daily more useful information about the uncontrolled impulsivity, the impairment in capacity to form relationships, and the ego and superego defectiveness" of those who have come to her attention.[14] This is probably an extreme example, but one does have to wonder what kind of relationship a person could have with others if this was what she thought about them.

Coplanning

The approach, or view of the task to be done, that I would contrast with the one discussed above is what I call coplanning. The helper using this approach starts from a very different assumption. She sees the vast majority of people as reasonable human beings, as far as anyone can be thought of as reasonable, but living in what is an increasingly compli-

11

cated world, which they either do not know how to or cannot manage. Many of them have tried solutions that do not work, leaving them angry, frustrated, apathetic, depressed, or ambivalent. Some may genuinely be sick—that is, out of touch with reality—and need therapy, but the helper does not assume this to be so unless the need for therapy becomes apparent. More often people are just confused. They simply don't know what to do, or what they are doing is making things worse.

Sometimes events have overwhelmed them. In an interesting article written, it is true, some years ago, a social worker predicted that within a few years everybody, not just the poor, the sick, or the oppressed, would be in need of help with at least three things—dealing with organizations (social security, the welfare system, a school board, a big hospital, a bank), playing a role for which one has not been trained (single parent, divorcee, adoptive parent, retiree, welfare client), and choosing a lifestyle. Although this has not happened as quickly as he foresaw, much of what he says makes sense.[15] Even rearing children is much more difficult nowadays than it was in the past. The world is a much more dangerous place. Children are maturing earlier and remaining dependent longer.

A Case Example

The Simpsons were a young couple with an eight-month-old baby. Although Mr. Simpson was employed at quite a good salary, they had moved to a damp, dark basement apartment, and because they had not paid their utility bills, their water and heat had been cut off. The court had investigated the Simpsons after receiving a complaint from Mr. Simpson's mother, who obviously resented her daughter-in-law. The court worker inferred from the way that the grandmother spoke of her daughter-in-law that Pearl, who was physically a most attractive young woman who had run away from her own home at the age of fourteen and taken refuge with the Simpsons, had been pregnant with Jo Ann when she married. Vernon had been twenty at that time, and Pearl only seventeen.

When the Simpsons left the baby cold, wet, and alone with a bad cold for a couple of hours one day, the court acted and gave temporary custody of Jo Ann to the child welfare agency.

The case was discussed at a staff meeting. Two workers saw the situation as one that called for parenting. Pearl, they said, had been a deprived child who had never learned responsibility. Even now the only mother figure in her life was antagonistic. Another worker was interested in the relationship between Vernon and his mother. Why, for instance, had the mother taken in a fourteen-year-old runaway girl to live with her and

12

Vernon, then seventeen and his mother's only child? Something here was very strange. Had she not foreseen what would happen?

Vernon, too, was totally unrealistic. He had told the judge that he had had lights and heat cut off because Pearl was running up utility bills, and he had proposed as a solution to their problems that he and Pearl get a divorce; he would marry his girlfriend, who had more sense than Pearl, and they would care for Jo Ann. He clearly had a character disorder and needed treatment for it.

A fourth worker suggested marriage or family counseling. Another worker saw no hope in the situation. She agreed that Vernon probably was psychopathic and would never be responsible. Psychopaths — people with character disorders — are extremely difficult to help because they are happy as they are and do not want to get well. Pearl was a teenage mother and should never have kept the child. The agency's efforts should be directed to freeing Jo Ann for adoption in order to give her a chance in life.

But the worker who was to carry the case, and to whom, as will be reported in another context, Pearl had said, "Now you simply have to help us," said, "The question I'm going to ask them is, 'Now that this has happened to you, what do you want to do about it? Do you really want Jo Ann?'"

This she did. Both Vernon and Pearl said yes, they did want their daughter. They had become so involved in their marital squabble that they hadn't realized what they were doing to her. Vernon's salary had been spent on his girlfriend. The worker said that one way Vernon could show that they really wanted their daughter was for him to be faithful in paying for her care. Vernon rather reluctantly agreed. And what did they plan to do about their marital situation? Vernon said that they got on each other's nerves. Would the agency hold it against them if they separated for a while? Pearl asked the same question.

This was a critical moment. It did not look, on the face of it, that their separation was a step toward establishing a home for Jo Ann, especially as Vernon's plan was to go live with his mother. It was, of course, their privilege to do what they thought best. Were they really saying that they each wanted Jo Ann but that they did not want her together? This they both strenuously denied. The worker then said that if this was true there were two ways they could show it. They could agree that theirs was to be a trial separation limited to not more than six months, and they could agree to meet in the worker's office every month to discuss how the separation was going.

They kept this schedule fairly well. Pearl reported that she had reenrolled in high school and was on the cheerleading squad, which she had missed earlier by getting married so young. Vernon accused her of "making it" with some of the boys, which she did not deny. Vernon missed one appointment and one payment for Jo Ann's care. The worker went to see him at his mother's house and found his girlfriend there. The worker asked him what his girlfriend's presence meant. Would he really be just as glad not to be burdened with a child? She was fairly sure that Pearl would contest any action to deprive her of her parental rights, and a girl was usually given to the mother. Vernon said he was still making up his mind. His mother was putting pressure on him to have nothing further to do with Pearl.

The next month, though, he reported that he was tired of his mother's nagging and being treated as if he were still a little boy. He was, after all, a married man. Could the worker help him find an apartment, and would she promise not to let his mother have the address? Pearl said that they had reached the fifth month of their separation. Wouldn't they have to decide soon? Vernon said that she could visit. The worker noted his expression as he looked at Pearl. She had found part-time work as a model and was attractive and well dressed.

The next month they came in together instead of separately, as before. Vernon asked if the agency would forgive him Jo Ann's board for a couple of months so that they could buy furniture for the new apartment they had found. The worker said no, not if they really wanted their daughter back. The judge, who was cautious in such matters, would want evidence of Vernon's responsibility, since he had been so irresponsible in money matters before.

Three months later Jo Ann was home. On the worker's first visit to the home, which the judge had insisted on, Vernon asked if she knew anything about constructing venetian blinds, which he said he would like to make for Jo Ann's room, and Pearl proudly proclaimed that she was pregnant again.

The worker was not blind to the fact that Vernon was a spoiled child and Pearl immature. But she thought that they should have a chance to grow up. Actually they both needed to "sow their wild oats" before their marriage could be stable, which, in the long run, it was. Of course they might not come through, but that was a risk the worker had to take. Vernon might have proved untreatable, proved, in fact, so unrealistic that he needed psychiatric care, which she might have helped him get. Pearl might have become a prostitute. The worker was also quite ready to help them find out that they did not want Jo Ann. Then adoption would have been a possibility. What she did was help them plan a journey on which they could find out if they wanted their daughter and could grow up if this was something they could do.

Coplanning is also helpful when someone wants to do or be something but cannot figure out how to get there. The helping person is in some ways like a travel agent. A good travel agent does not tell one where to go, but she can be of considerable help in suggesting how to get there; in suggesting alternative routes; in knowing something of conditions on the way to or at one's destination, so that the traveler might want to consider whether he really wants to go there; and, perhaps most useful of all, in helping him to estimate what his journey will cost. She may even have to tell him that he cannot do something he wants to do, as happened to me once, when my travel agent told me I could not fly from Turkey to Greece. The two countries were at war. Or maybe someone's passport is not valid for a journey to Cuba or Tibet.

Self-Discipline and Self-Knowledge

Helping is not an easy business, although it may be a most worthwhile one. It takes more than knowledge. I cannot promise that everyone who reads this book, even if they should "read, mark, learn, and inwardly digest" it, will become a good helper. Helping requires self-discipline and to some extent self-knowledge. The natural, impulsive, generous thing is not always the most helpful. Most of us shrink from being the bearer of bad news, or hate to see someone grieve and want to cheer him up, and feel that if we are not optimistic, we probably won't be good helpers. But in helping we may be called on to face the person we are helping with an unpleasant truth, or to allow a child to cry in a way that wracks our heart until he has, as we say, got it out of his system. We may even have to court someone's anger when we would much rather placate him and keep things pleasant between us. We may have to discipline ourselves to concentrate on someone else's troubles and not to let our own desires, fears, problems, defenses, ideals, likes, and dislikes interfere.

Acknowledging in ourselves tendencies that need watching is helpful. Do we, for instance, have a tendency to avoid unpleasant facts, to preach, to find easy answers to problems, to be liked by everyone, to want to be thought wise, efficient, or even helpful? It is not so much that these tendencies will prevent us from being a good helper, but we need to make allowances for them in our work. We may need to identify the kind of people whom we find it hard to help. I myself have difficulty with bossy old women and sometimes have to remind myself that an old lady I am trying to help is not my great-aunt Euphemia, who terrified me as a child. But those we dislike are not the only ones who may be difficult to help. I have to steel myself sometimes to be realistic with certain kinds of little girls, to remind myself that the troubled child I am trying to help is not the kid sister I always longed for but never had.

It is not that I cannot help these people. I can and do. It is just that I need to be aware that when I am trying to help someone, I bring to the task what I am, a human being who has his own likes and dislikes, who has had certain experiences that have made him what he is. There might be some, of course, who would disqualify me as a helper.

I have known some brilliant young women and men whose desire to control or to reform others was so strong, and generally unrecognized in themselves, that they never should be encouraged to go into a helping profession. I have known people who want to be child welfare workers because they are still in conflict with their own parents and who identify so strongly with children that they can do little more than indulge them. As admissions officer once in a graduate school of social work I turned down a young woman with straight As in sociology and psychology, over the protests of her instructors, because she did not really want to help. She had lost her husband through epilepsy, and all she wanted to do was to have a graduate degree so that she could get a job teaching people about that illness. She did not want to learn anything. She knew what she wanted to know already.

Sometimes, too, the self-knowledge and self-discipline that good helping requires would cost the would-be helper more than she would be willing to pay. And there are those who think that by learning to help others they can solve some problem of their own—which, by the way, is rarely accomplished. But these are perhaps exceptions. Most people can, if they want to, acquire both the self-knowledge and the self-discipline to become effective helpers.

Good helping does, however, involve one's self. One must be prepared for a good deal of pain as well as a lot of pleasure and even joy. The very word "compassion" means to suffer with someone, and empathy, which as we will see is an important factor in helping, requires that one really feels what another person is going through. Helping can also be exhausting. One can feel as Jesus is reported to have felt when a woman only went as far as to catch hold of his robe, that virtue (that is, strength) had gone out of him.

Helping Models

That good helping involves the self is one of the reasons why I have not given my understanding of the helping process any other name. Named models of helping, even Transactional Analysis, which does contain a great deal of truth, can be learned as a technique (I saw an advertisement lately which promised to teach it in a week). Helping is not a technique. It is an investment of one's self. The temptation with a technique, or a model, is to be more interested in its rules than in the purpose for which the rules were devised, which is to help people. I taught once in a school which declared itself to be Montessorian. I happen to think that Doctor Montessori was something of a genius and that most of the principles she set forth are sound. But in this school nothing could be done, however helpful, no adaptation made to the needs of British children, with Britain's (at that time) irrational monetary system, which counted in twelves and twenties rather than in tens, because "La Dottoressa" (Montessori), who taught children in Italy, where one hundred centesimi made a lira, had not authorized any new teaching tools.

Help then can involve little or big things; it can be long-lasting or short-lived; it can consist of material aid or counseling (words). Help takes place in a relationship in which the helper treats the helped as You and not It. When help fails, the helper may be as much at fault as the person she tries to help. Help can be given even if one does not know much about the other person to start with. The helper's purpose is simply to help and not to fulfill some other agenda, however worthwhile. Help needs to be clearly distinguished from efforts to influence or control. It can occur in situations which involve authority, but in these situations the helper does not have the right to take over another's decisions. She may be permissive but never indulgent. One useful approach to helping is coplanning. The helper should see herself as a generalist and the person she is helping as the specialist in his particular situation. Help requires self-knowledge and self-discipline. It involves the whole self of the helping person and cannot be learned as a technique. It can be exhausting and painful, but it also can be a source of joy.

17

CHAPTER 2

Taking Help

What It Takes to Be Helped
Perhaps the most important thing to realize at the very beginning about
help is that most people do not want to be helped in any significant way.
The great majority even of those who ask for help are at the same time
very much afraid of it. They may, in fact, actively work to render it fruitless at the same time as they ask for it.

These may seem extraordinary statements when so many people appear to be demanding help of one sort or another, when requests for
welfare services are increasing on every hand, and when one of the major
fears of the populace as a whole is, in America at least, that we are rais-
ing a generation who have been led to expect assistance from some
governmental unit rather than to rely on their own initiative. Yet it is a
fact that most people who are in trouble both want help and are terrified
of it. Indeed in most cases the fear of any kind of help that would really induce change or movement is greater at first than the desire for it.

We can understand this fear better, perhaps, if we consider what asking for help demands. The person who asks for the kind of help that
will really make a difference to him must, in fact, do four things. He must
recognize that something is wrong with or lacking in his situation which
he can do nothing about by himself. He must be willing to tell someone
else about his problem. He must accord to this other person at least a
limited right to tell him what to do or to do things for him. And finally
he must be willing to change in some way himself. This means giving up
whatever adjustments he has been able to make to the present situation-
-adjustments that may have and probably have cost him a great deal to
make and have become part of himself and wholly necessary to him—in
favor of a new kind of life, which he may have some reason to believe
will be more satisfactory but which, at the same time, is an unknown
quantity, full of possible dangers.

But the difficulty is greatly increased if up to the time of asking for
help a person's experiences of permitting another to take some control
of his affairs has been that he is taken advantage of, if telling another
has meant that his confidence is abused, or if his attempts to live a sup-
posedly more productive life have always resulted in defeat. And these

18

have been the experience of all too many of those who are in need of help.

Yet for the most part this tremendous demand made on the person to be helped has gone unrecognized. People who refuse help are still thought of as ungrateful when all they really are is afraid. Others are thought to be insensitive, not to know there is something wrong, or to lack simple common sense, when in fact they are acutely aware of the wrongness but even more afraid of what it would cost them to put it right. Many are stigmatized as content with unsatisfactory or degrading conditions when all they are is scared to act on their discontent. Again it might be said that one of the major medical problems of our time is the number of people who are sick and afraid to get well, not because they like being sick any more than the rest of us, but because being well would involve expectations of them which they are afraid they will be unable to fulfill.

Resisting Help

Is it surprising, then, that many people will do almost anything to prevent themselves from being caught in the process of receiving meaningful help? Is it surprising that many people meet an offer of help with suspicion or work hard to limit the kind of help they will receive?

Anyone whose business it is to help others will recognize quite a number of different stages in this struggle. First are those who apparently do not recognize at all that they lack anything or are in any kind of trouble. Those who truly lack this recognition are, I suggest, rather few, although in some situations people do repress unpleasant realities and lose touch with reality.

More often, perhaps, the person is aware of some sense of wrongness but, by putting the whole matter outside himself, either adapts to it by accepting his need to suffer and gets what satisfaction he can out of this, or persuades himself somehow that the problem is temporary and will go away if he waits it out.

Sometimes he tries to solve the problem by setting up certain conditions in which it is manageable, either consciously or unconsciously, in which case we call him neurotic. He may find, for instance, that he can live with the problem if he can claim special privileges from others by reason of his illness, or his more or less imagined status as self-sacrificing spouse, loved child, business executive, martyr, or even target of misfortune. He will not usually ask for help unless hard realities impinge on his privilege, and sometimes, even then, he will escape by denying this reality to the point that he becomes psychotic rather than neurotic.

19

Sometimes, although he apparently recognizes no need for help, he does in fact do so, consciously or unconsciously, but cannot take the second step, that of admitting it to another. Still, he needs help, and his only recourse is to act in such a way that help is forced on him, often apparently against his will. We are all familiar with the child who misbehaves in order to draw attention to the trouble he is in, although we often dismiss his action as somehow meaningless because "it was only done to get attention." Yet this is the child's way of bringing his distress to our notice. We are perhaps less likely to see an adult's behavior or even his criminal act as a plea for help, although experience has shown us that this is often what it is. Hierens, the murderer of Suzanne Degnan, scrawled on the child's mirror with lipstick a plea for the police to catch him before he did such a thing again.

This phenomenon is apparent in many court hearings involving neglect of children. The parents have often been offered all kinds of help before the matter was brought to court and have apparently either rejected it or proved incapable of making any improvement in response to urging, persuasion, or opportunity to do a better job. They are brought to court "as a last resort." The court may see its action as a regrettable act of force, but actually this is the way that the parents have chosen to yield to the demand that they be helped, a way in which they do not have to admit their lack of love for their children but can feel themselves to be deprived of their children's care against their will. Indeed if there have been adequate services which really offer help to a family before it comes to court, the chances are very small indeed that the court actually makes a decision against the will of the parents. Usually it does little more — although this little more is important — than to confirm the parents' will and give substance to it.

"Wish" and "Want" as Difficult Words

We are obviously caught here in something of a semantic tangle. The order of the court is clearly against the parents' expressed wishes. They may be very angry at it, and genuinely so. It is not a matter of the parents' having lied when they protested their love for their children. Human emotions are much too complicated to be expressed in such terms as "wish" or "want." We run into much the same difficulty when we use the terms "conscious" or "unconscious," which is why I find myself writing, as I have in the paragraph above, "consciously or unconsciously" as if I were uncertain which it was. A better phrase might be "consciously *and* unconsciously," for while it is possible to speak of a conscious act, such as a premeditated murder, and an unconscious one, such as blushing,

20

when we talk about a person's desires, his "wishing" or "wanting" something, we are talking about something that has both conscious and unconscious elements.

Nor can we solve the problem by talking about someone's "real" wish or desire, as we do when we say that what a person asks for at first is often not what he "really" wants, since in fact it is this that he "really" wants at that time but not what in time he will find himself to want. The truth is that to will something—and I shall use that word, among others, to express what I think people mean when they talk of "really wishing"—is not an emotion at all. It is an act of commitment to a certain course of action and involves being prepared to carry through with it. As such it is both conscious and unconscious, for both conscious and unconscious preparedness is necessary if the commitment is to be carried out. Quite often we find, for instance, an apparent commitment that is made with no reservations on a conscious level at all but which is utterly destroyed by an unconscious factor. A man may apparently want a job and do all that he can to obtain it, but when its pressures become too great for him, he may escape by developing an allergy to the materials with which he works. He does not do so consciously, and yet it could be said of him that his will to do the job was somehow incomplete. The same is true of the neglecting parent, who may genuinely "wish" or "want" to do a better job but does not actually have the "will" to do so.

Telling Someone about It, Being "Understood"
But even should a person get to the point where he recognizes his need for help, and go perhaps to considerable trouble to seek out someone who can help him, he is still very far from accepting help. He now has the problem of telling this person about his trouble. He may, of course, lack words to do so, especially if he comes from a culture which is not accustomed to discussing how one feels about anything. But even if he has the words and wants very much to communicate what he feels, and to have this other person "understand" him and his problem, he puts a special meaning into the word "understand."

He does not want the helping person to understand him completely, to know him in all his weakness. He wants the other person to understand his point of view, to see things as he sees them, to approve of him in some fashion, to accord him some respect. He may, therefore, under- or overstate his problem. He may tell only part of the story, again either consciously or unconsciously. Nearly always he will manage somehow to put the problem outside himself, to ask not that he be changed but that some other person be talked to and made to change. If he does admit

[handwritten at top: ask for it, they demand the kind of help they think is best, giving them some semblance of "control" or "handling the situation"]

[handwritten in left margin: People are often afraid to accept help. I Summon the courage to accept help, but when they ↑]

some other person be talked to and made to change. If he does admit some need for change on his own part, perhaps because he feels that he ought to, this is usually some part of himself he is willing to let go and therefore not too important to him.

Sometimes he will refuse to discuss the matter at all. He will uphold that he knows the solution to his problem, which he can accomplish by himself if only he receives a certain specified bit of help. One can recognize the phrase, "All I want (or need) is . . . ," which actually often means, "Give me this, which may or may not solve the problem for me—and don't dare tell me what I really need." Often someone who handles his fear of help in this way is very demanding and insists on his rights to a certain kind of assistance, so that he gives the impression of being greedy or overready to accept help when he is actually trying to ward off being helped. He is one whose courage has failed him at the point of asking for help. He wants help but is willing to take it only on his own terms, although these very terms protect him from really being helped. Again, however, he is not lying or deliberately asking for something which he does not need. For the moment, he really wants what he is asking for.

Demanding Help on One's Own Terms

This demand for help on one's own terms and no other is often seen among parents who bring their child to a psychiatric or guidance center. They are often quite surprised and even resentful when the psychiatrist or the social worker wants to see them as well as the child. They try to limit their participation to that of giving information about their child so that the psychiatrist may know how to help him. The last thing they really want to consider is the part they have played in the child's problem and their need to change in their relationship to him.

A related way of warding off help is to throw the whole burden of decision onto the helping person—"You tell me what to do." This way of avoiding the necessity for change is particularly difficult for some helping people to understand, since they naturally want to do things for people who want help and it does look, at least for the moment, as if the client really does want one to help. He is actually asking for advice, and up to a point he will take it. But since there has been no real change in the client's view of the problem or his readiness to do something about it, the helping person's prescribed remedies generally fail to do what they were intended to accomplish. Often, in fact, this very failure of the remedy to solve the problem without calling for any change in the person asking for help will be used to deny that the helping person has any knowledge of her subject, or "really understands."

22

This phenomenon is well known to anyone who has been a consultant. The client follows the consultant's recommendations in great detail. He is enormously cooperative. But the course of action prescribed fails to solve the problem, not because the consultant was wrong in what she suggested, but because the client accepts the consultant's suggestions as law to be meticulously followed. He does not make the suggestions his own. He does not adapt them to the particular situation in which he finds himself, and which only he knows fully—a fact which consultants sometimes forget in their eagerness to prescribe. And, as a result, the consultant's time is not only wasted; she is discredited as well.

A more extreme form of warding off help by thrusting decisions onto the helping person is to get that person to do what one needs to do for oneself—to find one a job, or look for a house, or inquire about a resource. This sometimes pleases the helper, who feels that she is "doing something to help," but all too often what the helping person does or finds turns out to be something less than the helped person feels that he needs.

Fear of Being Really Helped

Up to this point we have been considering the negative impulse, the fear of being helped, and it may seem to the reader not only that people who need help are highly ingenious and dishonest in defeating those who wish to help them, but that it is something of a miracle that help ever gets given at all. But quite clearly this is not so. Thousands of people do get effective help daily, although probably not as many as should. Even with all the protections people throw up around themselves, their need to be helped remains.

Nor are these protections in themselves unworthy things. They can, and are, and ought to be used to ward off all kinds of interference, patronage, or desire to control that may be offered under the name of help. The only reasons for dwelling on them at such length are that they also exist in a genuine helping situation and must be recognized and worked with, and because they are too often seen as moral faults which somehow could be conquered with an act of the will, instead of as the almost impulsive and quite natural defenses that they are.

How universal is this resistance to help? The very fact that it is not generally recognized might suggest that we have been generalizing here in much too total a fashion.

Do all people resist help? Are there not some who genuinely seek advice, whose need for help is so much greater than their fear of it that they are ready to place themselves unreservedly in the hands of another?

Is it not possible, even, that what we have been describing here is in fact the exception, the neurotic reaction, and that ordinary people do not go through this struggle? Most of us can remember times when we have been helped in which we can recall only eagerness for help and gratitude when it has been given. But if we think more deeply, we can also remember our doubts and fears, our difficulty, say, in approaching the bank for a loan or in sharing our problems with a counselor. One of the exercises sometimes demanded of social work students early in their learning process is to give an account of some occasion in their lives when they have needed or asked for help. To read these accounts is often a poignant experience, so real are the fears and doubts recalled. So far from these being the outpourings of the most neurotic students, the reverse is true. It is the more neurotic student, the student who can only live with a tightly controlled artificial projection of herself, what is sometimes called a persona, and the student who is unlikely to be able to learn to help others, who does not recognize that help is hard to take or confirms this fact, without perhaps realizing that this is what she is doing, by denying stoutly that she has ever needed or asked for help in her life. The process of taking help is so painful that many of us repress it or rationalize it in some way.

Many of the occasions about which these students write may seem comparatively trivial. Some have to do with seeking help from a teacher in high school or college when they found themselves "lost" in a course, some with such apparently unimportant happenings as being stranded with a car which stops running in an unfamiliar place. The majority have to do with borrowing money. Yet it would probably be too much to assert that there are not certain situations where the help to be given is so unlikely to touch one deeply or to demand any change in oneself that it is quite easy to ask. Some people have no hesitation in asking the way if they are lost. I myself would far prefer in most situations to be lost than to ask the way. In some situations, too — and asking the way should be one of them — the solution to the problem for which one asks help is so obviously something one cannot be blamed for not knowing oneself that it is not too hard to turn to the expert. It is not too difficult, perhaps, to consult a lawyer about the law or a scholar in some other field about his specialty, as long as the answer is unlikely to affect one too deeply. But most people are somewhat less than wholly frank with their doctor.

What about matters which do affect one deeply? Is it not possible that a person's need is so great that his resistance to seeking help has in fact been effectually answered before he comes to the helping situation?

There are such situations. They occur principally when a person is in a state of crisis that will make a major change in his life inevitable. There is, in this kind of situation, very little of the old and familiar to cling to. If help can be offered before new resistance can be formed, it may be accepted with some eagerness. But even here the process is not one of putting oneself in the hands of another to make one's decisions for one. It is a process of discovering in oneself new methods of coping with what is essentially a new situation, calling for new roles to be played. For a while, after a crisis, people are forced into activity, even in the form of protest. This short, vulnerable period, which may result in new ways of handling things, is all too often followed, if help is not given, by despair and finally by detachment from the problem or denial of it. The helping person is not always available at a time of crisis. Most people wait until long after a crisis before they seek help. They try to solve their problem alone until they become convinced of their own inability to do so. This is true even of such obvious help as public assistance. A study of the 1950s showed that 59 percent of families eventually applying for aid to dependent children did not do so until six months after the family crisis — death, desertion, or incapacity of the father — which made assistance necessary.[1]

Submitting Oneself to Another
In the vast majority of situations the wholehearted putting of oneself in the hands of another is more likely to be apparent than real. To allow another to make one's decisions for one is more likely to be a disguised way of resisting help than an acceptance of it. It is one way of avoiding making hard decisions oneself, and although there may be occasions where this is a sign of growth, it is more likely to be a sign of the opposite. The one situation in which it is a sign of growth is perhaps that in which the person has been trying to make decisions for which he does not have the equipment — perhaps trying to conduct his own case at law, or prescribing for himself medically, or needing to prove for himself facts that other researchers have established.

It might be argued, and is sometimes, that to submit oneself to the expertise of the social scientist is not, in fact, very different from doing the same with a lawyer or a physician, and that the person who more or less blindly does what a social worker or a counselor tells him to do is not so much resisting help as accepting the fact that he cannot manage his own life and is finding help in doing so. Why should making the decision to trust a doctor to tell me in detail what I should do to strengthen a broken leg be so very different from, say, trusting a marriage counselor or a minister to tell me in detail what to do to strengthen a broken marriage?

The claim of the social scientist or any other expert in living to the same status as the doctor is based on the assumption that in fact I can strengthen my marriage by putting myself unreservedly in her hands. But question must be raised about the possibility of this. It is not simply a matter of marriage being a much more complicated organism than a broken leg, which may not be in some senses true. Nor is it only a matter of the physical sciences being much older and of the physical scientists knowing much more about their material than the social scientists know yet about theirs, however true this may be at the moment. Such an argument would suggest that the social scientist might eventually attain this knowledge, whereas the difference is more fundamental. Nor does the apparently promising answer that a leg is a concrete thing with its own regenerative process, apart from my feeling about it, while a marriage needs for its betterment the involvement of my feeling, my unconscious as well as my conscious will, which cannot be prescribed for me, entirely answer the problem. My unconscious feelings do and may enter in very largely to what happens to my leg. I may have, for instance, an unconscious desire for my leg not to get well, to claim the indulgence accorded to the man with a limp, and this may greatly affect how faithfully I follow the doctor's advice.

The difference lies in the fact that I am asking the doctor's advice only on how to deal with my leg, and I know and can agree with him on what values are subsumed. This is a fairly simple matter—to have an operative leg or not to have one, or perhaps to have one that is partly operative. That what eventuates will have a great effect on the whole of my life is not denied, nor is the fact that I will have a number of decisions to make as a result of it. But these decisions I reserve for myself. I do not submit them to the doctor. As a matter of fact I do not believe, and she probably does not believe, that she is an expert in them. If she does, her relationship to me is radically altered. She is acting as expert in the whole matter of living, and I will have much more resistance to placing myself in her hands.

But when I ask someone to tell me how my marriage can be strengthened and determine to follow her advice, this distinction no longer exists. Any change I make involves immediately all my relationships with people. And it is these relationships that comprise the expertise of the counselor. Having once assumed responsibility for my feelings, for my conscious and unconscious will, she cannot in fact limit the control she will exercise, or her work will be incomplete. She may require me to make decisions for myself. Any but the most cocksure or naïve counselor would do so. But if she did so, she would in fact be denying the rightness of my total submission to her advice. She would be recognizing that this submission was a defense against really being helped and would try to overcome my resistance to accepting a kind of help in which I was more active.

A Problem of Values

Moreover, in accepting her prescription without myself really making decisions about it — in deciding, that is, to let her make my decisions for me — I am accepting her values, her belief about what a marriage should be like. I must in fact do so, since her knowledge of how to achieve a goal must be predicated on some concept of this goal and will prove inadequate if the goal is altered. Whether this is in fact possible is very doubtful. Values, which in this case mean the whole range of human preference, both conscious and unconscious, are not only almost incredibly complex but highly individual.

It can only be assumed that the values of the helped person and of the helper (whose values are in themselves partly unconscious) can be fully acceptable to both in very general terms, in which case we are attempting to adjust a very complex machine with a very blunt instrument, or that it is really possible to know a person in such detail that it is possible to predict the whole of his response to a given situation and tailor a prescription to it. This assumption, in turn, requires a belief that people are wholly mechanical beings, that their feelings, aspirations, even their consciousness itself are ultimately attributable to the laws of chemistry and physics. Although there are many who profess to believe this, it is an unprovable assertion and one that cannot be acted on with any certainty at all.

If, however, we make the assumption that there is something in humanity which cannot be measured or predicted, it is largely in the realm of values, or at least consciousness of values, that the difference must be assumed to lie. It would be precisely in the giving up of fine discrimination in this sphere that a person would give up the very thing that makes him or her human. To conceive of help as prescription in fact reduces it to the level of a control process directed at nothing more radical than adaptive efficiency. It leaves no place for love or joy.

Being Ordered to Take Help

The difficulty of accepting meaningful help, the resistance that can be put up to it, raises the question of whether, and how, help is possible when someone does not ask for it or when he is ordered to accept it. What happens then to our definition of help and our insistence that help and control are different processes?

There are four rather different situations that involve unrequested help. One situation, which is becoming much more frequent, is when a man, for instance, is convicted of drunken driving and ordered by the court to attend a clinic for alcoholics or, if his crime is child sexual abuse, a mental health center which may have a specialized program for offenders. To the normal reluctance to accepting help may be added shame in having to receive it and anger at what may look like punishment. It may—it probably will—be necessary to deal with these feelings before one can begin the specific help one hopes to give. But if these feelings are addressed, the chances of the involuntary client receiving help are quite good. The alternatives to his receiving help are clear, or they should be. He can, of course, refuse the help, or he can go through the motions and attend the required number of meetings, just as someone can be a model prisoner and earn a good-behavior release before reverting to a life of crime. The helper should be in the position of requiring certain evidence of help having taken place, perhaps a prolonged "dry" period or, in the case of the sexual offender, a full and frank apology to the child or some other sign of repentance.

Limits to Self-Determination

It is true that the offender's self-determination is limited. But this limitation is something that he brought upon himself and it does not mean that he is now subject to the helper's will and must do what she wants him to do. He must still make the decision of what he will do with the help offered, and the very fact that his choices are limited sometimes makes this choice easier. There is also the possibility that the help offered is what he really wants but has not been able to ask for.

Pearl and Vernon, the young couple discussed in the previous chapter, had made a valiant attempt to clean up the apartment they had let deteriorate to the point that their baby's life was in danger—water and heat had been turned off—but had found the job too overwhelming, and just before Vernon's mother was due to call, they had left the baby alone in the filthy apartment and had got drunk (although drinking was not one of their problems). The grandmother called the police, as they knew she would. They were held in jail overnight, and in the morning the juvenile judge awarded temporary custody of Jo Ann to the Child Protection Agency, which had been trying to help them see the seriousness of the situation but had found them to be rather resistant clients. As the

28

couple came out of court, the mother turned to the child welfare worker. "Now," she said, "you simply have to help us."

These young people needed the reality of the court hearing before they could admit that they needed help, and consciously or unconsciously they had sought it. Within nine months, held by the worker to meeting the court's requirements if they wanted their baby back, they had come to terms with their problem, had behaved responsibly by paying for their child's support, had found a new apartment which they kept clean and warm, and had their baby back.

Their recovery was not the result of control. The social worker did not tell them what to do. She kept before them the requirements of the court and the alternative, should they choose not to meet them or prove incapable of doing so—the termination of their parental rights. Control would have been part of the process if the worker had lectured them on being good parents, had sent them to classes on parenting, or, not understanding the role that the grandmother had played in their lives, had urged them to listen to her.

In a professional periodical there was an article recently describing a program for convicted child molesters. The authors took what seemed to be a positive delight in its unpleasantness—it employed aversion therapy, associating pictures of naked children with foul smells--and in the restrictions it placed on the offender's right to self-determination. It is possible to hold that child molesters must be prevented by all available means from repeating their offense, yet what was done to these men was forced rehabilitation and not help. And I am far from convinced that they could not have come to the same decision, not to molest little girls, in a way that would have left them their self-respect. One of the things that the article noted was that they were not, to the authors' surprise, weaklings or degenerates, but resourceful, capable people.

The Authority of the Helper

A second situation in which unsolicited help is offered is where there has been a complaint, usually of child abuse or neglect, and the social worker or juvenile officer has the duty to investigate and report what she finds. The person complained of has one option denied to those already convicted. He can deny the charges, disagree with the investigator's findings, and, if necessary, challenge them in the courtroom. This is his right, and he should be helped if that is what he decides to do. He is innocent until proved guilty. The protective worker has no authority over him except to investigate and report. She does, however, have, in some jurisdictions, one piece of authority that can be very helpful. She can, if the situation is not critical, offer help instead of bringing the case to court. The help she may offer will have conditions attached to it, and it will probably be time-limited, but the person complained of is free to reject the offer. He can do so, however, only at the cost of a court hearing. And in that hearing the social worker is not a prosecutor but one who presents the evidence as fairly as she can – not always an easy thing to do, especially if one is feeling indignant about what one believes is happening to a child.

Such a situation is also made more difficult because the child protective worker is the bearer of bad news. She has received a complaint, and the person complained of often starts with anger against the complainant. The worker has to learn to draw this anger to herself, where it can be dealt with. She does not make the client angry. The anger is already there. But the immediate problem of the client is not whatever it was that gave rise to the complaint, but the fact that the protective worker is standing on his doorstep, and this must be dealt with first.

When One Has to Intervene

A third situation is more difficult to define and, moreover, overlaps with the others. It is where a person plainly needs help but is unable to ask for it, and where the failure to get it will inevitably lead to some more or less major disaster – the delinquency of a child, or death from cancer, for example. Here we might feel a strong compulsion to offer help, and most of us would certainly try. Sometimes in fact the very offer will make it possible for the other to respond. But all too often the very fact that help has not been asked in so obvious a situation means that the resistance to it is very deep indeed.

Some such resistance may be cultural. Refusal to ask help of official agencies, even those like the school and the welfare agency which are primarily helpful rather than authoritative, is not infrequently found in areas where there is a deep suspicion of all parts of the "establishment," beginning of course with the police.[2] Here a helper may have to be quite persistent and to work quite a long time on the very business of people's fears of taking help. But help can only be forthcoming as these fears are overcome.

A fourth situation has to do with a phenomenon which we shall deal with more fully in chapter 3 – that of "choice" and "nonchoice." Briefly, in an encounter with any threatening piece of reality people can and do react in one of four ways. They may accept and use the threat constructively to gain new resolution or clarity. They may struggle against the reality and try to change it in some way. They may try to ward it off by escaping into some fantasy or rationalization. Or they may allow it to paralyze or crush them.

The first two reactions can be spoken of as "choice-reactions." They lead to some action, good or bad. The second two we can call reactions of "nonchoice." They lead to no action.

In the situation of the person facing a crisis and apparently doing nothing about it we do need to consider whether this is a genuine case of "nonchoice" or whether the ill that we foresee for that person has been chosen, perhaps in preference to some ill we cannot see or as a deliberate risk. If it is genuine nonchoice, we might try to intervene, not to prescribe what he should do, but to face him with the need for action of some sort.

This is a difficult and a skilled business. If we are going to attempt it, we need to have some skill in helping. We need to be sure, too, of the almost objective nature of the disaster that will arise out of not taking help. It is very easy to confuse such a situation with one in which the other person's need for help is really a matter of the would-be helper's opinion; where she disapproves, for instance, of the way the other is rearing his children, or where the result of what this person is doing will lead to something the helper does not want but the other for some reason does or is willing to accept.

Two Examples

Welfare workers in Maine once brought me two apparently similar situations, in that both of them involved elderly persons living alone in isolated areas. Mr. Black laughed when the worker suggested he move to a rest home in town. The worker asked him what would happen if he broke a leg. He had no way to call for help. He told her he had been a logger all his life and would not know what to do in town. We all had to die someday, he said, and he'd rather die in familiar surroundings, even if it should happen tomorrow. In town he might not break his leg, or die if he did, but he'd simply waste away, and probably quicker than where he was. He was probably correct. A number of studies have shown that to move an elderly person, especially against his will, to unfamiliar surroundings, even to a place where he will get the best of care, may shorten rather than prolong his life.

The other case was of a woman who appeared at first to welcome the worker's suggestion. She thought she would like having a clean bed and someone to take care of her somewhat. In contrast to Mr. Black's neat little shack, her cottage was filthy, largely due to a dozen cats which she had never house-trained. Nor had she cleaned up their mess. The worker was pleased with Mrs. White's decision, but on the day she called to take

31

her to see the rest home, Mrs. White said she had decided not to move. It would be too much trouble. During the next three months the worker tried again and again, and each time the woman agreed with the plans but could not carry them through. Finally the worker concluded that Mrs. White had no intention of moving and closed the case. By then winter had set in, and some hunters found Mrs. White frozen to death. The cats were nowhere to be found.

Mr. Black was fully aware of the risk he was taking and preferred the chance of a painful death in his beloved woods to an easier one elsewhere. The worker would have been wrong if she had tried to force him to move. Even if he had broken his leg and died the day after her visit, she would have had nothing to reproach herself with. Mr. Black had the right to die with dignity. But Mrs. White was incapable of making a rational decision. Even if her love of cats was the reason for her hesitation, and we do not know that it was, the condition of her cottage, her inability to carry through on plans, even her placid agreement with the worker's suggestions, should have alerted the worker that Mrs. White really wanted the worker to force the issue. Being free to make one's own decisions does not mean being free to make no decision at all when the outcome is likely to be a miserable, unforeseen, and unnecessary death.

Help Cannot Be Given but Only Made Possible

While intervention may be justified and responsible, all too often one's need to intervene is a matter of one's lack of belief in the right of individuals to manage their own lives. It may come, too, from the helping person's conviction that she is right and therefore has the right and responsibility to impose this rightness on others. Many people convince themselves that a person who is on the outside is less involved than the person seeking help and can therefore see things more clearly. To a limited extent this may be true. Sometimes there is a piece of reality which a person in trouble cannot see and which needs to be clarified. But for the most part it is not that the person to be helped does not see the reality, it is that he does not wish to face it or sees it so plainly that he is overwhelmed by it. He is simply at this time unwilling or unready to accept an alternative course of action, and unless we really do have the right and the responsibility to force him to do so and the skill to do this, we may be simply infringing on his rights to live as he sees fit and in the way he wishes to do so.

It is not hard, however, for a person with a strong moral code of her own, or for one who believes herself to be some kind of expert in social

32

work, psychology or sociology, to find some mandate to intervene in such a situation and to insist that she is acting from a wholly laudable sense of responsibility. Then, when she meets resistance, she attempts to push it aside. Not only does she usually fail to help in such a situation; in a sense, she poisons the ground. She controls rather than helps and forces the person she is helping to throw up all of his defenses against any real change, and she often makes it more difficult for that person ever to take more constructive help.

Actual physical "asking" for help is therefore not necessary, although it is generally helpful and makes a good starting point. One social agency uses an application form even for the kind of help one generally thinks of as being wholly unasked, the help offered to a neglecting parent who is facing as an alternative to taking help the removal of his child from his home. The recognition that this is help and that one can refuse it, if only at considerable cost, is a way of coming to terms with its difficulties. But readiness for help before it can be effectively given is a necessity. Help in the long run cannot be given. It can only be made possible.

CHAPTER 3

Choosing to Do Something about It

He Who Complies against His Will

It is perfectly possible, up to a certain point, to control the actions of another. People can be frightened, browbeaten, tricked, cajoled, gently persuaded, or argued into actions which will make them more acceptable to society. They may thereby become more comfortable for the time being in their daily lives and even apparently more at peace with themselves. Accounts of brainwashing and subliminal advertising have made clear how easily opinions and certain kinds of choices can be influenced. Hypnotism makes it clear that this is not entirely a conscious process, although it is generally held that the hypnotist cannot command behavior that is in conflict with what is rather loosely thought of as a person's "essential nature."

Sometimes, perhaps, it may be necessary to cajole, browbeat, or gently persuade someone to a course of action that will for the moment ease his situation, or avert an obvious danger, before he can be helped in another way. These situations are, however, rarer than they might seem and often arise not from the real need of the person being helped but from the unwillingness of the helper to bear the helped person's situation or to risk the mistakes her clients may make in the course of her attempts to deal with it.

Nor are commands, suggestions, persuasion, or even punishment entirely ineffectual means of helping a person who is ready to accept them, as we know in the upbringing of children, when the right of the parent to this kind of control has been accepted by the child. It is only when they are relied on in the absence of any readiness to make use of them that they prove to be barren, leading to no lasting change, to be self-defeating or actually harmful. It is at this point that we find "backslidings" — the helped person who "behaves beautifully" as long as the helper stays with him but then reverts to his former behavior when she leaves, as well as the person whose efforts always seem to misfire since unconsciously he is resisting plans made for him, and the person who reacts against what he has been expected to do and ends up in a state of rebellion. To no small extent it is true that

34

He who complies against his will
Is of the same opinion still.

[handwritten: We want one thing but also want it's opposite →]

Ambivalence

To understand why this statement is true, and the need for one or more acts of will on the part of the helped person before help can result in significant growth or change, we need to consider a phenomenon generally accepted in all psychological theory known as ambivalence. Ambivalence, literally "valuing both," means simply that all human emotions are a mixture of pleasure and pain, of positive and negative, of wanting and not wanting.

To say that someone is ambivalent is another way of saying that there is always a price to pay for all human experience. Every emotion or desire contains to some degree its opposite. It is not possible, for instance, wholly to love another person without at the same time sometimes feeling angry with that person for what this love is costing the lover, a fact that would make a lot of parents much more comfortable if they would only believe it. Nor is any but the most trivial decision an unhesitating one. There is always the other side to the question, the other possible choice, the other potential advantage lost because we have chosen to do this rather than that. *[handwritten: "what if"]*

It is not hard to see this principle operating in almost everything we may do. To go on a vacation, for instance, may seem entirely pleasurable. But the predominant positive feeling is still counterbalanced to some extent by the knowledge of the work accumulating on one's desk, or regret that one will not be involved in some decision that will be made in one's absence.

Normally this mild ambivalence presents little problem. Either the balance is very clearly on one side or the other, and we have little difficulty both in making up our mind and in living with our decision after it has been made, or the depth of emotion involved is trivial, in which case it hardly matters what we decide. Ambivalence is still present but can be easily accepted. But when the issues are large ones and, as they sometimes are, complicated and often nebulous, and the two sides of the question more or less evenly balanced, ambivalence may result in one of two conditions that may inhibit growth.

Either one can become paralyzed by one's ambivalence, so that one does nothing at all, or one may try to escape the choice by making a second kind of "nonchoice," a choosing of something that is not there, as a way around the problem. The first often gives the impression of stupidity, particularly in the word's true sense of being in a stupor. One

35

either obstinately continues in a course which will obviously lead to disaster, or one vacillates between the two possible courses and, in one's own words, "doesn't know which way to turn." The second leads to a fantasy life which becomes progressively less satisfying and cuts one off from making any constructive choice at all.

One normally thinks of such ambivalence as operating in what might be called "big" decisions, such as whether to enter into or terminate a marriage or whether to try to overcome a habit that one knows to be injurious. But often the actual decision that has to be made is apparently a small one. It is what the decision symbolizes, the feelings it arouses, that produces the paralysis or the escape. I know a woman whose mother once gave her a table not knowing that it was veneered rather than solid wood. I have rarely seen anyone suffer more over an apparently little matter than this woman did for ten days as she decided whether to let her mother know that the table was not what it seemed. On the one hand was a deep reluctance to appear ungrateful and to hurt her mother's feelings, complicated by a feeling that she had not always been as appreciative a daughter as she might have been; on the other was the recognition that she would have to live with the table for the rest of her life and a real reluctance to do so with a sham. This kept her awake for several nights and brought other projects to a standstill until the choice to risk being misunderstood by her mother was made—a choice which resulted, as so many similar ones do, in the solution of the problem, her mother wanting just as much as she did the table to be the real thing.

It is therefore out of ambivalence that people need to choose their way, and it could be said that the whole purpose of a helping relationship is to maximize the chance that this can be done. In terms of the four reactions we touched on in chapter 2, this process involves the passing from a condition of nonchoice (evasion of reality or being overwhelmed by the problem) to one of choice (accepting and using a situation or struggling against it).

Selective or Alternative Choice

Before we accept this statement too literally, we need to be very careful that we understand what we mean by the word "choice." It is misunderstanding of the nature of choice, both on the part of professional helpers and those who observe their practice, which has led to theories of extreme permissiveness both in helping and in education and has convinced many people that those who pretend to expertise in helping others are both unrealistic and amoral. Permissiveness may have its part in helping, particularly when the helped person's experience up to

Having the ability to choose is liberating but also holds grave responsibility as it often determines future outcomes for our selves and others

that time has been one of too great restriction, but this is in fact a side issue and has nothing to do with the kind of choice that is necessary in the helping process.

We use the word "choice" in ordinary speech in two different ways. One has to do with the selection of alternatives. I choose to wear a green or a blue tie. I choose to go for a walk or to stay home to read a book. I choose where I will live and the kind of job that I will do.

This kind of freedom to choose is undoubtedly both pleasant and in many respects conducive to a full life. It is the particular pride of democratic countries. In the early days of psychiatrically oriented social work this belief in freedom of choice was erected into a principle called "client self-determination," which was partly political (a belief that one person did not have the right to control another) and partly theoretical, stemming from Freud's early emphasis on the dangers of repression and a Rousseauistic belief that a person's own decisions about his or her affairs were more likely to be of value than the judgments of society.[1] Psychologically it lived in rather an uneasy relationship with early Freudian psychic determinism. It was thought of as at one and the same time inevitable (Bertha Reynolds once said that "it is no longer a question of whether it is *wrong* to try to make our fellow beings think and feel as we want them to. In the long run it is simply silly. The vital needs of their being will in the end determine what they shall feel and how they shall act"[2]) and, curiously enough, as a right that could be granted or withheld by the helping person.[3]

Later Helen Harris Perlman showed that much of this self-determination is an illusion.[4] Humans are much too much social creatures to be able to exercise any significant amount of self-determination. As Perlman pointed out, tradition and culture as well as law limit many of their choices. They are free, she says, to choose between ham and sausage for breakfast, but, for practical purposes they cannot elect instead caviar or gin. Yet, she points out, the little bit of self-determination left to people is tremendously important to preserve. It would be intolerable if it were thought right and proper to restrict even further, more than was absolutely necessary and without some showing of one's right to do so, the small amount of self-determination of this kind that people actually enjoy.

Commitment or Active and Willing Choice

The second meaning of choice has to do with much more than the selection of alternatives. It involves the whole of one's person, one's total reaction to a situation, and always includes a willingness to act on the choice that one has made.

37

Possibly the single word which expresses its essential quality most close-ly is "commitment," and yet, although active and willing choice may in-volve commitment in its positive aspect, it still remains a choice. Com-mitment is the choice to get well or to remain ill, to do something con-structive or even destructive about one's problem, to deal with one's cir-cumstances rather than let them overwhelm one.

There are a number of things to grasp about this kind of choice. First is perhaps that it bears little relationship to the amount of alternative choice that is available. A prisoner in jail has little opportunity for selec-tive choice. Prisoners cannot choose where to live, what to wear, what to eat, or what work to do. But they do have one very important choice to make. They can decide whether to make use of their imprisonment, which might be by learning a trade or even deciding to act somewhat differently in the future. They can choose to struggle against imprison-ment, perhaps by planning to break out or by getting their case reopened and proving their innocence. Or they can make a nonchoice and spend their time in daydreaming or be utterly crushed and embittered by the experience. Indeed one of the rather curious qualities of this kind of choice is that it seems to require some limitation of selective choice to become fully operative. Anita Faatz, whose analysis of choice in the casework process first drew attention to its special nature, says: "But to a degree far greater than we are usually willing to admit, and to an ex-tent that we are fearful to concede, the crisis in the helping process is more truthfully described as a process of helping the client achieve a new relation to the *inevitable*, instead of uncovering constantly new sour-ces of choice."[5]

This does not mean, let us hasten to say, that in order to enable ac-tive and willing choice one needs to restrict the area of alternative choice. The normal conditions of life do that quite adequately. And indeed, there is some evidence that in order for anyone to be able to make an active and willing choice (as opposed to a nonchoice) there must have been some experience in making alternative choices. The person with no ex-perience of choosing anything cannot as a rule choose actively and will-ingly, too. What is not necessary, and indeed is sometimes harmful, is too wide a range of alternative choices without the capacity to make them except impulsively.

There is a relationship between the two kinds of choices that does need to be recognized. Alternative choice may appear often to be moral-ly or emotionally neutral. To wear a green tie or an orange tie—what does it matter, except to satisfy a whim? But if the orange tie is worn in Dublin on St. Patrick's Day, or is chosen to please one's wife despite

38

being wholly out of fashion, the choice involved may be an active and willing one. It might be said, then, that alternative choice may in some instances be conditioned by active and willing choice, or be symbolic of it. Or it may mean very little at all.

What Faatz is saying is that active and willing choice must be made in real conditions, and not in an unreal world in which there is illusory freedom of choice, or in which the choice made will not result in natural consequences. It has also been shown over and over again that it is extremely helpful if the real conditions limiting selective choice—the law, the function of an agency, the "rules" of a service, the authority invested in a teacher or administrator—are explicit and inevitable in the sense that neither the helper nor the helped have the power to change them.

I have used the words "accept and use" to express active and willing choice in its positive aspect. People "accept" a situation, in the sense of recognizing its inevitability, and cease to struggle against it. But if they did this alone, if they simply accepted it as inevitable and made no use of it, they would not be making a choice—hence the doublet.

There Must Really Be a Choice

The second characteristic of active and willing choice is that it must really be a choice, in the alternative sense as well as an active and willing one. This may seem to deny all we have said about the difference between these two kinds of choices, but it does seem necessary to state that a choice cannot be a choice unless there are at least two things from which to choose. Many writers, and all too many practitioners, appear to be so impressed with the importance of "accepting and using" that they lose sight of the fact that one cannot assert a positive unless it is also possible for one to choose the negative in its stead. There is, and there must be, a choice between accepting and using the situation and struggling against it, or even resolutely refusing to do anything about it. There must be choice, too, in the ways one accepts and uses or struggles.

We can see this theoretically when we recognize that the one person who cannot sincerely affirm a "yes" is a yes-man, because such a person cannot say "no." We can see it if we realize that to risk something is in a sense to choose the possibility of it happening and then consider the plight of people who cannot "risk" or "choose" death by putting themselves in any situation in which they could possibly be killed. Such people could not cross a street or drive a car. They would be unable to "live" to any extent. One can only assert a positive if the negative is also possible.

The very concept of goodness itself presupposes the possible choice not to be good.

Yet one of the major weaknesses of a great deal of help offered today is that it does not offer a real opportunity for choice. It presupposes the positive, that is, the socially sanctioned or acceptable choice, and, by doing so, robs this very answer of much of its strength. The attempt to make someone good, however rationalized in terms of "influence" or "persuasion," is effective only where in actual fact the choice to be good has already been made.

From that point on the character-building agency has much to give. It is often less effective with the child who is not committed to good, which is one of the reasons why those agencies that express conventional middle-class "goods" find such difficulties in the ghettos.

And let it be said now that "to influence" and "to persuade" (in the sense of appeal to with moral overtones) are just as strong verbs as "to make" or "to command." There seems to be an illusion that somehow people are left freer to make their own decisions if they are persuaded or influenced rather than "made to" or "commanded," but in fact almost the opposite is true. If I am commanded or made to do something, I can at least identify the force that is being brought to bear. If necessary, I can rebel. But if the force being brought to bear is moral suasion or influence, I may either not realize that I am being controlled or find myself in the position of not being able to disagree without challenging the whole value system of the person trying to influence me. When I was young, a powerful relative would always end an argument with, "But it's God's will, my dear." Persuasion and influence are no less forceful than a direct command. They are only more subtle and, often, bitterly unfair.

The difficulty, of course, with allowing a real choice is that we so much want people to make what we think of as a positive choice that we do not dare risk the possibility of their making what seems to us a negative one. Even the possibility of their doing so often feels like treason. This is particularly so when we are very sure ourselves of what the positive is and are much committed to it. Churches perhaps make this mistake more often than any other body, but they are far from being alone in doing so. Schools, juvenile courts, child protective societies, and even other agencies who have learned to value growth and change often cannot bear to see their clients choose wrongly. They feel a responsibility to see that they choose correctly.

Sometimes we forget how difficult it is to know what is right for another person. It is no disparagement of a general good to say that it may be impossible for another to choose it at this time. It may even be quite in-

we do not want others to make a "bad" choice, so we try and "persuade" them toward one that is positive

appropriate to his need. This is the frequent mistake made by those who, recognizing, for instance, that probation is "better" than prison or reform school, which is in fact generally so, will not permit a probationer to choose to break his probation. I have seen a teenage girl commit a serious delinquency for the sole purpose of convincing her wooly-minded and idealistic probation officer to send her somewhere where she would be protected from the impulses she could not handle on probation. In fact to prescribe for another what choices he can or cannot make, except in very general terms or for his immediate protection, is a form of presumption. And this is true whether the criteria used are moral or psychological—whether we tell a person we are helping that he is not free to sin or that he may not remain unadjusted.

Positive and Negative Choice

To identify "positive" with the accepting and using choice and "negative" with the choice to rebel is possible only if these words do not carry an implication that the "positive" choice is always better. While in general this may be so, there are clearly situations in which the opposite is true. If one is sinking in a quagmire, one does not accept the situation. One struggles to get out. Rebels are necessary to society, and where there is social injustice or repression, the "negative" choice is much more positive than the "positive." The words should therefore be freed from any moral connotations and should be understood much as they are in electronics, as indicating moving toward or away from accepting and using the situation.

Many people need to make a negative choice, in perhaps both meanings of the word, before they can make a positive one. Often the negative has to be tried out first to see, as it were, where it leads. One of the most successful pieces of helping I have ever seen recorded was of a puritanical, suspicious grandmother, full of fear of her granddaughter's puberty, haunted by the knowledge that her daughter, the child's mother, had gone wrong and inclined to blame her own leniency for this, and yet caught up in her love and pity for the child and a longing to be reconciled with the daughter she could not forgive. This woman ended by recognizing her own part in the story with the rather dramatic statement, "I'm not hardhearted, only hardheaded, I declare," and was able to enter into a much more understanding and warm relationship with both daughter and granddaughter.

Yet, after the first interview, in which she came to understand that no one could or would reform her granddaughter for her, she tried to solve her own problem the next time the child disobeyed her by marching her down to the cellar and taking the carpet beater to her. It was only in reliving this experience with her caseworker that she was able to make the choice to face and to allow to develop her real love and warmth for the child.

Whaling a thirteen-year-old girl for a minor disobedience is not generally thought of as a positive act and was clearly contrary to the values of the child welfare worker who was trying to help this woman. She could quite easily have used the incident to lecture the grandmother, to make her feel guilty, even to give up trying to help her anymore. The result of such a response, with a woman whose culture approved rigidity rather than leniency, would as likely as not have been even more severe beatings, if only to prove the worker's censure wrong. And if they were severe enough, no doubt the beatings would have solved the immediate problem of the child's rebellion, although not the grandmother's unhappiness nor the real problem of the relationship. But when the grandmother told the story, the worker recognized in it the woman's first real attempt to find a solution for herself and a step toward getting well. Her exploration with her of what the experience meant to her and how desperate she must have felt was what led to her ability to change.

A person who makes a negative choice is much nearer making a positive one than the person who makes none. And this perhaps calls for some clarification of what we mean by a negative choice. A negative choice is never the nonchoice, the decision, if it can be called one, to remain in ambivalence or to escape into fantasy. That kind of nonchoice is utterly defeating. It is, incidentally, what a helped person goes through when he is put under pressure to make a positive choice and cannot do so. It is what we mean by failure. It is static and leads nowhere.

Negative choice is, on the other hand, dynamic. It is the resolution to alter the situation, to do without help, "to go it alone," to fight, to do things in antisocial and unapproved ways. And if it is real negative choice, and not a blind impulse of rage — though the two are sometimes hard to distinguish — it involves a willingness to accept the consequences of one's acts. When we say that negative choice must be permitted, we do not mean what the "permissivists" so often seem to mean by free choice — that negative acts may be indulged in with some sort of guarantee that they will not result in unpleasantness in return.

Within the helping relationship itself expression of anger, or negative choice, may not carry unpleasant consequences. This freedom to express negative feelings is necessary because the helping person must permit it to be experienced. Moreover, if she is concerned with the person she is trying to help, and not with her own feelings, she is not hurt by the helped person's anger or criticism and has no need to retaliate or punish. She may even wish to set up opportunities for the helped person to express negative feelings in a safe environment, as the play therapist does with dolls a child is permitted to torture. But where the negative choice is exercised in the real world, the client must take responsibility for his choice. He cannot be protected against the consequences of his act.

What is often not recognized is how close a person who makes a negative choice is to making a positive one. Those who care for children in Children's Homes, for instance, have long discovered that it is the rebellious child who gave them the most trouble who often comes back ten years later to express his sincere gratitude for what was done for him, while the conforming child who does this is rarer. Some of the world's greatest sinners — Saul of Tarsus and Augustine of Hippo — have become the world's greatest saints. The opposite of love is not hate. It is indifference. Hate and love are very close to each other, as we might expect if we understood the ubiquity of ambivalence. As the old popular song has it, "I hate you because I love you, and I love you because I hate you." A large proportion of murders are of persons to whom the murderer is related in a love-hate relationship — husbands, wives, and sweethearts — and to hate someone it is necessary to care about what they do.

The Right to Fail

Failure = making no choice

The distinction between negative choice and nonchoice can perhaps be seen more clearly when we consider failure. Failure is, as we have said, what happens when one is incapable of making a positive choice. It is also, curiously enough, what happens when we cannot make a negative choice either. I learned this some years ago when I was academic adviser to a young woman who had been a brilliant student in high school but was now, in college, inexplicably failing her work. She felt entirely miserable and unable to account for her bad grades. She was working hard, but nothing ever seemed to come out right. I feared that she might be ill, either physically or emotionally, and was able to help her decide to go to the student health service. There she talked to a psychologist. A week later she was back in my office with her head held high, obviously quite a different person. She had decided to quit school and to go back home to be married. She felt this to be the right decision. Previously she had given in to her father's expectation of her, although, as she emphasized, she had agreed and thought that she really wanted a college education and, even, postponement of marriage. Indeed, she said that coming to college had been in part her idea, to escape from her boyfriend's importunity as well as to please her parents. Now she was

43

able to face her parents' disappointment because she had decided that she was now grown up and had a right to run her own life.[6]

To her parents, at least at first, this was a negative decision. Many a university teacher would, too, have seen the problem as one of helping the young woman succeed in her courses. The psychologist, however, knew that the more important problem was whether she really could or wanted to succeed and helped her to see that apparent failure was actually a victory for her.

An active and willing choice can only be made by the helped person himself. It is an intensely personal thing and involves much more than the conscious self. It cannot therefore be brought about by argument or persuasion, although a logical consideration of alternatives may have a small part to play in it. It is sometimes in facing the logic of a situation that feeling becomes crystallized; as often, however, logic has nothing to do with it. Such a choice often occurs at the darkest, most confused moment when one is faced with apparent defeat, and, as such, it is not unlike Kierkegaard's "leap in the dark." But the insistence that it cannot be made by any other than the helped person himself has nothing to do with permissiveness or with a moral or political theory of self-determination. It is a simple fact.

Risking the Wrong Decision

That to help involves risk, both that help may not be taken and that the outcome may be entirely different from what the helped person planned, is a corollary of this fact. Kenneth Pray once said of the casework process that the worker, with all her knowledge, cannot determine — cannot even predict — the outcome.[7] There are, of course, ways of both predicting and ensuring limited or temporary goals that have to do more with adaptation than with growth and change, chief of which are careful diagnosis and treatment, but these are control processes which have relevance only in the context of the major choice, and as such are often subjected to strange surprises.

The most unlikely people prove capable of accepting help and doing something about their problems; equally unlikely people who appear destined to succeed unaccountably make a mess of it. The happiest, most poised and competent child I ever met came from a background so disorganized, so loveless, and so culturally deprived that it appeared impossible to find any hope or light in it; was herself of low mentality judged by any objective test; and had been subjected to about the worst set of child welfare procedures and placements it is possible to imagine. While it is possible that the many social workers and psychiatrists who at some

44

time worked with the child missed some important diagnostic fact, this fact must certainly have been one whose significance is as yet unknown to either of these professions. Indeed, if we knew why some people are able to use disaster and suffering to strengthen their hold on life and others respond to the very same stimuli with apathy or evasion, much of our problem would be solved. Perhaps there is some factor that we have not identified. Why some young people flourished and others "went into a decline" was not understood until the discovery of Koch's bacillus. Many forms of depression are now treated chemically. Possibly the difference between those who can turn apparent defeat into victory and those who cannot is the final human mystery to which no answer will ever be found. All we can do at the moment is to create the kind of conditions that have proved on the whole most favorable for victory rather than for defeat.

Some would object that Kierkegaard's "leap in the dark" is as likely to land one in the lap of the devil as it is in the hands of God. In a sense this is true of the kind of choice we are discussing. I do not know how Kierkegaard answered the objection, but I presume that he must have considered that it was more likely that one would find God than the devil. The same, I think, has to be assumed about choice. People, if freed to make willing choices, generally choose the good. If they did not, helping would be a purposeless business. One does have to assume that human beings have in them some natural tendency to maturity of some sort, to be able to cope, to come out on top and solve their problems, just as they have in them a tendency to grow physically and mentally.[8]

The Turning Point

There is one more characteristic of what we have called active or willing choice that is worthy of note, and that is its repetitive nature. We have spoken of an act of choice as if it were a single act at a certain moment of time which settled once and for all the helped person's problem, and there is some reason to do so. There is often a moment of crisis at which the decision appears to be made. This turning point can be identified with extraordinary preciseness in some situations. In a carefully structured helping process it can almost be predicted as likely to occur at a certain stage in time. Anita Faatz goes so far as to write: "No matter what the service, no matter how it begins, whether voluntarily or otherwise . . . there is but one crucial moment of time that matters, and this is the moment in which the self chooses between growth and refusal of growth, life or the negation of life; when the organism, in short, chooses to live and turns its energies from the negative fight against what is to the vibrant immediacy of what it can do, no matter."[9]

We can recognize the same kind of phenomenon in some religious experiences. But here we have not only learned to mistrust the conversion that is apparently too wholehearted and too complete; we are aware that the decision has to be reaffirmed again and again, and we also recognize genuine conversions that take place more or less imperceptibly. Similarly, in the helping process the decision is made again and again, as Faatz explains when in her somewhat mystical language she says of the "moment" of which she writes that it is "as well a moment which recurs again and again, never to be wholly settled or determined, but in constant process of becoming, as is the life process itself."[10]

There is also the problem that the initial choice is made in a particular context — in this case the helping situation — but the effects of the decision have to be carried out in a wider or a different field. The person being helped by another must carry out his decision in the wider sphere of all his relationships. There is a constant need both for new affirmations and for reaffirmations which have to do with doing as well as with feeling. Both stem from the original choice, but to some extent this choice has to be made again and again. The one thing which we can be sure of is that by virtue of its having been made once, it will be more possible to make the tenth and even the thousandth time.

Nothing that we have said, however, should lead us to the conclusion that, because this choice is a highly individual matter and can only be made by the person directly concerned, all the helping person needs to do is to leave the helped person free to make it. Nothing is more cruel or less productive than to tell someone that the choice is his and, so to speak, to tell him to go into a corner and decide. If that were possible, he would have done it long ago.

Our job is not to make the choice for him. We cannot do this in any case. But it is our job to provide him with a medium, a situation, and an experience in which a choice is possible, in which the fears that beset him can to some extent be resolved, in which he can find the courage to commit himself one way or the other, and, maybe, the practical tools that will enable him to put his commitment into action. This medium is what we call "the helping relationship," the major characteristics of which are explored in chapter 4.

46

CHAPTER 4

The Helping Relationship

A Meeting of Two People

The medium which is offered to a person in trouble through which he is given the opportunity to make choices, both about taking help and the use he will make of it, is a relationship with a helping person. The helper may be a professional or a friend sought out for advice. She may be someone expressly provided for this service, as is a probation officer, or someone in a position of authority which involves functions other than helping, such as a supervisor or parent. She may on the other hand be sought out because of her knowledge or position, as a physician or a minister, or simply be someone believed at the moment to be able to offer something. But in one way or another an encounter takes place and a relationship begins.

This relationship, if it is to be helpful, has as its primary purpose the enabling of what we have called active and willing choice, although it may also be directed toward the offering of a specific kind of help—money, or physical assistance, or advice. If it is to do either or both successfully, it must have certain characteristics, some of which will be readily apparent from our discussion up until now. That these concepts overlap will be evident; nevertheless, each is perhaps necessary to understand the whole.

Mutual

It may seem unnecessary to begin by saying that its most important characteristic is that it is a *mutual and not a one-way relationship.* There are things which the helped person brings to it and things which are brought by the person offering help, and its success or failure may depend as much on the latter as the former. Yet this fact, as we have seen, is by no means general knowledge, and if things go wrong the natural tendency of the helper is to place all the blame on the helped person. While taking help is hard, giving it successfully is also difficult. It requires, as we have said, self-knowledge and self-discipline, as well as some knowledge of the principles of helping.

47

Not Necessarily Pleasant or an End in Itself

A second characteristic of the helping relationship, which is indeed part of its difficulty, since none of us likes to be anything but loved and respected and often expect to get out of helping something of this feeling, is that this relationship is *not necessarily consistently pleasant or friendly.* While there must be some sense of working together on a problem, and although in the end there is usually something that might be called trust in the relationship, even this is not always so. Sometimes real moving takes place in anger and reaction.

This is well illustrated in Glasser's *Reality Therapy*, where his refusal to accept his delinquent girls' excuses and rationalizations often provoked anger that helped the children come to terms with their problems.[1] It is quite obvious in many child-parent relationships, even in the punishment that "clears the air."

The attempt to keep the relationship on a pleasant level is one of the greatest sources of ineffectual helping known. It results in insincerities; in attempts to please the helper; in staying exactly where one is, or deepening a pattern of evasion; in overdependence; and in actions taken without any real readiness for them.

A mistaken understanding of the hesitancy with which most people approach an offer of help, coupled, perhaps, with a realization of how powerful a force "liking" and trust are in inducing change once it has really begun, has given rise to the all too common concept that no helping can take place until something called "rapport" has been established. Helpers sometimes spend much time in making friends with people before they get down to business with them. They give children treats or tell them stories "to establish a good relationship" with them. But the kind of relationship that is bought in this way is not the kind of relationship on which true helping is based. It is often nothing more than a protection to the helper from having to take the full impact of the helped person's struggle. The child, for instance, who cheerfully goes with the nice social worker to a foster home all too often is prevented by the worker's very niceness from expressing and coming to grips with his doubt and despair. He has in fact been disarmed, deprived of his natural weapons to deal with his problem. He has been snowed into accepting something for which he is not prepared.

Aristotle once said that if one pursued happiness, one was unlikely to find it, a statement that can easily be verified at Miami Beach or any other large resort. Happiness, Aristotle upheld, is the result of what he called a "virtuous" life — that is, an engaged and active participation in affairs. The same can be said about a relationship. Seek it as a goal in

48

itself and generally it will elude one. But a relationship will grow wherever one person demonstrates to another both by her actions and her words that she respects the other, that she has concern for him and cares what happens to him, and that she is willing both to listen and to act helpfully. This is the kind of relationship on which helping is based, and it cannot be manufactured. It begins at the moment that any two people meet. It grows as they work together, but it cannot be forced or hurried.

Another effect of the belief that the helping relationship must be a pleasant one is the fear that some helpers have that the relation will be damaged if they are forced in any way to do what the client will not like--reduce his assistance grant, tell him something he does not want to hear, impose any conditions on him, or make an unfavorable report to some other person. This is particularly common where a social worker must bring a client to court. Instead of being honest with the client about what has been found and helping him face what is likely to happen to him, the social worker all too often virtually pretends that she has had nothing to do with the matter, that any unpleasantness is somebody else's fault, even that she is secretly "on the client's side" against the judge and would, if she could, help the client to evade the court's decree. This approach is not only plainly dishonest but encourages the client in a non-choice and robs him of his ability to do something about his predicament. It involves indulging him exactly as one might spoil a child and, moreover, treating him like a child. It is also one of the things that give the impression that helping people are amoral, that they condone bad behavior rather than, as they actually do, feel for the person who has not been able to do what he should but recognize with him clearly that he needs to do something different.

A relationship that can be destroyed when the helping person has to be firm, or honest, or obey the law, or hold the helped person to the real situation as it exists is a relationship built on false premises. It is not worth preserving, and the attempt to do so at the cost of honesty only perpetuates something that is meaningless in the first place. Laws that insist that a social worker's report to a court should be confidential and concealed from the client are based on a false concept of the helping relationship and are very bad law, since they deprive the client of his right to know the basis for the decision that is to be made about him.

The search for a good relationship has in it another danger, too. It ignores the fact that relationship begins the moment helped person and helper meet. The helped person begins at once to explore the quality of help he will get. He puts out his problem to find out how the helper will react. He struggles to express himself. But if the helper's interest is on the relationship she is building and not on what the helped person is saying, she will miss much of what is being said. I have seen a child struggle to tell her social worker, in five or six different ways, each more desperate than the last, how unhappy she was in a foster home and fail to get through because her social worker was so busy "building relationship" that she could not hear the child.

Most helping relationships become in the course of helping pleasant and friendly, and full of trust. And they cannot be mean, rigid, sadistic, cold, unfeeling, or unconcerned. Concern for the helped person is, and must be, always present. But this concern is what the helper brings. She has no right to expect, in return, agreement, gratitude, or liking. She may and probably will find these in the majority of her encounters. But if she goes out seeking these, she is seeking something for herself, not for the people she is serving. The desire for "good" relationships, rather than for productive ones, can be a major obstacle to one's ability to help.

Feeling as Well as Knowledge

A third characteristic of the helping relationship is, however, that it is *one of feeling as well as of knowledge.* Some would-be helpers, either uncomfortable with feeling, afraid of being drawn too deeply into the helped person's problem, or impressed with a false concept of what it means to be a professional, try to maintain a relationship that is detached, cold, "impartial," or "objective."

The coldly "objective" person betrays by that very word what it is that she does to people. She treats them as objects, people she can study, or manipulate, or make in some way to change. The person who really wants to help is committed to treating people as that part of the operation whose feelings and opinions matter, who will be doing the things which give purpose to the relationship. This is the reason why an objective science *about* people or social conditions can never offer all that is needed to teach how to help people. An objective science works *on* people. The helping process is a method of working *with* them or even being made use of *by* them to find something for themselves. This is what makes it possible for some helping professions to talk of helped people as clients even when the relationship has not been initially sought by them.[2] They truly attempt to serve their client's interests.

The helper, however, who is objective—and this is perhaps a slightly different use of the word—has avoided one obvious pitfall. She has not thrown herself into the situation in a wholly undisciplined way, becoming swayed by every wind of feeling and taking sides either for or against her client. She is not wholly an amateur as I would be, for instance, if I tried to take part in a game of professional football, not knowing what was going on and being pulled out of position by every move of the ball. I need, however, more than a knowledge of the game to be an effective player. I need skill, strength, a sense of anticipation, an ability to be part of a developing movement. Just not to be pulled out of position is at best a negative virtue.

Helping is always a matter of both knowledge and feeling. One cannot do without either. The true professional is at the same time objective and full of feeling--a paradox, perhaps, but nevertheless one true of any true professional in the arts. It takes rigorous practice and hard objective learning to become a great dancer, but the dancer who does not dance with feeling betrays that fact at once.

Helping Must Have the Single Purpose of Facilitating Choice and Action

A fourth characteristic of the helping relationship is that it has a *single purpose* which controls everything that happens within it, that of *facilitation, choice and action*. The defined purpose of this relationship is to help a person, or possibly a group of persons, to make choices about a problem or situation and about the help he or they are willing to take about it. It can be said as simply as that. Yet this is one of the most difficult things to achieve. All too often when we set out to help another, we have all sorts of secondary purposes, conscious or unconscious, in mind, such as satisfying our own conscience, proving some theory, advancing some cause, or showing our skill in helping.

How intrusive such a second purpose can be is not generally recognized. We can all see the obvious cases. If the helper has a need which the relationship is being asked to satisfy, if she needs to control others, or to feel superior to them, or to have them like her, it is not too hard to see how these needs can distort what happens in the relationship. We can also, if we imagine ourselves to be comparatively free of these needs or to be able to keep them under control, stigmatize them as selfish and therefore see that they can have no part in helping. It is not, however, these rather obvious "second purposes" which are the most difficult to control. It is rather our good interests which often get in the way--our desire to be of help, our feeling for justice, our need to try to build a better world, our concern for the honor and dignity of the organization which we represent, or, if our desire to help springs from our religion, our desire to evangelize and spread the gospel. These wholly praiseworthy objectives can distract us from the business at hand and prevent us from listening to what the person we are helping is saying. They all too

51

often shift our concern from the way in which he can come to grips with his problem to what we would like him to do about it.

For several years I taught groups of public welfare workers in short courses in the summer. They made remarkable progress in learning to help people, and in general I was able to observe each year more clients helped in a way that resulted in a radical change in ability to deal with their problems. Only one year was there a regression. This was the year in which the 1962 amendments to the Social Security Act were implemented in part by requiring written social summaries of each client's situation.

Although these summaries had a good purpose and undoubtedly helped workers plan more wisely what could be done to help, the centering of the welfare worker's attention on the possible meaning of this and that fact came between client and worker. The worker became temporarily much less able to hear what the client was telling her about his situation and what he thought he was able to do about it. Opportunities for constructive choice were missed because the helping person's interest was not on what was happening in the here and now, but on some overall picture of the client's total situation. Clients became aware that the worker was no longer responding to what they were trying to tell her but was thinking of something else.

The surprising thing was, however, that when the workers stopped being concerned about their summaries, when they stopped asking questions to try to uncover facts, when they concentrated on what the client was telling them and only tried to compose their summaries after the interview was over, the summaries were fuller and generally much more useful. The clients had actually told them all that they needed to know.

Much the same is true of our concern for justice or morality or for a better world. If we are thinking of these when we are face to face with a person we are trying to help, our attention is on something other than his problem. Unconsciously we are trying to use him to fulfill our purposes and not his. We have abandoned our belief that only he can make a decision that will have real meaning to him. We lose him in our enthusiasm for something which, however important, is not part of his present struggle.

If we can postpone these concerns, at least until he is out of the room, we will in general find that what has happened between him and us has conduced to our other interests, too. If it has not, we are faced with a choice. Which do we really want to do--help this person discover a way of meeting his problem, reform the world, or promote morality? If our interests in the second and third are such that we must restrict our help-

Be in the here and now.

ing to whatever will produce the kind of result we want, then we must recognize that our helping will be of a different kind and perhaps should not be called helping at all. We may quite justifiably desire all three and work on them in different situations, but in the helping situation the client's need must be the sole focus of our concern.

Even more the same pattern is true of our desire to be of help. This desire can be a major trap. It can entice us into doing things for people they can and need to do for themselves. It can make us try to force decision before the helped person is ready for it. It cannot allow people to move toward and away from taking help, as all people need to do, and it is, despite its apparent altruism, basically a need of the helper rather than of the helped person. Just as it could be said that one of the conditions for helping someone come to a positive decision is not to wish it too passionately oneself, so it can be said that one of the conditions under which help can be given must be that the helper does not too passionately wish to give it. This does not mean that she is indifferent or does not care. It means that she cares so much that the help given is real help that she will not insist on it being given when it is inappropriate.

Where Control and Helping Meet: Helping is Not Control

Therefore a fifth characteristic of the helping relationship is that it *helps but does not control.* A difficult situation is apparently created when the helping person has, it might seem, a double loyalty, where she is at one and the same time a helping person and an agent of social control. Social workers are often expected to act in this twofold capacity, and in some fields, such as child protection or probation, it would appear to be inherent in the job. Indeed there is an increasing tendency, in the United States at least, to emphasize the fact that the social worker is employed by the community and not by the individual, and that all social workers are to some extent involved in enforcing the values of the culture. One writer, for instance, believes what is known as the "hard core" or "multiproblem" family requires in order that any change be made is that the worker sees herself and behaves "as the instrument of social control and social change" although not "the personal embodiment of the 'right' attitudes and values." She becomes to her client "the ego-ideal, the personification of the core-culture."[3]

It should be apparent at once that this writer is not concerned so much with a helping process as he is with one of control. Are, then, such social agencies instruments, primarily, of control rather than of help? Is there a place in them for the helping process?

social control... but, it should NOT dominate our motives to help.

→ we cannot discount the importance

There is no doubt that a good deal of most constructive help, as opposed to control, is offered by social workers who work in what might be thought of as "social control" agencies, and, as we have already made clear, the kind of choice with which help is concerned is not dependent on freedom from social restraints. But, if the social worker is also concerned with implementing these restraints, does not the interview have exactly the kind of double purpose we have said that it cannot have?

It would be useless to try to escape this question by asserting that this is a book on helping and not on social casework, since social casework obviously includes a helping function, and our statement is that helping must be the sole purpose of the helper-helped relationship. Nor can we take refuge in the assumption, often made by those who are unhappy about the apparent authority involved in some social casework roles, that a person "really wants," in being helped, to do what society wants him to do.[4] While this is sometimes true, it is obviously not always so. It also introduces two assumptions that we have been at considerable pains to discount — that there is something that a person "really" wants that is different from what he sees as the solution to his problem in the present, and that the solution to human problems is more or less limited to adaptation to social demands.

It would be even worse to suggest that the help given by agencies with social control functions is in some sense not "real," since by every criterion we can establish for real help — change of attitude, clarity, decisiveness, and ability to translate choice into action — some of the help given by these agencies is the most "real" of all. One of the best helping agencies I know is a woman's prison, another a juvenile court. It might be said, based on experience, that the limitations imposed on the client by the apparent other purposes of these agencies are important factors in the help they give.

Yet to have another purpose in the helping relationship does in fact do all we have said. It does distract. In trying, as it were, to kill two birds with one stone, we all too often miss them both.

✗ The solution to this apparent paradox lies in a more careful examination of to whom this other purpose belongs. It is the law, or the agency empowered in some way to enforce the demands of society, and not the helping person herself who has this purpose and creates, or makes apparent, a reality which is outside both helper and helped. It is not I who demand that you should do this or that. It is the law, or the organization which I represent. I may in fact agree with it and probably do in general, since this is where I work; but this is incidental, and my business with you is the undivided one of helping you make decisions in relation to this reality. You may decide to deny it or to struggle against it, but if so, there are consequences, which I did not create and which you will have to cope with. Ultimately the choice is yours.

This distinction may be difficult. Yet it is very important. The function of the helper is not to maintain the control but to help the offender come to terms with the reality of what society expects of him. This is in part what we mean when we say that ours is a rule of law and not of persons. It is not I who tell you that you must not neglect your children, or get drunk, or cheat your neighbor. It is the law. Even the moral law is not of my fashioning, however much I accept it as binding on me. It is something outside both of us which as a helper I can help you look at and choose or deny with as much clarity as I can. If you deny it, then there are consequences, which I will try to help you see.

In some situations the same person may be responsible both for helping and for setting the conditions which the law, or some other expectation, will demand of a person. A judge may be in this situation. So may a teacher, who wants to help a student but still must require a certain performance if the course is to be passed. A business executive may want to help a worker, but cannot permit inefficiency. These people are not prevented from offering help, as long as they are able to disassociate their two roles. What the law, or the course, demands must remain a given, a reality which, in her helping role, the very person responsible for its interpretation can help the other look at and accept or struggle against. This can be done.

It is not easy. It requires a willingness on the part of the helper to be undefensive about the authority she has, to admit, even, that she may be wrong, but that this is where she stands in a situation. It may, and sometimes should, include helping the person helped to change the law or the regulation which the helper represents, to appeal and to present his case. But for the moment this is the law and my interpretation of it. I can understand how hard this may be to you but I cannot do anything else but hold to it at this time.

An Encounter in the Here and Now

The importance of identifying one's role as a helper, and disassociating it from other roles, such as preacher, reformer, teacher, researcher, or executive, focuses attention on the helping situation itself — the actual meeting between two persons or groups. One of the important things to realize about it is that it is limited in time and space. Although the helping that takes place in it may affect the helped person's whole life, a sixth

Some help requires clients to adhere directly to the law

55

characteristic of the helping encounter is that it *takes place in the here and now.*

Two or more people come together, at a certain place, at a certain time, for a certain purpose, and under certain conditions. What they say, or refrain from saying, and still more what they feel, is often as much conditioned by the particular situation as by their wider problems. The person who tells you of his marital problems is as much concerned, at that moment, with how you will react as he is with his struggle at home.

He has, in fact, a double problem. He has to be concerned not only with the problem for which he wants help, but with the problem of getting help. And often the second problem may take precedence, temporarily, over the first. Thus a person in trouble may float "trial balloons," or try flattery, or test the helper to see if she really means what she has said. What he says about himself will almost certainly be distorted, not necessarily deliberately, but by the very fact that he is sharing something with another.

The process is a very natural one. All of us, in all our contacts with people, care about what others think of us. All of us care, indeed, what we think about ourselves. We create what is known in politics or business as an "image." Moreover, we use this image to try to manipulate others. It may be an image of strength or one of helplessness or despair. It may be of rectitude or nonchalance. Whatever it is, it is our protection against being fully known by another – that almost ultimate threat – as well as the way we have found to deal with others.

In one sense it could be said that no real helping can take place until the image is dispelled and the real self can be shared. But it cannot be abruptly broken. It must be yielded bit by bit, explored, found unnecessary. And always some of it will be there. Indeed the kind of image that a person projects tells us a good deal about the kind of problem he has and how he goes about solving his problems.

The image a person projects indicates the way he is trying to get help, or to ward it off, or to limit it to what is acceptable to him. And since in order to be helped one first has to make a decision about taking help at all, what he is saying and doing is, so far from being irrelevant, the very material of which help will have to be built.

It is important, therefore, that the helper is aware of what is happening in the here and now. She cannot accept what the helped person says solely as bits of information to be stored for future use, as those who try to follow too strict a system of diagnosis and treatment soon find out. Not only what is said is important, but why and when and, obviously, how. One of the most neglected questions in helping is, "Why are you

56

telling me this now?" and this question may need three different emphases: Why are you telling *me* this now? Why are you telling me *this* now? and Why are you telling me this *now*?

The same is also true of what the helper says and does. Not only does the helper have her own image to project, but what the helped person says or does not say may be a direct reaction to what the helper says or does. That is why an account of an interview needs to be so much more than a collection of facts about the client or his problem if it is to be fully understood. It must contain what both helped and helper said and did.

Conditions and Limits for Help

A seventh characteristic of the helping relationship is that it has conditions and limits. The "here-and-nowness" of the helping relationship means also that it can be separated out of a person's total experience and given special artificial characteristics of its own. In a sense this may seem to be impossible: both helper and helped bring to the relationship the whole of their past life experience simply by being there, and its repercussions may affect the whole of the helped person's life. But it does exist as a special occasion, and this gives the helper, or the organization for which she works, the opportunity to set certain conditions that may help both helper and helped focus on what needs to be done.

Among these conditions is time, much used by clinical social workers who offer severely time-limited sessions or time-limited courses of treatment. There is nothing so frightening or debilitating as unlimited time. It is the saving grace of many human experiences, including childhood, formal education, a vacation, and the process of being helped, that they will end. If they did not, if one had, for instance, to remain in school until one knew everything there was to know, or to be helped until one was entirely well, it would be intolerable and no one in their senses would engage themselves in such a project. Time in the form of a deadline is extremely useful in helping one concentrate one's efforts on a particular goal. Few students would complete a paper if they had unlimited time in which to do it.

In facing the problem of the child in foster care whose parents apparently are not making any effort to regain custody nor are willing to give their child up for adoption, we have found real value in being clear from the very first that the child's parents have a year, but no longer, to decide what they want to and can do about the situation and to work on implementing their decision. Before we imposed a time-limit, the child was often left in limbo, as it were, year after year, always hoping to go

57

home someday, and seeing his or her parents perhaps two or three times each year. With the time-limit, however, and with the parents given three options—to work toward taking their child back, to decide that they can never be parents to their child and that he or she would be much happier with another set of parents, or to prove themselves responsible and supportive part-time parents—nine out of ten family situations can be clarified and the child be assured of some permanence in life. Not only can firm decisions be made; they can be tested in practice and child and parents helped to accept what is, in fact, reality. This is so much better than what some agencies do, which is to resort to the courts if the parents are not ready to take the child back after a year or so, when psychologically no decision has been made. This is a good example of what we mean by "co-planning." The agency helps the parents achieve what they believe they want to do, or discover that they either cannot or do not really want to do it, but the agency does not decide what they ought to do. It also builds into the process times at which the parents' progress can be reviewed, which is helpful in nearly every helping situation.[5]

Also important are those factors which limit the scope of the help to be given or the power of the helping person over the person helped. These may be external criteria, such as the law or the regulations under which assistance may be given, which often, as in public assistance in the United States, limit the welfare worker's discretion to refuse or to reduce a grant as much if not more than they restrict the size of the grant she may give. Or they may be in the nature of contracts or agreements--it is this I am asking help for and not this or that, and you have agreed to help me only with this at this time. Being helped is such a frightening thing that some people only find it possible to risk taking help if they are aware, to some extent, of how far the helping person will press them, although the result of being helped in a limited area may turn out to be upsetting to the whole.

All too often, however, especially in such programs as public assistance, before social services and financial assistance were separated, asking for money has meant that the asker has subjected his whole life to the review of the caseworker, who feels compelled to help him in all sorts of ways the client has not foreseen or may not want. Although the helper who would do so is not likely to be a good one, a clear understanding of the conditions of help is useful both to helper and helped.

Limiting the scope of help may also help the helped person partialize his problem, that is, concentrate on one bit of it instead of trying to handle a "whole sea" of troubles all at once. A partialized problem is quite often one that a person can do something about when he is helpless before the whole. If he can start work on even a little bit of the whole, he may gain courage to tackle a little more.

This setting of special conditions that exist only for the helping relationship, or for a part of it, is sometimes called "structuring" the relationship. The term can also be used for a single interview. Its rationale is the not unreasonable expectation that the helped person, once having had the experience of finding himself able to handle himself in a protected situation, may gain the confidence in himself or in helping persons to handle his problems in a wider sphere. It is the same rationale that we use when we allow a child, for instance, to manage his own clothing budget in a family setting, where he cannot make too disastrous a mistake, in the expectation that he will thereby be better able to handle a more total budget when he no longer has us behind him.

Likeness and Difference: Something New

An eighth, closely allied, characteristic of the relationship is that *it must offer something new*. This is obvious. If it did not, there would be no reason for the helped person to make a decision now when he had not been able to do so in many identical situations. But it is not as simple as this. To introduce difference into a situation in such a way that it proves a moving rather than a paralyzing factor requires that there be a good deal of likeness, of shared experience and understanding, on which the difference can be based. Indeed the whole helping process has sometimes been described as a skilled use of likeness and difference. The helping efforts of many untrained or occasional helpers is apt to contain much too much difference in the form of blame, unsolicited advice, commands, or moral precepts. This might be called inappropriate difference.

For many years helping theory tended to emphasize likeness rather than difference. Carl Rogers' nondirective counseling does not go this far, but it does put the counselor in a nondiffering position. Popular feeling to some extent has followed this bent. Parents are urged to be "pals" to their children, to minimize the difference of age and responsibility. We deplore "the generation gap." Much has been made of the impossibility of the middle class understanding the feelings of those in poverty, or of whites trying to help blacks. During the 1960s and 1970s there was a good deal of talk about the need for "indigenous workers" — persons with the same background, including lack of education, as the people they were helping — who were assumed more likely to understand and be trusted by the poor. They are rather rarely heard of in the 1990s. Occasionally one hears of an individual who is really helpful to those who are in similar circumstances. Velma Barfield, for example, was a source of strength to her fellow prisoners on death row before her own execution for murder. But for a person to hold that only someone like himself can help him denies the essential likeness of all human beings.

While there is some truth in the statement that people from widely different cultures or age groups find difficulty in understanding each other, the problem is one of imagination more than it is of similar experience. It is not necessary to have experienced the same problem as the person one is trying to help. Despite the experience of Alcoholics Anonymous, who have built a very successful method of helping on an initial likeness, it is not necessary, obviously, to have had an illegitimate child to help an unmarried mother. It is not even necessary to be a woman. Nor is it necessary to be of the same class or color as the person one is helping. None of these more or less artificial likenesses is necessary to helping. They have to be created when there is in those who normally handle the problem a lack of imagination and respect for the person being helped. What one needs to help a criminal is not to have committed a crime, but to know what it is like to be tempted to do so, or to have the imagination to feel the tensions and frustrations out of which crime is born.

There is even a danger in having had experiences too much like those of the person being helped. Initially it may be an advantage in establishing what we have called likeness. But there is no more harmful helper than the person who has successfully solved a problem, taken credit for it, and has forgotten what it cost her to overcome it. Such a person often expects other people to solve their problems in the same way as she has done. "I solved it. Why can't you?" Often, too, such a helper is threatened by a helped person's doubts or anger, even by his discussing the problem. If the helper's victory over the problem has been achieved with the help of some repression, she cannot allow the questions she herself had and repressed to become live options again.

Alcoholics Anonymous's apparent reliance on likeness alone as a major factor in helping is perhaps the exception that proves the rule. In my opinion what makes their work both possible and productive is their insistence on the role of a force—divine grace—outside either helper or helped.

We need therefore both likeness and difference. Specific suggestions for the introduction of specific difference into the helping situation will be made in a later chapter.

Do NOT just explore the positive choices available

Working with Negative Feelings: Choice Truly Offered

Again it may seem almost too obvious to mention, but a ninth characteristic of the helping relationship is that it must be one in which *choice is truly offered—not, of course, unreal or manufactured choice, or choice stripped of its consequences, but what we have called active and willing choice.* This means in practice that the relationship must be one in which negative as well as positive solutions can be examined.

It follows that negative as well as positive feelings must be allowed expression, without the fear that these will lead to blame, or shock, or the withdrawal of the helping person's interest, concern, or esteem.

People generally need more help with their negative feelings than they do with their positive ones. We can illustrate this statement by likening a person to a car or a trolley with at least a moderate tendency to proceed down a road. People, we have said, must be presumed to have some innate tendency to grow, to go forward, to make constructive choices in their own interest. But a person in trouble is like a trolley which has stalled. *unable to move forward*

While it is conceivable that the engine has worn out, there are two much more likely explanations for the trolley's failure to advance. One might be that the road is indeed too rocky or steep, in which case, when we come upon it, the sensible thing to do is to try to remove some of the rocks. It is indeed good sense to be sure, in any situation, that obvious rocks, such as lack of money, or physical illness, or lack of education or skill, are either removed or recognized for what they are and, if possible, a path found around or over them.

In many situations it will be found that although the way appears to be clear, and the engine not seriously damaged, for some reason or other the trolley fails to move. What has actually happened is that the forward motion of the trolley is pressing against a strong spring of negative feelings, that is, of fear, guilt, anger, or despair.

We can now draw our diagram thus:

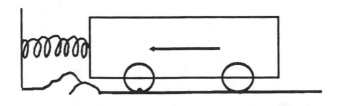

We will have to admit, though, that the stanchion or post to which the spring is attached (on the left of the diagram) has no real existence. It and the spring are actually inside the trolley itself and are preventing not the whole trolley moving but, say, a wheel turning or a piston completing its stroke. Nevertheless, diagrammatically, the figure will serve and the result is the same.

The usual impulse of a helping person, finding such a human "trolley" that appears to be stalled, is to get behind it and push. That is, positive feelings are encouraged, and the person urged or exhorted to move. But the result, if our diagram has any validity, will be a small positive movement, it is true, but at the same time a tightening of the spring, thus:

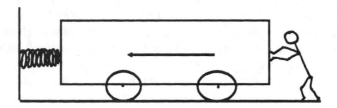

Resistance to help is therefore increased, and either the whole mechanism breaks down, which is what happens in mental illnesses of various kinds, or, when the helper stops pushing, the trolley backslides, sometimes to a position further back that it was before.

Any engineer, faced with this model, could tell us that the sensible thing to do is to remove the spring, or, if we cannot do so, to uncoil it in some way so that it no longer holds so much tension in it. This requires looking at it, which, in our analogy, means allowing negatives to be expressed, discussed, and seen for what they are, which is usually far less ominous than they were feared to be.

The analogy is not perfect, but it may help us to see why, in human helping, it is not possible to proceed on a basis of simply "accentuating the positive and eliminating the negative," despite the popularity of such writers as Norman Vincent Peale. Their very popularity in America explains in fact why it is so often necessary for the helping relationship to deal with negative feelings. The whole of American culture tends to ignore negatives. An optimist is highly regarded, a pessimist somehow thought of as someone who is dissatisfied, or even disloyal. There are hundreds of Optimists Clubs in the United States, and no Pessimists

Club, to my knowledge. A person in trouble will find little difficulty in finding people to support his positive feelings, to push his trolley, to tell him to look on the bright side of things, to "snap out of it," or to "be thankful for small mercies." Only the true helping person will be willing to help him with his negative feelings, with the things that are really blocking his progress, which everyone else cheerfully chooses to ignore.

The importance of working with negative feelings is illustrated by what happens when someone faces a disaster, such as the loss of a spouse or a child, or one's savings, health, or job. The first reaction is usually shock, which may last for as long as a month. One wise doctor I know, when he has to tell someone that he has a terminal illness, asks the patient to return in a month to discuss the situation. By that time the most common reaction is protest and anger against the people involved and against Providence itself. "This isn't fair. What have I done to deserve this?" "This wouldn't have happened if my husband had listened to me." "Why didn't you spot my condition earlier?" A friend of mine, a clergyman, told me once that when his beloved wife died after a long bout with cancer, to his amazement his first reaction was to be angry with her. "She has no right to leave me."

The protest is followed, in many cases, by despair, which may last indefinitely or be partially solved by detachment, denying that one cares. "I can manage." "I'll be all right." People then go on, as it were, on two cylinders, "making do," having insulated themselves from their pain and grief. Although they may not recognize it, they are emotionally handicapped.

But with some others something very different happens. They seem not only to survive the disaster but actually to gain from the experience. While we would never wish suffering on another person, and would indeed try to relieve it as much as we could, we do have to admit that sometimes suffering does ennoble some people. We probably know someone to whom this seems to have happened.

The big question is, of course, What is the difference between those people who turn disaster into victory and those who succumb to disaster? There are, of course, many possible answers—temperament, heredity, a person's past experience, all of which may make a difference and probably do. But in a study (which, to my regret, I can no longer identify) of two groups—four-year-olds who suddenly found themselves in the hospital without their parents, and young women in their twenties who were widowed—the factor that correlated closest with mastery of the situation was the extent to which the persons were allowed to express their protest. Those would-be helpers who told them to cheer up or accept what had

63

happened actually made it less likely that they would gain from the experience. Several young widows have told me that this was true of their experience.

If, too, we diagram the process, we may find that one cannot go directly from despair or detachment to mastery without going back through protest. Often, in fact, one has to reactivate a protest that has been repressed, which may further disturb the person a while.

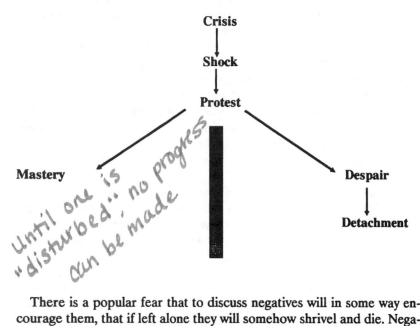

There is a popular fear that to discuss negatives will in some way encourage them, that if left alone they will somehow shrivel and die. Negatives would be encouraged if by discussing them we meant sympathizing with them, sharing them to some extent, or being sorry for someone on account of them. But, as will become more apparent later when we discuss empathy and sympathy, to discuss something with someone is not to encourage it. It is rather to see it for what it is and to cut it down to size.

Psychiatrists, it is true, recommend that one not discuss or explore negative feelings with a person suffering from depression but, rather, encourage him, and this recommendation may seem like a rather important exception, for how do we know that our apparently "blocked" person may not be a depressive? But it is more a caution against identification with negatives and against dwelling on them than it is a recommendation that negatives not be explored. There may, however, be some situations where, contrary to usual experience, a person has had his negative impulses reinforced by friends, relatives, and neighbors, perhaps because he has sought this reinforcement, and whose greater need is to discuss the unseen positive. These are not usually hard to detect. The person seizes on the negative, demands one's agreement with it, displays it, one might almost say flaunts it. At the same time he is unwilling to consider any realistic discussion of it. He needs it too much.

One cannot say that this type of negative is not a "true" negative, since to ascribe to emotions truth or falsehood is to make value judgments one cannot support. But it is true that this kind of negative is somewhat different from the negative feeling that one does need to discuss or explore. Perhaps we should use different words for them. The negative that needs uncovering and discussing is one of which generally the helped person is afraid or ashamed. It may be denied, or even repressed. It is thought to be unacceptable, like having rejecting feelings about one's child, or fearing a necessary operation, or being guilt-ridden for something one has done. The depressive, on the other hand, is using his negative feelings, sheltering behind them to resist getting well, even sometimes wallowing in them. We might reserve the term "negative feelings" for the first and call the second "negative projections" to indicate the use that is being made of them. The second category would then include the negatives that form such a part of the paranoid's world, which it is also unwise to discuss or explore.

The need, however, to permit the expression of what we have called here "negative feelings" should be apparent. It is one of the reasons why the helping relationship cannot always be pleasant and why the effort to make it so is so often unhelpful. One cannot express negative feelings and keep a relationship pleasant, particularly if one of the negative feelings is anger, and even more particularly if this anger is directed against the helping person or the organization she represents. Fear, guilt, and despair are all ugly emotions. We tend to discount them or cover them up.

Being Nonjudgmental

The need to be able to express negative feelings in the helping relationship is also the basis of the tenth characteristic of the helping relationship as a whole, which is that it *must be nonjudgmental.* This aspect of the relationship too has often been misunderstood, and thought to mean that the helping person must be willing to condone any kind of behavior.

But bad behavior is not condoned by the nonjudgmental person. She is not there to be a judge. If she were, it would not be a true helping situation. She may, or should, point out that a proposed course of action is illegal, or even generally thought of as immoral, if such an observation means anything to the person being helped. She may help someone see the probable consequences of his action, but in general the most productive response is something like, "Will that really solve your problem?" or "How will that seem to you ten or twenty years from now?"

Wrong and even immoral actions are so often desperate, if wrongheaded, attempts to meet a perfectly legitimate need, and to reprove them often makes the would-be transgressor more intent on trying them out.

The tendency to judge, to approve or disapprove, is in general only a way of asserting our superiority over the person with whom we are dealing. While in an imperfect world society finds it necessary to control actions both by punishment and reward and by social approval or disapproval, and I may find myself, most unwillingly, in a position where it is my duty to apply these sanctions, this is no reason why I should take this burden on myself when it is not my responsibility.

If I have any knowledge of how hard most decisions are, how little I can know the conditions under which they must be made, and if I am aware that I have never been in exactly the situation which this person has had to experience, common sense might prevent me from wanting to be judgmental. Particularly it might warn me about being judgmental about feelings, for this is a totally fruitless exercise. A person can help, in some instances, what he does about a situation, but not what he feels about it. To tell someone that he ought not to feel "like that" about something is like telling a person with a broken leg that it ought not to hurt and that it is his fault if it does.

Yet this kind of judgmentalism is all too common in our helping. It goes along with the belief that help should be given only to those who are "deserving," whereas it would seem more sensible to say that it is the "undeserving" who are likely to be in the most trouble and to need help most.

The need of the helped person is to find practical ways of doing differently. He is not helped by a reinforcement of moral judgments of which he is in all probability only too aware. He needs to look at the feelings which led him to act as he did and to find out what he can substitute for them, and this is often impossible if his chief preoccupation is his shame or guilt. New beginnings have to be made within the framework of feelings that he already has. He cannot be entirely different

66

from what he has been before. He must be able to look at himself, and this he cannot do if he sees himself as entirely bad.

For this reason alone the helping relationship cannot be that of self-appointed saint with a sinner, or self-appointed judge with an offender, or, its modern equivalent, self-declared adjusted person with the maladjusted. It must be a relationship between two fallible human beings, each of whom could, in the last analysis, have done what the other did if circumstances had been different. It is true that one is probably stronger than the other, or better educated, or more intelligent, and we can only hope that this one is the helper. It is also true that the helper may hold a position which elevates her above the other and gives her some authority over him. These are often useful "difference" factors. But the likeness must come first, and a common humanity and fallibility is the basis of likeness.

The helping relationship is, however, only the medium in which help is offered. It is not help itself. To be able to establish the kind of relationship described here is half the battle, but not all of it. Something more dynamic needs to come into the relationship. One needs to do more than avoid some of the crasser errors of undisciplined helpers. One needs to be able to help. This leads naturally to a discussion of the helping factor itself.

CHAPTER 5

The Helping Factor

Various Theories

There must be something which the helping person brings into the relationship through which help is actually given. The relationship we have discussed cannot do this by itself. We have already described it as a resultant and not something that can be created apart from what goes on between helper and helped. We cannot set up such a relationship and then sit back and expect help to flow from it without some positive action or contribution on our part.

Quite clearly too the helping factor is something more than the material things with which help often deals, such as money, a job, housing, or medical care, although it is a mistake to think that these things are unimportant. It was one of the misapprehensions of many nineteenth-century helpers that to give material things was wrong, or at best a necessary evil, and that all meaningful help was conveyed through psychological reinforcement. Octavia Hill herself believed that all material help to the aged was a mistake.[1] We can read only with some distaste of the early settlement worker who was "as liberal with his sympathy as he was chary of meat and coal tickets."[2]

Yet the psychological factors in helping have had such a hold on the thought of social workers in the United States that a false dichotomy has been created in many places between tangible and intangible help, and some states have tended to justify a low standard of material assistance by emphasizing the supposed excellence of their counseling services.

A job, a house, an opportunity are very important to people. They may be completely necessary to the solution of their problems. Yet, there is something more to helping than this. While there are obvious situations in which they are all that are needed, in which case helping would seem to consist solely in their provision, in the majority of situations something else has to happen, either in the actual giving or possibly before it, if a person is to make full use of them. And even then their mere provision can be done in such a way that their use is enhanced or limited. The dignity of the application procedure, the concern shown for details, the promptness of their provision, even the setting in which they are given, all contribute to or deduct from their helpfulness.

There have been many attempts to isolate or define the primary helping factor. The nineteenth century, by and large, relied on moral exhortation, friendliness, and encouragement, as in the classic nineteenth-century statement: "Let the moral sense be awakened and the moral influence be established in the minds of the improvident, the unfortunate and the depraved. Let them be approached with kindness and an ingenuous concern for their welfare; inspire them, with self-respect and encourage their industry and economy. . . . Those are the methods of doing them real and permanent good."[3]

Later a more rationalist approach relied on careful case study and appropriate treatment, which in general meant manipulation of the environment and the supplying of influences which the helped person was thought to lack. Some attention was also paid to the participation of the helped person in plans made for him.

A little later, in the late twenties and early thirties of this century, it was believed that listening alone was perhaps the primary helping factor, and American social work went through "the era of the mouse."[4] The helper became little more than a mirror against which the helped person projected his concerns. It was thought that if the helped person could verbalize his feelings and his problems, he could look at them more rationally. Carl Rogers' nondirective counseling became the principal model.

Knowing "Why"

With the advent of psychoanalysis, interpretation of unconscious motives was given first place. It was believed that the rationality of the conscious brain, brought face to face with the apparently infantile reasoning which the unconscious seems to employ—its tendency, for instance, to identify wholly unlike things—would reject this irrationality in favor of more sensible behavior. Insight would lead to change.

So deeply is this concept ingrained that many people will uphold that one cannot modify one's behavior unless one knows exactly why one has misbehaved in the first place, which is clearly not always so. Some understanding of one's motives may be very helpful in coming to a decision, but many of a person's most fruitful decisions and commitments are made without knowing exactly why. Incidentally, this belief, somewhat misunderstood, has led to one of the least fruitful exercises of the beginning helper, the constant asking of the helped person "why" he did something, or "why" he feels this way, when he either does not know, or is afraid to tell you, or, more likely still, has provided himself with a whole set of rationalizations to prevent himself from facing this problem.

Anyone who has ever asked a naughty child why he did something and has been greeted with silence or "because . . ." will recognize what happens.

The same belief once caused a class of mine to insist that the purpose of an interview with a delinquent girl we were studying could be no other than to find out "why" she ran away from home. They were quite shocked when I said that this might be quite helpful, if it could ever be known, although I doubted that it would ever tell us more than the precipitating factor. The actual causality would be probably almost infinitely complex and involve many factors outside both their and Mary Ann's control, a recognition which is being increasingly made by students of epidemiology. If they were interested in trying to create conditions in the community which would minimize delinquency, such an analysis might have value.

But this was not the purpose of the interview as it was held. It could have only one present purpose. That would be to find out ways by which Mary Ann would be able to handle her impulse to run away again.

I do not mean that the epidemiological approach, the desire to control or alter conditions so that other Mary Anns might not need to run away, is something with which a social worker should not be concerned. I do mean that to help Mary Ann in the here and now the knowledge of her action's complicated causality is probably not enough. There is always a temptation in helping to think that if one knows why something has occurred, one can correct it. But this is simply not so. Even if Mary Ann could say, and even be convinced, that she ran away because of any number of factors, there is still her will, her image of herself, her fears, and the reality of her present situation to take into account. Humans are not simply rational creatures, and a fourteen-year-old girl perhaps not always an exemplar of logical thinking.

If Mary Ann were a very sick child, or if her impulse was such that it was uncontrollable by any conscious act on her part even with some change of attitude on the part of her parents, psychotherapy with interpretation might have been necessary. The need for this would have shown up, perhaps, in a more total disorganization than this girl was presenting, or in her failure to make use of the helping process that most people can use to some extent. Even here her problems might have been solved by psychiatric treatment not involving interpretation.

Her particular behavior might be amenable to conditioning or to drug therapy. This solution would involve a "why" of a sort—knowledge at least that her condition could become manageable if certain tensions were relieved, which is not so much a "why" as a "how." Sometimes by *causality NOT always the most effective "solution"*

handling one factor in a complex situation a person may be brought to a condition below, as it were, the critical point at which symptoms appear.

This situation is, however, very different from the probation officer coming to her diagnosis of why Mary Ann behaved as she did and then interpreting this to her. Of much of this kind of psychosocial diagnosis, especially if not made by a psychiatrist, one can only say, "So what?" It might perhaps help the worker make some suggestions to Mary Ann's parents about how they might treat her to avoid exacerbating her problem—that is, if they were ready for this help.

But it would have done more, or less. A preoccupation with causality would have failed to engage Mary Ann's capacity to face her situation and to do something about it herself.

Particularly is this true, as Glasser points out in his *Reality Therapy*,[5] if the causality of an action becomes an excuse for not doing something about it. It is all very well to know that one behaves badly because one has been rejected or unloved. There is no doubt that to be rejected makes it harder to behave well. But it does not remove the responsibility of a person to do something about his behavior.

Reality, Empathy, and Support

Doing something about her impulse to run away is what Mary Ann needs to struggle with now. To help Mary Ann do this the probation officer must start with the reality of the situation, the fact that she has done something illegal; the possibility that the judge might send her to a correctional school, or let her go home only under supervision, which she might find difficult to bear; even the fact that she might find it impossible not to run away again. In order to decide what she wanted, what she could bear, what use she could make of whatever was decided, and what help she needed to do this, Mary Ann would need to be held to facing these facts and possibilities.

She would also need to be free to discuss and explore her feelings about them, and in fact be reassured that her expression of these feelings would not get her into trouble. Part of these feelings might be anger, at her parents, at the judge, or at the probation officer. The last is particularly likely if the officer has done her job in holding Mary Ann to the reality of the situation; but since this anger is something which Mary Ann cannot help feeling about the situation, and since to repress it, or "bottle it up," will only make it more important and harder to deal with, it may need to be expressed.

71

Lastly, if Mary Ann is to take help in her situation, she must know that the officer will be available to her, will not turn against her when she is troubled, and will provide as far as she can what Mary Ann needs to carry out her decisions.

This situation may serve, despite its particularity, to help us see what it is that the helping person must convey to any person in trouble. What has to be conveyed can be phrased as a "statement" which the helping person makes, although it is much more than this. It is not simply something said. It is something conveyed by words, feeling, and action. But in terms of a statement it could be phrased in three sentences, as follows:

"This is it." (Reality)

"I know that it must hurt." (Empathy)

"I am here to help you if you want me and can use me,"[6] or, more succinctly, "You don't have to face this alone." (Support)

These three sentences in turn may be expressed in terms of what is actually offered through them. In this form the helping factor is composed of three elements which we may call *reality, empathy, and support.*

Such an analysis may seem extremely simple. If these elements indeed make up the helping factor and all that a helping person needs to do is to be realistic, empathic, and supporting, then it may be thought that there is little to it. Anyone ought to be able to help. The analysis is, however, a very simple way of expressing a very complex matter, and like many simple statements, religious, philosophical, or scientific, it is extremely hard to put into practice. The relationship, too, between its parts is of great importance to the whole.

Yet, these three elements are always necessary in any helping process, and the three together do in fact constitute the helping factor. I know of no piece of helping that cannot be analyzed in these terms, and no piece of unsuccessful helping that does not show a weakness in at least one of these elements. Either reality, or support, or empathy, or more than one of these, has been lacking, misunderstood, or, perhaps more frequently, not fully carried out. Reality has been partial, empathy and support conditional.

It might be wise to examine first each principle by itself and then try to bring them together. The order in which they are presented here does not necessarily mean that one introduces them, in helping, serially or in this order. One may start with an expression of empathy or even of support, and in any case they are interwoven. One does not stop where another starts. But if there is an order, reality often does come first.

72

Reality

Reality means a number of things, some of which have already been touched on. It means, first, not discounting another's problem, not taking it away from him by believing it unimportant. This is a thing we are particularly likely to do to children, whom we cannot believe, for some reason, feel as deeply as we do. How often we say, "Oh, they'll soon forget it," or "They're too young to be affected much," when everything that we really know about them points to the fact that their despair, their fear, and their anger are not only intense but can leave permanent scars. To be real, on the other hand, means to face the problem with someone in all of its ugliness or terror. It means doing him the honor of taking his problem seriously. And, with children, in particular, but with adults also, this is the first requirement if a relationship is to grow. One cannot have a relationship of any depth if one does not take the other person seriously.

Another form of taking away a person's problem is to solve it for him or to insulate him from it. We either produce a quick solution or we help him to evade it, to forget it, not to come into contact with it.

Often we do this because we see that the problem is painful. The helped person is disturbed about it. We wish to spare him this disturbance. But, while it might be necessary to allay some forms of disturbance temporarily, disturbance has about it some of the qualities that are now recognized in a fever. It used to be good medical practice to allay all fevers. Now there is growing understanding that a fever is the body's way of fighting an infection.

A child once, in a Children's Home, was very much disturbed by her mother's visits. The social worker suggested solving the problem by restricting the mother's visits. The child said, with a good deal of anger, "What you don't understand is that this is something I need to get disturbed about."

People need their problems if they are to solve them for themselves. Sometimes they need to be disturbed. Not to permit them to become so, when they are trying to tackle their problems, is to encourage nonchoice.

False Reassurance as "Nonreality"

A common form of nonreality is reassurance. Reassurance, or rather false reassurance, is an attempt to palliate reality by telling the person in trouble that "things will be all right" when there is no reason to think that this will be so, or when the present hurts so much that this is wholly unimportant. We can recognize obvious cases of it. No wise parents today would tell their child that the dentist won't hurt. The dentist very well may hurt, and the parent be proved a liar. But we still, some of us, will tell a child that he will be happy in a foster home when this may not be so and when in any case all he can think of at the moment is his pain at leaving his own parents.

We use this kind of reassurance for two reasons. In the first place, we cannot stand the child's present unhappiness and are willing, although we may not know it, to try to dispel it even at the cost of greater unhappiness later. And, in the second, we are apt to be a little defensive because a foster home, in this case, or some other service, is what we have to offer him and we do not like the idea that he might not like the only thing that we have to give him. It makes us feel very inadequate. I have seen a welfare worker "reassure" a client that the termination of her grant does not really matter, since she ought to be able to get support from a recently located absent husband, when her lights and gas were to be turned off that afternoon. "Pie in the sky" is no substitute for bread in the here and now. False or unrealistic reassurance does not strengthen a person's ability to handle his problem. It effectually disarms him and robs him of the anger or despair he may need to deal with it.

Another reason for false reassurance is our natural protectiveness toward those we consider vulnerable or lacking in real strength. We feel that the person we are helping would be hurt by coming face to face with the truth. As such, it appears to us at the time as a wholly kindly and helpful action. There may be some instances in which the helped person could not possibly face the truth, but more often the helping person is only too glad to have a good reason not to face the helped person with the truth. She fears the helped person's reaction and her own inability to deal with it. The genuine cases where the truth is so horrible that it would be more harmful than helpful are rather rare.

Protecting People from the Truth

To protect someone from the truth is to make a very serious judgment about him. It is to say that he is incapable of being helped with his real problem. As a minister expressed it to me once, it is to deny him his chance for an "abundant life," fully experienced.

The truth, too, is often much less harmful than what the imagination puts in its place. Some years ago I was approached by a teacher who was concerned about a fifteen-year-old boy, the adopted son of an apparently stable and loving family, who had begun to run away. There seemed to be nothing in the home to suggest a need to escape from it, and although the boy was adolescent, he did not appear to be particularly rebellious. The boy was plainly running "to" rather than "from," and when I was told that the town he was running to was his birthplace, I was fairly safe in assuming at least tentatively that he was doing what so many children away from their own parents have to do, which was to answer the question, "Why did my parents give me up?"

I therefore asked the teacher why the boy's parents had done so and was told that the boy was illegitimate. I asked whether the boy knew this and was met with the rather indignant statement that the teacher was sure that no one had ever mentioned it to him. She thought, I believe, at the moment that I was suggesting that someone had taunted him with his birth and thus caused him to run away.

It was quite hard for her to take when I suggested that if she wanted to help the boy, someone had better tell him the truth. It seemed like a horrible thing to do. We wrestled with this for quite a while, acknowledging what it might cost him and the possibility that I was wrong in my belief, and in the end we decided that she would at least try telling the truth. This she did, very honestly and bravely.

To her surprise the boy was greatly relieved. As the boy expressed it, "Of course she had to find another home for me." Later the boy confessed that he had been for several years tortured by two alternative fantasies. One, derived from a film, *The Bad Seed*, which is based on the theory that evil is inherited, was that both of his parents had been executed for murder. The other, derived from an advertisement, and comical if it had not been so tragic, was that he had an unbearable odor about which "even your best friends won't tell you." When for a moment he was able to talk himself out of the one fantasy and see it for what it was, the other would rise to plague him. The truth was far less dangerous than the untruths he had imagined.

We are much too ready to assume that another person cannot bear the truth. Only when an untruth has become so necessary to a person that he or she cannot live without it is it wise not to face the truth. We must remember, however, that reality is only one of the three helping elements. It cannot be introduced without empathy and support.

Reality as Difference

We sometimes call a piece of reality deliberately introduced into a helping situation a piece of difference. It may be a fact. It can conceivably be an opinion, although we need to be careful that it is not a prejudice or a personal point of view irrelevant to the helped person's need. Unskilled workers are, as we have said, full of inappropriate difference, and they introduce pieces of difference in inappropriate ways.

How do we know when difference is appropriate? How do we avoid perhaps robbing someone of an illusion that he needs? We do need difference, something new, in the helping relationship. I would suggest at least four criteria.

The first, and perhaps the most important, of these is that there is sufficient likeness — understanding, common purpose — to assure the helped person that the difference is not a personal attack. Perhaps the most successful piece of consultation I ever did was with an agency that had been severely criticized for its practices by a number of authorities and had become quite defensive about its program. I was asked to its campus as one who understood and shared many of its ideals. The difference I introduced was even more extreme than that of its other critics, but it was difference expressed in the context of common goals, of respect for their efforts, even where misdirected, and of appreciation for the good things they had done. This time the agency listened and changed even faster than anyone could possibly have hoped. People can, after all, say things to other people who know that they love them that they could not possibly say to a stranger.

Secondly, the difference must be expressed in the helped person's terms. In this case I could express my difference in terms of the agency's own goals. I could show them that their methods were not accomplishing what they themselves set out to do. Often the most useful little bits of difference can be expressed by using the helped person's own words. A welfare worker was interviewing a deserting father, who rather naturally was trying to excuse his desertion. His statement was that he could not bear not being master in his own house. "You know," said the worker, "that's the strangest way I've ever heard of being master in your own house, to run away from it."

Thirdly, there is a somewhat elusive quality about the person who is ready to accept difference. There is an element of challenge, of projecting an image and watching to see how you are going to respond to it. This was very obvious in the deserting father's words.

This is perhaps the least concrete of our criteria. It is a sense one gets, an understanding of the process of image projection, a knowledge that a projection is being made for a purpose. The helped person is really saying, "Will you buy this image of me?" and if you do, you only strengthen the image and make the real self less accessible. I heard a mother once tell a counselor how reasonable she was in her demands on her seventeen-year-old son, and how unreasonable he was. "And he never gets in by nine o'clock." The counselor's quiet statement, "But you know, seventeen-year-olds don't get in by nine o'clock," was a fruitful piece of difference. The mother was able, with its help, to see that she was not making reasonable demands but was terribly afraid of what her son might be doing at night.

The last criterion has to do with empathy and support. It is briefly that one has no right to introduce difference or reality unless one is prepared to help the person one is helping with the shock. Reality by itself is harsh. It can be very destructive. It is only reality approached with empathy and support that is a true helping process. Indeed we might restate the whole method of help as "facing people with reality with empathy and support." To face someone with reality and leave them to handle it alone is cruelty, not help.

Problems in Using Reality

The fear of not being able to handle the repercussions is one of the chief obstacles to introducing appropriate difference. I find myself that as I grow older and, if not more confident, then at least practiced enough to know that I can survive, and even be of some help, whatever a helped person's reaction, I grow bolder and more helpful in the introduction of difference. I still have not had the courage to do as one social worker did and to say to a client who was trying to manipulate her or reassure himself by surliness and sarcasm, "You know you are the most unpleasant client I've ever had to deal with."

I would not recommend this much difference to any but the most experienced helper, and not then unless all four criteria were met. Yet in this case it was appropriate and proved a turning point in help.

Obviously to tell even a very small percentage of those one is trying to help that they are unpleasant people would be a very poor rule in practice. In most cases it would result in the very reverse of helping. How, then, could this woman risk it? Obviously it could only be done when she was sure that Mr. Smith recognized her desire to help. Just as people can tell "home truths" — in itself an interesting term — to those who are sure of their love and interest, so a helper can risk difference with someone who trusts her. Again, it had to be true. Mr. Smith had been behaving in an objectively unpleasant way. He had in fact been making a stream of petty but mildly offensive allegations about the whole office staff. But there was a third element present. The worker recognized his unpleasantness as part of his persona, the projected unreal self which he was using to stifle his doubts. There was an element both of uncertainty and of challenge about what he was doing. It actually demanded an answer, and if the answer had been a placid acceptance, its value as an escape from reality would have been strengthened. This was also true of the mother with the seventeen-year-old son. What she was really asking was, "Is it all right for me to treat him as if he were much younger?"

The ability to distinguish between an unreality of this type and the unreality which the helped person really believes and in fact cannot live without is a matter of some skill. To tell a sufferer from a functional heart disease that his illness is imaginary, which is objectively true, would in most cases be disastrous. He knows that he is ill, cannot prevent himself from being so, and has the same pain and shortness of breath as the person with actual heart damage. It is largely a matter of listening carefully to the feeling behind what is being said, of catching that element of challenge and doubt, and of being aware that the helped person will always, to some extent, project a persona in his effort to protect himself from you. Sometimes one can pick it up through an inherent contradiction in what the seeker for help may say. Sometimes one may have to say to someone, "You say you enjoy doing this but you don't sound like it." Body language, too, often betrays what a person is feeling. So does tone of voice. The classic example is that of the counselor who told a mother that her child needed more loving if he were to behave better. The mother came to the next session dragging the child into the office and said, "You were wrong. I've half killed this brat loving him and it hasn't helped a bit."

Playing Devil's Advocate

Another form of difference which can sometimes be of help, providing again that it is kept within a framework of likeness, consists in the speculative assumption of exactly the opposite of what the helped person is asserting, so that he may gain strength in demolishing your argument. This is in fact the function of the devil's advocate in a canonization procedure. What a devil's advocate says is, in effect, "Have you considered the possibility that we're on the wrong track altogether? Let's look at that possibility." This is a form of difference that can only be used when the helped person is fairly sure of himself; when, in fact, all that he needs is to move from a tentative statement to a forthright claiming of what he knows and believes. It cannot be used when a person is struggling to make sense out of chaos, or when he is searching for an answer. It requires, too, a clear understanding of the helping person's authority and purpose. It is not an argument as much as it is a way of examining and strengthening the basic presuppositions on which one is acting.

stay direct

Reality and "Tact"

Reality also means not being indirect. Helping persons, unfortunately, have acquired something of the reputation of being rather "wily birds" who tread delicately and never quite say what they mean. This is sometimes described as "tact" or "consideration," but so easily becomes either evasion or a way of gently manipulating someone else to do what you want him to do and at the same time think that it was his own idea. I have even heard helping described as doing exactly that. But clearly this is far from the kind of helping with which we are concerned. "Tact" may be a good word when it means telling the truth with concern for another's feelings, but all too often when one says, "I told him tactfully that . . . ," one means, "I hinted that it might be so because I was afraid to say so directly." There are some things that cannot be said "tactfully" in the sense of gradually or evasively. They can only be faced for what they are.

One area in which the reality of the situation needs to be very clearly expressed is that of the helping relationship itself. Generally this means what we described in our account of Mary Ann — what will or may happen, the probable consequences of actions, the authority and rights each person has in the situation, who can tell whom to do what, and the conditions under which help is being offered. Concealed power is both unfair and generally unhelpful. The worker from the juvenile court who minimizes its authority and presents it as only wanting to be "of help" without making clear that it will enforce this "help" is trying to buy relationship at the cost of the truth, and she will end by having neither.

Do Not Justify Reality

A further requirement of reality is that it must be presented as it is, without attempts at justification. One of the things we all do when it becomes our duty to present or enforce an unpleasant reality is to try to justify it. "It's for your own good." "We have to be fair to everyone." "I'm sure you'll find out eventually that it is wise." The moment one does this to reality, one robs it of its primary helping value, which is that it exists outside both helper and helped person and is something that they can both look at together, as a fact, and without a predetermined mental attitude toward it. To justify, or to explain, means that one claims the reality as "good" and that the helped person is wrong in being angry at it. While some objective explanation may sometimes have some value if for nothing else than to establish that the reality really does exist, the helper has to be sure to stop short of presenting the argument for it, when there are also arguments against it. To argue that a reality is good weakens it. It raises the possibility that it could be different and nearly always ends in a wrangle between the helped and helping person about what might be instead of about what is.

Helper and helped person need to be on the same side of reality. In the following diagram on the left the reality actually comes between the helper and the client. In that on the right the helper looks at reality together with her client and helps him decide what to do about it.

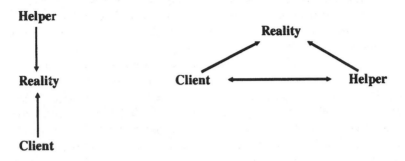

The Right to Fail

But there is one use of the word "reality" which helpers should avoid. Unfortunately, the word is often used in professional social work literature to mean the social worker's estimate of the client's capabilities. A course of action is seen to be unreal if in the social worker's opinion the client is attempting something beyond his power. But this assessment, although it may be common sense, is not reality for the client. It is merely a judgment on him. What is real is what such plans would cost him and the very real possibility that he might fail.

These need to be discussed. But, as David Soyer points out, people have the right to fail and may not in fact be satisfied with a second best until the impossible has been attempted.[7] Sometimes, too, people surprise one. To elevate into reality a diagnosis, however careful, is presumptuous and is in all too many cases a disguised form of protectiveness. The history of art, athletics, and many other fields is full of stories of those who have overcome apparently impossible odds in the pursuit of an idea.

Being Nice

Reality is perhaps the hardest of the three elements to hold to for any sensitive person. None of us likes to be the bearer of bad news. We do not like seeing people hurt, and reality often hurts. Americans in par-

80

ticular find great difficulty with it, since American culture
premium on considerateness and on not "hurting people's feel
makes plain speaking very difficult. If anyone doubts this — and
cally many Americans think of themselves as outspoken — one n
compare American and British book reviews or political comment.

There is a deep tradition in our culture of being "nice." Really to face
reality with someone often feels like being "mean," although it can be
tremendously helpful. Even professions which have something of a tradition of "toughness" and "no nonsense" about them have apparently
developed a need to show themselves gentle and understanding.

I once had occasion to teach a number of adult probation officers.
Before we began, I was apprehensive about their reactions to being in-
structed by a social worker who, a few years before, would have seemed
to them "starry-eyed" and a "bleeding heart." I thought they would find
my material on empathy very hard to take but that they would have little difficulty with reality. Exactly the reverse was true. These men were
willing to go to all lengths to try to understand their probationers, and
to do things for them. They counseled with them, found them jobs, ob-
tained medical care for them. The one thing they found it almost impossible to do was to tell them that they were on probation and that if they
broke its conditions, the judge could and might send them to prison. Yet
it was around this fact that they could have given the greatest help — if,
that is, they had used this fact not as a threat but as a reality with which
the probationer needed help.

Empathy

In order to help someone else with reality one has to show empathy
for him. Empathy is the ability to know, or to imagine, what another person is feeling and, as it were, to feel it with him without becoming caught
in that feeling and losing one's own perspective. It is not, let us be very
clear, a way of softening reality. It is not the jam with the pill, or the
praise for part of another's work that enables one to come out with blame
or correction where it is needed. It is not in any way something "thought
up" by the helper but a response on her part to what the helped person
is going through.

Empathy, Sympathy and Pity

Empathy needs to be clearly distinguished from two other responses
to people in trouble. While words are somewhat difficult here, since we

put connotations on them that make them difficult to define, we shall call these other two responses sympathy and pity.

The three responses have sometimes been described as feeling "like" someone (sympathy), feeling "with" someone (empathy), and feeling "for" someone (pity), but I find these prepositions somewhat difficult. The real difference between them lies in the amount and the kind of difference from the helped person that the helping person maintains.

In sympathy there is little difference. The helping person feels as does the person she is helping. She shares the same feelings, identifies herself with his interests, becomes aligned with him, loves and hates the same things. The helper who feels empathy, on the other hand, understands the feelings that the other has about the situation, knows how uncomfortable and even desperate he may be, knows, as we have said, that "it must hurt," but does not claim these feelings herself. In the middle of all her understanding and the feeling this may engender in her, the helping person remains herself, with her own grasp on reality. The helper who feels pity also retains her difference. She does not get overwhelmed by the troubled person's feelings. She does so, however, only by insisting on her superior fortune or merit. Emphasis is on the difference between her and the person she is helping, and the likeness, or understanding, is for the most part lost.

The difference between these feelings can perhaps best be illustrated, somewhat facetiously perhaps, if we consider three reactions when a man who strongly dislikes his wife confides in another man. The sympathetic person would say, "Oh, I know exactly how you feel. I can't bear mine, either." The two would then comfort each other, but nothing much would come of it. The pitying person would commiserate but add that he himself was most happily married. Why didn't the other come to dinner sometime and see what married life could be like? This, in most cases, would only increase the frustration of the unhappy husband and help him to put his problem further outside himself, onto his wife or his lack of good fortune. The empathic person might say something like, "That must be terribly difficult for you. What do you think might possibly help?" And only the empathic person, of the three, would have said anything that could lead to some change in the situation.

Sympathy, as we have described it, is not entirely useless. There is some value in the precept to "rejoice with those that do rejoice and weep with those who weep." It is good to know that one is not alone and there are others who feel as you do. But this is really a function of support rather than of sympathy, and the empathic person who feels for one in what one is going through is able to give a lot more help than the person who simply shares one's distress. I can remember a social worker who met a client's distress over her son's behavior by saying, "Oh, I know exactly how you feel. I cry myself to sleep every night over mine." The client left angrily saying, "She's in as bad a way as I am."

This may seem like an exaggerated sympathy. But this is one of sympathy's problems. We often hear it said that one can have too much sympathy for such and such a person (or such and such a group of persons). This is perfectly true. Sympathy can very easily become a weak emotion, and it can confirm a weak person in his weakness. But the person who, on this account, is suspicious of any attempt to understand others, who sees such an attempt as somehow a sign of weakness, has not understood how empathy differs from sympathy. Empathy is both a strong and a strengthening emotion. Because of the difference that the person who has empathy retains, she never condones or confirms weakness but enlists the troubled person's feelings in the attempt to overcome it. One cannot have too much empathy. But—and here, perhaps, is the rub—empathy very easily slops over into sympathy. Sympathy is much the easier emotion. It is very easy to get caught in someone else's feeling system and to begin to identify with it. Young and inexperienced helpers find maintaining the distinction one of their hardest tasks.

An Act of the Loving Imagination

I have spoken of empathy as an emotion, and purposely so. It is, of course, formally an act, but an act based on feeling. The best description I know of it is an "act of the loving imagination."

Both "act" and "imagination" are important words here. While empathy requires imagination and therefore knowledge, and it is possible that the most important contribution of the kind of specialized knowledge of an individual's likely behavior that we call "diagnosis" is to make empathy more likely to be appropriate, empathy is much more than knowing intellectually what another must be feeling. It always involves the ability to enter into this feeling, to experience it and therefore to know its meaning for the other person and the actions that are likely to flow from it.

There is in fact a paradox here which it is very hard to explain in ordinary, rational terms. How can one at the same time feel an emotion and yet remain separate from it, which is what we have said that empathy demands? It is all too easy to do one or the other, but not both, either to give up empathy for sympathy or to rely on knowledge without feeling. Yet both to feel and to know is necessary if the purposes of empathy are to be fulfilled. Nothing carries less conviction, or is likely to fall so wide of the mark, as an attempt at empathy that is purely intellectual. The purpose of empathy is to convey feeling, not knowledge. But because feeling is communicated by so much more than words — by gestures, tone of voice, facial expression, and bodily posture, which are too complex to be capable of dissimulation — an assurance of feeling can only be communicated if this feeling actually exists. We can therefore see plainly that this kind of genuine feeling and separateness from it are both necessary, but not a purely rational explanation of how they can be combined or how one acquires the ability to combine them.

Can Empathy Be Learned?

These difficulties have caused many people to assert that empathy cannot be learned. It must be a natural gift. Or possibly it is something that one only acquires in practice. In my experience, however, the facility can be trained, if not fully taught. While there are certainly people who have a natural empathy for others, there are also those who can release a great deal of loving imagination once they can free themselves from stereotyped reactions to people and once they become aware of their tendency, in some situations, to respond negatively, or sympathetically rather than empathically.

To learn empathy one has to be free from the kind of blocks that are thrown in one's path by liking and disliking people, by lining oneself up either for them or against them, instead of just caring about them, whether one likes or dislikes them. And this comes largely from self-knowledge. It is not so much that a person stops liking and disliking as it is that he or she learns to control the consequences of such feelings.

Empathy also depends on knowledge, and on encounters with people who are quite different from oneself. Many well-to-do people find it hard to be empathic with the poor, because they never meet them on a social or equal basis. The same is true of whites and blacks. To hear how another feels, expressed frankly and without equivocation, can be a shock but also a reality on which empathy can be built.

Knowledge of social conditions and some of the causes of feeling can also be of help. But some would-be empathizers become overwhelmed with the amount of knowledge they feel that they need before they can empathize at all. They feel that they cannot possibly know exactly how the other person feels, especially if they have never experienced a similar situation. They are quite correct. To think one could do so would be presumption. But empathy does not in fact need to be too precise. There is always something of the tentative about it, an acknowledgment that feeling must be present, and probably within a given range, and an invitation to the helped person to express his feeling more precisely. That

84

is why the statement which we have used to typify empathy is not, "I know how it hurts," but, "I know that it must hurt."

Again, the empathy which is needed, at least in the beginning of a relationship, is largely directed toward the struggle through which the helped person is going, his fear of help, his wanting and not wanting to get well, the frustrations of his efforts to solve his problem by himself, and this is common human experience, although not always recognized as such. Later perhaps one needs to expand to the wider problem, but by that time the person you are helping has usually given you quite a bit on which to proceed. Empathy is not something which the helping person constructs entirely by herself. It comes more by degrees, in a process of dialogue. It is needed in some degree initially, however. At this point it is an unlocking act. In the framework of the trolley diagram we discussed in the last chapter, it is the key which unlocks the casting so many of us have constructed around the spring of our negative feelings.

There are times when one can convey empathy in a subverbal manner, but generally it does need to be expressed verbally. I find that many young helping people can feel empathically, but they find it difficult to put their feeling into words. There is, of course, some risk in empathy. Like reality, it may trigger unforeseen reactions, both in the helped person and the helper, since it does deal very directly with feeling. Often it can start on a very simple basis, about having to wait for the counselor to be free, or the weather, or the difficulty of putting feelings into words.

Often the most immediate and important occasion for empathy has to do with the helping situation itself. This is particularly so when the helping is unsought. One of the first things a protective worker—that is, a social worker who investigates complaints about the neglect of children— has to realize is that it is her presence that constitutes for the moment the client's most immediate problem. It is with the feelings about her visit that she needs to empathize first, even sometimes to insist on, so that these feelings do not get displaced on to the original complainant, where they are much harder to handle. And often it is this initial empathy that literally unlocks a door.

An Example of Empathy

An example of empathy which may illustrate some of its characteristics came to my notice in a welfare case. Mrs. Brown, a recent widow, informed her welfare worker that she was withdrawing her application for financial aid for herself and her young daughter, since she had accepted the invitation of Mr. Timms, a notorious womanizer, to share his house. She announced this quite aggressively and had a good deal to say about the inadequacies and insecurities of a relief budget. She had clearly braced herself against the argument which she expected to encounter and was presenting her decision as already made. She was taken utterly by surprise at the welfare worker's comment, "That must have been one of the hardest decisions you ever made in your life."

A number of factors contributed to this remark. The worker knew that to argue would result merely in a battle of wills which Mrs. Brown would inevitably win. She knew, too, that from the moment this battle was engaged, Mrs. Brown could never change her mind. To do so would be to admit defeat. She was also aware that Mrs. Brown probably knew all the arguments which the worker could possibly use. If she did not, her neighbors would undoubtedly have let her know them.

At the same time she felt, underlying Mrs. Brown's aggressiveness, the need to stifle still existent doubts. The very way that she cut off argument and denied her need for advice showed her fear, and this process the worker was able to recognize and to feel for. She may, too, have felt that Mrs. Brown was not a person who made an immoral decision easily. But she did respect the fact that Mrs. Brown had come to what Mrs. Brown herself believed to be a firm decision, and she accepted her client's right to be angry about the inadequacy of the relief budget.

She did not allow either her own distaste for Mrs. Brown's decision or her defensiveness about her program to stand between them. And finally she kept her attention on her client's feelings and not on her own wish to see Mrs. Brown choose differently. Thus, respect for Mrs. Brown, an ability to feel for her at this critical time in her life, and a knowledge of some of the dynamics of the helping process combined to produce a very simple statement, at the same time spontaneous and based on an acquired self-discipline, which allowed Mrs. Brown to change.

The statement opened the door to Mrs. Brown's doubts and fears. She asked to look again at the relief budget. She found it to be rather less rigid than in her anger and disappointment she had thought it to be. She asked questions which she had been too angry to ask before. She herself brought up what her decision would cost her in terms of her own conscience. She said it would cut her off from her church, which was one of the things that she valued. Finally she told the worker that, with the loss of her husband, she had to find something to depend on, "and I don't know but that the church and you are a little bit stronger than Mr. Timms."

This instance, although primarily an example of empathy, also begins to illustrate what is meant by support. Empathy opened the door, but both empathy and support were necessary to complete and sustain the change.

Support, No Matter What

The third element in the helping factor is support. This has two aspects, material and psychological. Material support, the means to accomplish the task, may or may not be present in the helping situation. It is not generally part of either psychotherapy or problem-related counseling. When it does occur in these, it takes the form of technical know-how of some kind, whether this be marital techniques or where to find a school for one's child. In some helping it is, however, the most visible part and is thought of by many people as all that there is to help. It is what helping gives, whether this be money, opportunity, or know-how. Nor, as we have said, can it ever be considered unimportant. People need money, opportunity, education, and technical assistance to implement their decisions.

But people also need psychological support. They need to know that they are accepted and that the helping person will not give up on them. She will not be shaken in her desire to help. Even if helping proves impossible, she will still care about the person she is helping, "no matter what."

Support Even When Help is Not Possible
Particularly she will not desert the person she is trying to help because that person disappoints her or makes what she believes to be an unwise or immoral decision. It is true that there are two or possibly three situations in which this decision or failure may mean an inability on the part of the helping person to go on being the primary helper. One situation occurs when the decision, or some limitation in the helped person, removes him from contact with the particular source of help with which he has been working. A student may fail and be required to leave a school; a child's behavior may be such that for the protection of others he must leave a Children's Home; or a client may no longer be eligible for assistance. Or, the nature of the problem may be revealed by a person's act or decision to be such that he needs a kind of help which the original helping source is not equipped to give. The person being helped may need psychiatric care, or a sheltered environment, or some particular form of training or counseling which can only be given elsewhere.

There is also always the possibility that the helped person's problems may be such that no one knows at present how he can be helped. His resistance to help may be so strong or his ability to act so lacking that no skill that we have at present would be enough to provide any help. He may need, for his own protection or that of society, to be institutionalized, or control measures may have to be substituted for help. This decision would, however, have to be made with the greatest reluctance and with the knowledge that the helped person had not so much proved himself unhelpable as we unable to help him.

But even should one of these conditions separate helped person and helper, the principle of support means that the separation is not accompanied by rejection. The helping person still cares. She still respects and is concerned about what happens to the other.

Sometimes indeed it is in this very act of separation that helping really begins. I once knew a child in a Children's Home. She was a most unfortunate person, fat, dirty, low in intelligence, and from a family whose moral standards were appalling. Attempts to help her had met with little success, and most people found her quite repulsive. It was hardly a surprise when she became involved with a man who, because the child was a few months under sixteen, was charged with statutory rape. Nine Homes out of ten would at this point have written off a child whom they had shown that they could not help and who, since there was some publicity, had also embarrassed them. Some even today would have accompanied their rejection with a lecture on her ingratitude, although, one might hope, not with public disgrace.

The trial was to be held in a city some distance away. Dorothy clearly could not continue to live at the Home, and the normal procedure would have been to discharge her and to have her placed in a detention home to await the trial. Her housemother, however, approached the superintendent and said, "My other children can do without me for a while. Dorothy needs me now as she has never done before." The superintendent, agreeing with her, made arrangements for the housemother to live with the child in a motel during the trial and until Dorothy's subsequent commitment to a correctional school.

It was, not unnaturally, to the housemother who had shown concern for her at her worst that Dorothy turned after she left the training school. It was she whom she consulted over the problems of working and marriage. Six years later Dorothy's younger sister, who had remained at the Children's Home, became restless; Dorothy, hearing of this, offered her a home. Investigation showed that Dorothy, although still somewhat primitive in her housekeeping, had quite a decent home to offer.

Measured in terms of the distance Dorothy had traveled from her own beginnings, the Home had done more for Dorothy than it had for the hundreds of "nice" children it had reared. And it had done it at the point that its efforts had seemed in vain.

It goes without saying that support is also hard to practice. It is very easy to reject those who have let one down, especially where this has been accompanied with anger, blame, or ingratitude. One can moreover believe oneself either moral or realistic, according to one's taste, in doing so. Trying to help Dorothy after she had behaved as she had could so easily have been thought of either as condoning her behavior or simply as a waste of time. Her background and her intelligence did not suggest the possibility of her taking help at this point. Some girls might not have done so, but one might still raise the question whether they had been offered so solid a support.

To Support Is Not to Condone

It is extremely difficult for human beings to get away from the idea that to care about a person in trouble is to condone what he has done. It does not seem sufficient to allow someone to suffer the consequences of his act or to take his punishment for it. We seem to need to reinforce societal sanctions by disassociating ourselves from those who have offended against them, instead of seeing these people as those who need our help the most. Recently there have been some signs of improvement in this reaction, but also a backlash against it.

Part of this is reaction against unrealistic helping. To be concerned about a delinquent is not to approve of delinquency. Nor is it to excuse it, to throw all of the blame onto conditions or onto society. Poor conditions, poor heredity, undoubtedly make it harder for acceptable decisions to be made, but not all people make such decisions under these strains. The helper whose support is a disguised form of exculpation, who believes that the delinquent had no choice but to act as he did, is being unrealistic. She is indulging rather than helping.

But in part our unwillingness to try to help rather than to punish the delinquent is our fear of ourselves. It is a strange reflection on how delicately balanced our "good" and "bad" decisions must be that we get so angry at the bad ones. This anger has its roots in fear. We fear that we too may be tempted. It has long been known to psychiatrists that those who are most violently opposed to some social ill are often those to whom it is secretly most attractive, and that the faults we see in others are often the ones we are most prone to ourselves.

Support may be indicated in a number of ways. Sometimes the mere fact of being there is sufficient. Sometimes it is indicated by physical contact, particularly with a child. Sometimes it includes a direct offer of help, or making clear that one is available. Sometimes it is a matter of giving someone an introduction, of "breaking the ice" for him in facing a new experience. One must, however, remember that the statement is not simply, "I am here to help you," but "I am here to help you if you want me and can use me." Support is not taking over or forcing help on people. It is at its best when it is consistent but unobtrusive. But at the same time it must be unconditional.

Using the Elements

Reality, empathy, and support, then, are the three elements of the helping factor. They still do not tell us how to help in any given situation, which is perhaps something no one can tell another, but they do give us some idea of how we need to approach the problem. But even here they are not prescriptions. No one can go into a helping situation saying to herself, "I will be real. I will be empathic. I will offer support." The very effort would distract her from listening to the person she wanted to help.

But they do offer a way of looking at our own helping efforts. In every helping situation that has gone wrong, or been less productive than one hoped, it is good to ask oneself three questions:

1. Have I been able to face reality with this person, or have I glossed over the truth or offered false reassurance?
2. Have I been able to feel and express real empathy, or has empathy been lacking, or limited ("You can share your feeling with me as long as you don't feel so and so")?
3. Have I offered real support, or has it been conditional support ("I will continue to try to help you as long as you don't do this or that")?

An honest answer to these three questions often shows us what has gone wrong.

All three elements are necessary to each other. Reality without empathy is harsh and unhelpful. Empathy about something that is not real is clearly meaningless and can only lead the client to what we have called nonchoice. Reality and empathy together need support, both material and psychological, if decisions are to be carried out. Support in carry-

90

ing out unreal plans is obviously a waste of time. The three are in fact triune, and although in any one situation one may seem to be predominant, all three need to be present.

CHAPTER 6

The Helping Person

Before we can discuss specific suggestions or "rules" for helping—the
application, that is, of these principles to practice—one of the things we
need to pay attention to is the kind of person who will be a successful
helper. Only a person can give life to rules, and without a person behind
them, rules are of very little value.

Clarifying Issues Regarding the Helping Person

Much has already been implied about the helping person. We have already eliminated as successful helpers the coldly objective "student of
humanity," the person whose major interest is knowing about people
rather than working and feeling with them. We have warned, by implication, against those with strong personal needs to control, to satisfy their
own conscience, to feel superior, or to be liked. We have also issued, as
it were, incidental warnings against confirmed optimists, against those
who have solved their own problems and have forgotten what it cost
them, those whose own solutions have been precarious or have involved
repressions, those whose major interest is in justice or morality rather
than in helping, those who are afraid of hurting others' feelings, and quite
a number of others. These constitute a powerful accumulation of negatives, and it may be thought that helping can only be done by some sort
of extraordinary saint, rigorously denying herself and at the same time
perfectly adjusted.

If this were so, we would be even worse off than if we had accepted
the doctrine that help should only be offered by those extensively trained
in social and psychological diagnosis and treatment. There are probably fewer well-adjusted saints than there are competent diagnosticians.
But fortunately we do not have to be a saint to be a competent helper,
and indeed the kind of saint most people would envisage from this
description would not be a good helper at all. She would lack warmth
and spontaneity and might find empathy very difficult.

92

Helping is Not for Everybody

We do have to recognize that helping is not everyone's gift. There are those whom helping does not interest at all, and there is no particular reason why it should. There is much else to do in the world. The world needs helpers, but it also needs people who are more interested in machines than they are in people, and those whose competence and interest are in research or in pure knowledge. These people are not helpers, but they often contribute to our knowledge of help.

There are others who are interested in helping but who harm instead of help. They use helping more or less as an excuse to satisfy quite unrelated needs, such as to control, to be liked, or to feel superior to others. Many of these people should not be put into helping positions.

One Does Not Have to Be Utterly Selfless

But here I think we have to be careful not to insist that the helping person be utterly selfless. To do so would be most unrealistic. There must be some satisfaction in helping, other than that of the wish to serve.

It would also be dangerous. As Erich Fromm points out in his *Art of Loving*, the person who "does not want anything for himself" or "lives only for others" is often a neurotic. Such people lack "self-love," which, as Fromm says, is the opposite of selfishness and alone enables us to "love our neighbor as ourself."[1] There is nothing wrong in getting pleasure out of helping. Indeed one usually does best what one likes doing. At the same time while most of those engaged in helping have something of a desire to serve, their choice of helping as the form of service they will perform probably means that they have in some measure those very needs which, if carried to excess, would disqualify them from helping. People who want to work with children usually like to be loved by them. A person who tries to help a community organize itself probably gets some pleasure from the changes for which she is responsible and the feeling of power that this gives her. A consultant rarely minds being referred to as an expert, and many a good helper has felt that serving others does not do her conscience any harm.

Where then is the difference? Is it simply a matter of degree? I would suggest that it lies rather in the ability to postpone personal satisfaction in the interest of the person one is helping, to accept one's reward where one finds it, not to insist on it, and not to let one's desire for it get in the way of the primary business. As someone who loves children, and one who loves to be loved by them, I might know that in the course of my work I will find a number of children whom I can love and who may even love me in return. But I can also be aware that in a particular case

93

a child may need to struggle against me or to hate me, and I hope that in such a situation I could postpone or subordinate my own need to that of the child. This is far from denying that I have this need. The dangerous person is not the one who frankly delights in children and gets great satisfaction from them. It is the one whose desire to be loved by children makes it impossible for her to face them with an unpleasant reality. It is the one who cannot let the child leave her to go on to another helper, or share the child with other people (including, sometimes, the child's own parents).

A person is much more likely to be able to defer her own need, or to allow it to be met where it reasonably can, if she is aware of it. It does not take her unaware, and she is not afraid of it. Although sometimes her need may have considerable force, she knows that she can handle it under most circumstances, which is probably all that we can say of any of our needs. Some needs are more or less obvious. Others, such as the need to control, or to be thought wise and compassionate, we tend to hide from ourselves. Others still we may have repressed, and to recognize them may involve us in considerable risk.

Self Knowledge: Being Unafraid of Oneself

Self-knowledge is a necessary part of being a helping person. But self-knowledge in itself is not enough. There has to be as well a quality of not being afraid of oneself. I put it this way rather than using the term "accepting one's self," which is used by some writers, as this may carry the connotation to those unfamiliar with it of being satisfied with what one is and being unwilling to try to change. The two things are not the same. One may not particularly like oneself. One may try to change or improve and yet not be afraid of what one is, may accept the fact that at this time this is how one reacts or behaves. The person who is afraid of herself denies what she is; the unafraid recognizes her own weakness.

To be unafraid is the quality of not having to deny one's own feelings, nor prevent their natural expression by keeping a tight control over them. A person who has learned not to be afraid of herself does not have to create an image of herself that denies how she actually feels. She does not present herself, for instance, as the "oversweet" person whom we can usually recognize to be quite hostile underneath, and whom we would really like better if she could occasionally get angry or say an unkind word. The person who knows herself and is not afraid of what she knows is not threatened by the anger, the dependency, even the seductiveness of the person she is trying to help. She does not have anything to prove or to protect. She will not find the helped person's problems triggering

94

unexpected and perhaps unwelcomed reactions due to her own repressions.

This suggests one other group for whom helping is not an appropriate type of service — those for whom this self-knowledge would cost too much to acquire. All of us, to a certain extent, throw up protections against feelings we do not want to acknowledge. Sometimes these protections are unnecessary, and although it may be at first painful to learn to do without them, one finds that one can do so. But sometimes these protections are necessary to us, and to give them up, as one might have to, in order to help others is simply too much to pay.

There is nothing wrong in such a decision. One of the apparently most promising social work students I have known had to make this decision for herself when she found that to discuss with a neglected child his feelings about his parents was too painful for her to bear. It brought up too many memories she had repressed about her own parents. If this was what helping demanded of her, she would have to choose another career, and this is what she most sensibly did. Her repressed feelings about her parents would be no handicap to her in almost any other profession. In a helping profession they were.

And yet it was probably because of this very problem that she chose to work with children in the first place. She was, although she did not know it, unconsciously aligned with children against adults. But to become a helping person with children whose feelings about their parents were ambivalent, she would have had to consider both sides of this question. This would have cost her an inordinate price. She was wise not to pay it. What would have been unwise and harmful to those she was trying to help would have been to go on trying to help without being willing to pay the cost that helping entails.

One Need Not Be Perfectly Adjusted

Psychoanalysts have traditionally held that a training analysis is necessary before one begins to practice this specialty. The primary purpose of the analysis is to uncover any distortions of reason to which the student may be prone because of her own unconscious mind. To this extent it is somewhat analogous to the process of becoming unafraid of oneself, which all helpers need to do. But, unfortunately, this necessary preliminary has given rise in some circles to a belief that what a helping person needs is to be cured of all of her problems before she can be permitted to help. At the end of the training analysis, so runs this thinking, the student will be "well adjusted," and thus ready to help.

95

That this normally happens must be open to doubt. Analysis may be a method of solving certain deep-rooted problems, but it is not a general tonic to the personality. Many psychiatrists, skilled in their work, are patently not too well adjusted themselves, despite a training analysis. The claim to being well adjusted, however, is sometimes made and gives rise to other claims — that the analyzed person sees things clearly, is alone unswayed by an irrational unconscious, and therefore has the right to tell others what to do or to serve as an example for them.

The same is sometimes claimed for other helping persons. Helping people are supposed to need to be perfectly adjusted people, without problems of their own. Otherwise one can turn on them and say, "Physician, heal thyself." But this again suggests a misunderstanding of the role of the helping person. While she obviously cannot have problems of her own so pressing that her major preoccupation is the effort to help herself, she does not heal by example or by reasoning better than the person she is helping, except perhaps in the specific situation the helped person is distorting, which nearly anyone else could do. She is simply someone who, because she does not need to protect herself in a helping relationship, can make available reality, empathy, and support to the person she is helping. Moreover, because these things demand an interchange of feeling which must be felt to be sincere and immediate, spontaneity and ordinary, fallible human emotions are more characteristic of her than controlled, carefully thought-out responses.

Spontaneity Within Discipline

I wrote earlier of a response which was "at the same time spontaneous and based on an acquired self-discipline." In doing so I may have left a paradox dangling. It may be hard to see how a helping person can be both disciplined and spontaneous.

Obviously a good helping person does not behave impulsively or even, sometimes, in what we would think of as a natural way. To take but one example, it is normal and natural to reassure an unhappy child, and in any casual contact we would not only do so but be insensitive and unnatural if we did not. Yet there are situations in which to reassure a child robs him of his ability to deal with his problem, to express his anger and despair, and to accept our support. I have seen a little girl of five struggle with her despair over leaving her mother and with the fear that she had in some way been the cause of the family breakdown, and in this struggle lose for herself eight foster homes in eighteen months, principally because a kindly but not too knowledgeable caseworker reassured her, to stop her sobbing, that she would be loved in a foster home. This happened to be the one thing she could not bear. Love from a stranger only deepened her sense of her mother's lack of love.

How, then, could the response which this worker needed to make, but did not, be thought of as spontaneous? Perhaps an analogy could be drawn from other fields, and this might also help us look at the meaning of true professionalism. The professional dancer, for instance, has acquired a great deal of self-discipline, some of it quite painfully and slowly and, in terms of the normal impulsive gestures an untrained person would make on a dance floor, quite unnatural. But, as she becomes a professional, she does not have to think each move out beforehand. Her dancing, within the framework of the discipline she has acquired, becomes entirely spontaneous, and she puts into it, we say, "all of herself."

Much the same happens in helping. The beginning helper is often overwhelmed by the realization that her natural impulse may be to do or to say something that would be harmful. She restrains herself. She strives to be objective or to learn rules and principles. Her responses are intellectual rather than feeling ones, and she feels that all the joy, the natural warmheartedness, has been "professionalized" out of helping. Others, still acting impulsively, may observe her and feel the same. At the moment they are right. But as the helper becomes more at home in a helping relationship, as the habit of concentration on another's needs becomes second nature to her, as the knowledge she has acquired about how people take help or deal with their problems becomes her normal and natural way of looking at other people, and as she learns no longer to be afraid of her own feelings, she begins to find a wide area for spontaneity. She is no longer concerned about saying exactly the right thing—a frequent fear of beginning helpers—and knows that if she can stay with the other person in feeling—that is, feel with him but maintain her difference—what she says will be appropriate.

There is a great deal of popular feeling about the professional helper. Although we do not deprecate the teacher, the nurse, the physician, or the minister who has undergone rigorous training in order to be able to serve others, we often feel quite differently about the professional helper.

There are a number of reasons for this. Helping is something we all like to think we can do without any training. All it needs is a warm heart and common sense. We have a firm belief that helping should be spontaneous, "from the heart," and that to think about it spoils it. We fear the coldness of "organized charity" or tax-supported programs. And somehow we object to people making a living out of helping, although we do not object to the minister, the doctor, or the teacher doing the same thing.

Quite why this is so is hard to say. Part, I think, is due to our own pleasure in helping. We do not want to be denied this pleasure or to be told that our helping is insufficient or possibly harmful. We resent, as it were, the person with the license to help. Part may be our identification of helping with Christian "love" and our feeling that love ought to be something spontaneous and impulsive, although that is actually the kind of love (eros) that is self-seeking rather than seeking the good of the other (agape). Certainly our culture has put emphasis on irrationality in all types of love. And partly we may have met professional helpers who do seem to us cautious, cold, impersonal, and insensitive. But the "professional" worker who is any of these things is not a true professional. This seeming professional is someone who perhaps knows that all too often both the undisciplined will to help and the harsh judgment on others are self-serving emotions. But she has not learned to put anything in their place. She is also the most likely to insist on her own professionalism.

My own experience is quite different. The warmest, the gentlest, the most sensitive helpers have been those who in pursuit of helping have subjected themselves to the most rigorous training, both of their minds and of their feelings. They have cared enough to learn.

Getting Professional Training

This discussion of professionalism raises the whole question of how much training, if any, and of what sort, is necessary in order to become a competent helping person. Part of the purpose of this book is to suggest that much can be learned about helping by the person who does not plan to undergo extensive professional training. And yet as we face the need not only for knowledge of the helping process, which might be supplied in part by this book, but also for the acquiring of self-discipline, to say nothing of a disciplined spontaneity, which this book quite clearly cannot provide, there are bound to be some doubts about the matter. Can one hope to acquire self-discipline in the school of experience?

I think I would have to answer that if someone intends to make helping her career, if she hopes to be more than a competent helper, one of the highest class, then she would be advised to take professional training, either in social work or in some other discipline that is concerned with helping the helper look at herself in practice. Without going into detail about what this training should consist of, which is not our purpose here, certain things could be said about it. It should be a continuous structured experience, not an accumulation of little bits of knowledge, and an experience in which the helping person herself experiences a helping relationship with teacher, adviser, or supervisor. One of the principal ways of learning what to give help is like is to be a receiver of help. Indeed it has sometimes been said that as one receives help, so one is likely to give it.[2]

Again, such a course of training needs to contain, or even to be built around, a deliberately sensitizing experience, in which the student is enabled to examine her own feelings and her reactions to others. This usually involves some kind of group experience. And, thirdly, the whole experience should contain some form of fieldwork, under supervision, not so much to give experience in practice—this can be gained elsewhere—or even to try out theory in practice, but as a chance to try out for oneself, in a setting established for that purpose, how one actually performs in the stresses and strains of the helping relationship.

If training is for a specific profession, as it most usually is, then a fourth element needs to be added—that of specific knowledge of services and how they work, of social conditions, of normal and abnormal psychology, both individual and in groups. Because we have upheld that specialized knowledge in this field is not an absolute prerequisite to beginning to help at all, it does not mean that it is not an important tool for the professional helper. In some form or other knowledge about people and about society is an important tool in all forms of helping.

Yet this kind of training is not and will not be available for a great number of people in full-time or part-time helping. Some of these people may be able to rely in part on good supervision, which may supply the important experience of taking skilled help. Others will not. They may be helped by short-term courses, or even by books such as this one, but their chief learning will have to come from experience. It will not come, however, unless this experience is pondered, unless there is an attempt at honest self-appraisal in terms of one's ability to do what is demanded of one and some clarity at least about what needs to be done.

What short courses, in-service training, and books may do is stimulate the process of self-appraisal, bring in some new ideas which may enable one to look at the process from a fresh point of view, warn against some persistent dangers, and offer the thinking person some framework of theory and some vocabulary in which she can couch her thoughts.

Despite this emphasis on the need for training, however, one does have to admit that there are many people with little or no training who are capable of really skilled helping. Both of the examples we used to illustrate empathy and support in chapter 5 were the work of "untrained" people, although both had had long experience as well as some short-course and in-service training.

The welfare worker whose empathy helped Mrs. Brown reconsider her impulsive decision showed a combination of knowledge of the helping process, acquired self-discipline, and the ability to feel. The houseparent who helped Dorothy in her hour of apparent defeat found the ability to do so in her religious convictions. It was her strong sense both of her own sinfulness and of her having been forgiven that made it possible for her to transcend her shock and disgust and to offer Dorothy something of what she herself felt that she had received. Yet quite clearly the same religion, although not perhaps the same implications drawn from it, could have caused in another woman an almost totally opposite response. It could have resulted in an unyielding moralism based on her hatred of what she saw as sin. There must have been something in this houseparent, as there must have been in Mrs. Brown's worker, which enabled her to make use of her knowledge and her belief. The little training each had received may have sharpened these workers' skills, but they also had something in their temperaments on which this training could build.

Three Important Characteristics: Courage, Humility and Concern

Many attempts have been made to describe the qualities of the person who is, or is likely to become, a successful helping person. Most begin with a liking for people and continue with a plethora of human virtues, such as patience, dedication, and flexibility, and end with a sense of humor. They become little more than a description of an ideal human. Therefore I shall select only three characteristics which I believe are not usually sufficiently stressed but which the helping person needs rather more than does the nonhelper.

Courage

The first of these qualities is courage. This may sound a little surprising to those who have in their mind somewhere a stereotype of the helping person as somewhat meek and mild and perhaps more "feminine" than "masculine" in temperament. It is true that helping makes use of a number of qualities that are traditionally ascribed to women — sensitivity to feeling, interest in people rather than in things, a willingness to serve rather than to dominate or to control. On the other hand, the desire to control others by psychological rather than physical means has been held by some to be a predominately feminine characteristic, and the helping professions have both suffered and gained from a long line of extremely powerful women. Social workers might like to make up their own lists.

These so-called feminine qualities are sometimes a problem to the young male worker. Actually they have little to do with masculinity. One of the most sensitive and indeed one of the most tender helping students I have ever taught was a tackle on a Big Ten football squad before he sought training as a helper. At first he wanted to work only with adolescent boys, but he also had to be responsible for whole families in foster care. The crux in his learning came one day when he came into my office, saying, "I refuse to order panties for Thomas's little sister. That's not what I came here to do. What would Coach think of me if he knew?" I said, "Then she'll have to do without." Faced with this he admitted that he thought that previous workers had dressed the child much too plainly, and was it all right if he chose a dress for her that brought out the color in her blue eyes? He was delighted, a week later, at her pleasure in her new clothes. And once having come to terms with his almost "maternal" feelings he was much gentler in his work with his boys.

I hope that in deciding, for the sake of convenience, to refer to helpers as "she" I have not helped perpetuate a myth. Both men and women can be sensitive and gentle, and this is, I think, beginning to be recognized when it comes to the care of children. But stereotypes die hard. I was told by a leader in the field when I graduated from a school of social work that there was no future for a man in child welfare, and I was once denied the right to teach a casework class because as a man I could not possibly be sensitive enough. Yet I have spent my life in child welfare and taught casework many times.

Helping Requires Courage

Any implication, however, that helping does not demand courage of the highest order is very wide of the mark. It takes great courage to share with another the reality of his situation, and it is lack of courage which so often prevents us from doing so. We do not want to face the bitterness of his despair. We would rather do anything than be the person who brings reality to another.

It takes real courage, too, to hold to one's own grasp of reality in the face of a client's pleading—a courage, perhaps, of one's own convictions. Especially is this true when the person we are trying to help is an expert manipulator. We can so easily be snowed by plausible requests, which, once granted, lead to the weakening of the whole system of reality in which alone help can be forthcoming. It also takes courage not to be defensive of our programs or of ourselves when we are attacked. It takes

101

courage to bear anger and even to court it deliberately, as has to be done sometimes if the anger is to be expressed. None of us enjoys people being angry with us.

It also takes courage to take the risks both with oneself and others that helping inevitably demands. The personal risk involved may be that of failure, or being confronted with an emotional situation one has no idea how to handle, or having one's own comfortable world upset, or being blamed or abused. But perhaps the greatest personal risk is that of assuming responsibility for bringing into a situation an element which may help but which holds within it the possibility of harm.

Taking Risks

How a person actually uses help is always unpredictable. What we think may help could conceivably lead to retreat or breakdown, and the more we become engaged in what may really change a situation, the greater is the risk involved.

We can see this in the instance of the runaway boy we discussed in the last chapter. To tell this boy of his birth was an obvious risk. It might have resulted in a great deal of pain and hurt with nothing gained, or it might even have destroyed what little confidence he had in himself. We might have been wrong in our belief that this was what he needed to hear or wrong in our estimate of his ability to take help. The teacher was right to be hesitant. The alternative, however, was to leave things as they were, with the child obviously troubled and needing to run away. We had to make the decision to risk doing harm in the hope of doing good, but we could have equally well decided to leave, not so much well alone, but a moderate ill alone, for fear of what our intervention would do.

This kind of decision often faces the helping person. There are obviously some risks one does not take. Sometimes, if it is available, one may try to get expert help in appraising the situation. When, for instance, the caseworker had to decide whether to take a child to see a mother she had idealized and was fighting the worker to be with—the same child mentioned earlier whose struggle had cost her eight foster homes in a row—knowing that her feebleminded mother would not even recognize the child, and that this would be a shattering blow, the caseworker sought the aid of a psychiatrist to help estimate Shirley's essential ability to sustain shock. Yet she might not have had this help.

The alternatives in this situation were to risk real trauma for the child or to have her continue a struggle based on her unreal picture of her mother. All attempts to dispel Shirley's illusions about her mother by

102

talking, either by the psychiatrist or by her social worker, had failed. In this case the risk was worth taking, although it cost Shirley ten days of desperate sobbing before she could face up to the truth that she could never live at home. She was then able to give up her struggle and to make quite a good life for herself in a foster home. But it might not have been so.

Sometimes the risk involved is simply that of relationship. Too often a helping person fears to introduce some piece of difference, or let someone know her position, for fear that this will cost her her relationship with the person she is trying to help. A relationship, however, that cannot bear reality is generally not worth preserving. However pleasant it may be, it is not achieving anything worthwhile. For instance, a woman who had been receiving welfare for many years, and whose case record was inches thick, had her case reviewed by a class which included her caseworker. The class decided that the woman needed to be faced with the reality that, as the woman's children were growing up, she would soon find herself ineligible for Aid to Families with Dependent Children and that she had done nothing to prepare herself for the future. Even her caseworker agreed, but when I asked the caseworker if she could face the woman with the truth, the worker replied, "No, I couldn't. It would spoil my relationship with her."

Perhaps the best criterion for deciding to take a helping risk, outside of expert knowledge of the person's ability to respond to challenge and the degree of discomfort in the present situation, is the presence or absence of what might be called "drift." Drift is the gradual but consistent worsening of a situation. A boy in a Children's Home gets into a descending spiral of child-adult and peer relationships; a husband and wife drift apart. By not intervening, one is not letting the situation alone. It will not stay where it is, and a crisis of some sort needs to be precipitated.

Risks in the helping process need to be taken responsibly, with as much weighing of alternatives as is possible and a full realization of what is at stake when we intervene in such a way. Yet in my experience I have seen much more potentially good helping go to waste through not taking perfectly reasonable risks than I have seen damage done by taking them. This is true even of children, whom we normally think of as unable to face a harsh reality, and whom we naturally want to protect.

It Is All Right to Be Afraid

Helping people may also sometimes involve one in physical risks, although these are not too common. This risk does underline, however, that what is involved is not the courage of the person who is insensible to danger or insensitive to hurt, but rather the courage of the person who is afraid and yet does what she knows she needs to do.

I began my professional helping career in a children's protective agency, which involved bringing the fact that a complaint had been made about the care of their children to some pretty disturbed parents. To do so is for many people one of the most frightening demands of a helping profession. To stand on someone's doorstep as the bringer of bad news, to face and sometimes to court anger, to be abused and sometimes threatened, is not an easy thing, and many a worker, myself included, has left the office silently praying that no one will be at home and has circled the block two or three times before knocking at the door. A few people, however, find no difficulty in this task. They march up "bravely" to the door, state their business, sweep aside and generally manage to nip in the bud the parent's expression of anger. Quite possibly these people are simply denying their fear, which means that they are actually so afraid of being afraid that they have to act as if no fear were involved. But even if they are wholly unafraid – if indeed anyone can be – they are so only because they are unable to feel with the person whom they are supposed to help. Their ability to help is small. It is only the person who can be afraid and not be afraid of her fear who is in a position to help.

Humility

The second quality the helping person needs to have is humility. The word is of course a difficult one. It has a negative connotation for some which suggests a lack of self-confidence, a failure to claim what one knows and is. It often suggests a deliberate and hypocritical self-abasement in the manner of Uriah Heep. But it can also mean not claiming to be what one is not, being content to play one's part rather than insisting on taking the leading role when it has not been assigned to one, and refusing to assert a more or less specious superiority over others or to claim the right to control their lives. As such it is opposed to arrogance and presumption and is a genuine virtue.

Nonjudgmentalism

Humility shows itself in a number of ways in helping. Perhaps its most obvious manifestation is what is often called nonjudgmentalism. This is essentially the refusal to set oneself up in a seat of judgment to which one has not been appointed. It does not mean giving up one's power of

acknowledging we have made mistakes too

discrimination between what is good and bad, but it does mean not using this judgment to belittle another person, either directly to his face or in making plans for or about him.

Where judgment becomes dangerous is where it ceases to be a judgment on an act and becomes a judgment on the person who commits it, which involves a claim to know his motives or his character. To say that someone does not deserve to be helped is to make the kind of judgment that no one has the knowledge, or the right, to make about another. And, significantly enough, such judgments are usually made by people who actually know very little about the conditions in which such acts are performed.

It has long been the experience in welfare programs that the same citizens who are most vocal in their belief that welfare recipients are lazy, dishonest, or immoral as a class will insist that the clients whom they know well, and who are objectively no more industrious, honest, or moral than the average person, are exceptions to the general rule, victims of circumstance, and deserving of help. Moreover the immorality of the remainder will be greatly exaggerated and will be based on a very few instances, as in the general belief in the United States today that relief clients are responsible to a major degree for the increase in the number of illegitimate births, when in actual fact only a very small fraction of illegitimate children ever get on relief rolls.

This crass kind of judgmentalism may not affect the helper too much. It can be written off as the ignorance and the prejudice of the person who is not engaged in helping. Where judgmentalism deeply affects helping is where it obtrudes into the helping relationship, where it results in a decision to give up the effort, or cuts off expression of feeling, or causes the helping person to decide that the helped person is incapable of making decisions for himself and must be coerced or influenced to do what is right.

All these are, in effect, belittling actions. They assume that the helping person knows better or is better than the person she is trying to help, and that this knowledge or superior morality gives her the right to make such decisions. The person who has successfully solved her own problem and forgotten what it cost her is particularly liable to judgmentalism of this kind. She rapidly loses patience with the person who is struggling to do what she believes, now, anyone ought to be able to do and which she herself has done. Also liable are those who have genuinely found it easy to be good, at least in a limited way, because they have never had to face the particular temptations with which the helped person is struggling.

On the basis of their ability to withstand lesser strains, they cannot imagine that they would ever give in to greater ones.

Not all judgmentalism is, however, in the moral sphere. There can be a "scientific" judgmentalism that is just as severe and just as inhibiting to the helping process. This is the judgmentalism that arises out of the claim to know what is right or wrong for another and what is wrong with him.

The helpers of the 1920s and 1930s who took up psychoanalytic theory with such vigor reacted against the judgmentalism of the puritan tradition and remained for a time free from scientific judgmentalism because of two factors. One was their belief in psychic determinism, which made it, in the words of one of them, not so much wrong as silly to try to control others. The other was their very genuine awe in the face of the newly revealed complexity of human emotions which psychoanalysis revealed. Both of these safeguards have now vanished. It is a danger inherent in the claim to be scientific that one comes to believe in time that one really knows what is right and what is wrong for another person. Awe vanishes in the intoxication of beginning to understand. While what results is scientism rather than true science, there are today as many scientifically judgmental helpers as there are those whose judgmentalism is of a moral cast. These are those who fundamentally consider all their clients ill, who stress their weakness and dysfunction, who are quick with negative diagnoses, and who all too readily assume that their knowledge of what should be done gives them the right to take over, to protect their clients by making decisions for them, or to use one or more forms of more or less subtle coercion.

Humility and Serving Others

Humility means more, however, than refusing judgmentalism. It is more even than knowing that the more one knows, the more one ought to be convinced that one knows very little indeed. It is more than knowing that one can very likely be wrong, more than rejecting the assumption that because one knows a little one has either the right or the ability to decide for other people, more even than being able to say and feel sincerely, "There, but for the Grace of God or good fortune, or environment, or a happy childhood, go I." It is all of these, but it is also the willingness to allow oneself to be used by the helped person as his needs dictate, and not as one's own need to help demands.

We need again to be careful of terms. To be "used" by another person does not mean to be exploited by him. To allow oneself to be exploited is only to make the other person's problem worse, to provide

106

him with an unreal way of solving his difficulties. To allow oneself to be used in this way would be to contradict one of the implications of courage. To "allow oneself to be used" by another "as his needs dictate," however — the whole sentence is important — means the willingness to let the helped person decide to what extent and under what conditions he is willing to be helped. It does not mean necessarily agreeing to help under these conditions, or even refraining from pointing out that help is not possible under them. Nor does it mean refraining from offering what help is available, or even, if the need be desperate, intervening in an attempt to get help started. But it does mean, ever and always, treating the helped person as the important one in the relationship, the one whose opinions, feelings, and ideas matter, serving his interest, allowing him all possible freedom to be what he wants to be.

It means also being willing not to be the primary helping person in the other's life unless it so happens that this is what the other needs. It means being able to release him to another, or to play a minor role in a team effort. It may even mean playing a role that is unpopular or lacking in immediate satisfaction. In trying to help people with certain character disorders, for instance, one helper may have to be the one who deliberately holds the client to reality and stimulates the anxiety, which the person seems to lack, while another gives empathy and support and, so to speak, "picks up the pieces." Here the triune nature of help is partitioned, and the lot of the representative of reality may be hard.

Humility also means giving up pride in a "finished product" of helping and being content with being able to say, "I helped him at such and such a time, or with this little bit of the problem." It certainly means giving up the need to be thanked or recognized.

Trusting the Process

One of the hardest forms of humility the helping person needs to acquire is the knowledge that it is not she herself who is doing much of the helping. Quite apart from the fact that it is the helped person who has to make the final decisions and who, in the popular phrase, "is helping himself," the helping person is, as it were, the agent of a process rather than the creator of it. It is true that she puts into it reality, empathy, and support, and that these are not easily supplied. It is true that she approaches the helped person and his problem with courage, humility, and concern — not altogether common virtues. It is true that she can quite easily prevent or pervert the process and that there are skilled and unskilled helpers.

But if these things can be done reasonably well, and particularly where the relationship is well structured—that is, has a purpose, some regularity in time, and a clarity about its conditions—help will be forthcoming. The helping person will not have to exercise close control over what happens. She will not have to take the initiative in creating helping situations as much as she will take the opportunities which the helped person offers her. She will not so much assert her personality as respond to the personality of the other. She will rarely do things which she can look back on afterward and say, even to herself, "This is what I did to help and only I, perhaps, could have done it."

This is what is really meant by "listening" to another and "staying with him in feeling." It does not absolve the helper from the need to respond in an appropriate and even a courageous way. It is not a reason for passivity. It is rather that in helping one becomes aware that as the other person encounters reality, or limits, and as one is able to show empathy for him, and support him, something begins to happen to him in which one participates as much as one can but which is not dependent on one's own qualities. Anyone other than oneself could just as well be there. This is quite a humbling experience.

Its main effect in helping is to temper the helper's need to try to accelerate the process or to force results. As such it is the source of another virtue often ascribed to helping persons—that of patience. It is surprising how often in helping, just as one comes to the conclusion that nothing is happening, the helped person finds help for himself.

Concern

The third quality of the good helping person is what might be called concern. I use this term rather than the more usual "liking for people" both because it is more than "liking" and because "liking" is in itself a difficult word.

Concern, Liking, and Disliking

To "like people" may mean a number of different things. The cheerfully extroverted "good mixer," the person who enjoys crowds and inconsequential chatter, may be thought of as "liking people," but that person's relationship with them is a superficial one, and he or she is rarely a good helper. People who enjoy working with other people to some other end, such as salespeople, may also "like people," but usually they enjoy them as objects and not as persons. When we mean by "liking people" that we see only the good in them, that we never get angry at them, and that there are not some whom we cordially dislike, then we are asking of ourselves an unreal sentimentality or a dangerous self-deception. "Like" and "dislike" in this sense are matters of taste and experience. They arise from roots often quite deep in the personality, and although they are sometimes irrational, they are often not under conscious control. The problem is not so much to change them—one may doubt if this can really be done—as it is to transcend them.

A student of mine once found herself supervising a woman she thoroughly disliked. This made her quite uncomfortable. She felt that she ought to be able to like her and tried very hard to do so, looking for her good points, for reasons and even excuses for the other's behavior. This made her feel so guilty when, in spite of all she could do, she felt waves of dislike for the woman that she soon ceased to be able to hold her to any standards in her job. I had to point out after a while that her efforts to like this woman were seriously affecting her ability to help her.

It was only when this student could acknowledge and cease to be afraid of her dislike, which incidentally would seem to have been, if not deserved, at least not unnatural, and yet could assert truthfully that she did want to help, that she came to understand that what the helping person develops is a feeling to which liking and disliking are wholly irrelevant.[3] This is what is meant by concern.[4] It means to care what happens to another person quite apart from whether one finds him attractive or unattractive. The housemother who helped Dorothy did not find the child attractive. She did not like her in any ordinary sense of the word. Yet she had a deep concern which showed up like and dislike for the personal and somewhat selfish emotions that they are.

Concern and Concepts of Love

The quality of concern is sometimes called, quite simply, "love," both by secular philosophers and by theologians. This again is a slippery word and can involve us in quite erroneous concepts. We need the Greek distinction between different kinds of love. The kind we are speaking of is very close in meaning to that of the Greek word "agape." Indeed a careful reading of the most famous passage on agape, the thirteenth chapter of Paul's letter to the Church at Corinth, will show that so far from this being a general exhortation to "love" our fellows in some rather vague way, Paul is attempting a precise definition of this quality. Even the Latin word translated in the King James version as "charity"—caritas—means caring for, or concern.

Some of the qualities Paul ascribes to agape — its not being puffed up, or easily provoked, or insisting on its own way — bring it close to what we have called humility. Others, such as its endurance, are close to what we mean by support. In a more secular context Erich Fromm, in his *Art of Loving*, calls what Paul describes, rather surprisingly, "brotherly love" (which tends to equate it with the Greek *philia*) but catches some of its meaning when he describes it as "the sense of responsibility, care, respect, knowledge of any other human being, the wish to further his life."[5] He makes clear that it transcends differences in talents, intelligence, and knowledge, but he falls short of adding Paul's "love never ends" and ascribes this characteristic to what he calls "motherly love." The mother, he says, makes an "unconditional affirmation" of the child's life and needs, and this, he points out, instills in the child a love for living and not merely the wish to remain alive. This is close to what underlies the whole theory of helping: that love, or concern, stimulates to some degree the capacity for love and concern in the helping person. Where Fromm's definitions may mislead us is that he equates "motherly love" with inequality, so that his "motherly love" always includes some element of superiority and protectiveness. This may be an element of "motherly love" but not of the love, or concern, that the helping person needs.

Loving but Not Liking Our Enemies

It may seem that we are requiring of the helping person a kind of "freeing love" which is a high spiritual quality unlikely to be possessed by a normally fallible human being. In one sense this is true. It is only this kind of concern and the empathy which springs from it which brings the apparently impossible command to love one's enemies within the realm of practicability. It is only by transcending like and dislike that one could possibly "love" those one "dislikes."

We do not do this by changing "dislike" into "like." We are not asked to like our enemies, but to be concerned for them. Unnecessary disliking is a pity, and, when that dislike is based on moral judgmentalism, it is destructive to helping. But we should distinguish between disapproval and dislike. That "there is so much good in the worst of us and so much bad in the best of us that it ill behooves any of us to find fault with the rest of us" is good sense. To say that we ought to like everybody is not.

Yet I do not believe that concern, as we have used the word, is outside the range of any person who has learned not to be afraid of herself and who has some measure of humility. She does not, as we have shown, have to be self-denying. Nor does the helper have to achieve an idealistic liking for people. She can and will retain her natural taste and dis-

110

crimination, but in her helping she must not so much forget them as become so concerned about the person she is helping that they no longer have the power to sway her.

Liking and disliking are in fact rather selfish emotions. We tend to like those who flatter us, agree with us, or make us "feel good." We tend to dislike those who are most like our own worse selves—that part of our character that we have repressed or overcome. If I have a tendency to be bossy, but am careful not to be so, I will probably dislike bossy people.

Concern is, in the final analysis, a much more enduring and stable emotion than either liking or disliking. It is more honest, because it does not have to conceal dislike. It is also more inclusive. One does not have to like a person to help him.

Courage, humility, and concern may then give us some characterization of the helping person. Other qualities such as dependability, patience, integrity, or a sense of humor are of course also desirable, or perhaps simply facets of these. Intelligence and imagination can be of help. But the helping person is an essentially human being, with many of the faults that all of us share. There is nothing ascetic or infallible about her or about her knowledge. She is disciplined but no automaton, sensitive but no seer, knowledgeable but not necessarily intellectual, unselfish but not self-denying, long suffering but no martyr. When we meet her we will probably like her but not, perhaps, be too impressed.

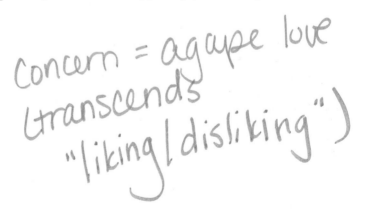

concern = agape love
(transcends
"liking / disliking")

CHAPTER 7

Suggestions for Practice

The suggestions made in this chapter may appear to constitute a set of rules or techniques for the practice of successful helping. In one sense that is what they are. They can be listed and numbered; even, if necessary, memorized; and the helper who has followed the argument of this book so far, and who has acquired some of the qualities of a helper and some of her self-discipline, may be a better helper if she remembers some of them.

The objection to calling them rules or techniques is that they do not guarantee, by themselves or apart from an understanding of the whole, any measure of success, if indeed this can ever be guaranteed in the helping process. They cannot be put into practice without the feeling and the attitudes from which they are derived. They are meaningless outside a relationship that is realistic, empathic, and supportive. They require that the person who practices them have courage, humility, and concern. Nor do they offer a blueprint of how an interview should be conducted, point by point. An interview based on rules and techniques would become a mechanical thing, devoid of the very element of feeling that makes it of help.

Yet they are all important things to do and to remember and are offered as such. Their numeration and the emphasis given to each in the text is a recognition of this fact. They do, of course, overlap sometimes and lead one to the other, but this is only natural. Some of them, too, are repetitive, and yet there also seems some value in putting them together here. I have tried, too, in most cases to give examples that may show how the suggestion may work in practice. Most of these examples, although not all, are drawn from the practice of social work, since it is here that my experience lies, but they are equally applicable to other methods or settings of helping.

Seen in this light these suggestions, rules, or techniques can be listed as follows.

1. Start with the request as it comes to you.

As we all know, what is requested may not be what the helped person eventually may come to want. It is, however, at the moment his evaluation of it—either what he wants at this time, or what he is willing at this time to discuss with you. It is what he is putting out for you to take hold of and his first definition of the kind and type of help which he both expects and is willing to take from you. Although eventually he may alter his request, or you may help him define it differently through the introduction of new ideas or difference, this can only be done in the context of your having looked at and listened to his original request.

To infer that the original request is not a real one is to show disrespect for the asking person. The only exception to this rule would be when the request is, by its very nature, patently either an invitation to pursue the asker's reasons for his request or some kind of "trial balloon" to see how one will react. Thus, if someone asked me if I knew a good way of committing a murder I would probably tell him no, and at least wonder why he felt impelled to ask this of me. The same might be true of statements which are really concealed requests for help, like an apparently unconnected statement that women are not to be trusted, which obviously conceals feeling about something that is troubling the speaker. Here I would say something like, "some woman must have let you down," as a way of bringing the problem down to the particular.

Conversely, it is important to recognize the point at which an answer to the problem presented no longer is what the helped person wants.

A woman, obviously troubled about her relationship with her granddaughter, asked for financial help for her. But when a budget was worked out, it was obvious that the grandmother was willing and able to supply all the child's needs except those that had to do with her granddaughter's beginning adolescence—cosmetics, clothes, sanitary supplies. Only then could the grandmother come to see that it was not finances that really bothered her, but the child's becoming sexually mature. She feared that her grandchild would repeat the child's mother's pattern, which the grandmother had been unable to control. Yet, when this was implied earlier in the interview, the grandmother rejected it out of hand.

Often the shift is not arrived at by this process of reason but becomes apparent in the asking person's dissatisfaction with the answer apparently arrived at. In the example above, for instance, it was the grandmother's reaction to the smallness of the amount the agency could offer, due to her desire to help the child, that enabled her to move on and to discuss her deeper fears.

2. Respond to feeling rather than to literal content.

To suggest that the helper respond to the helped person's feeling rather than to the literal content of what he says may sound rather contradictory after we have insisted that one must accept the terms on which help is asked, but it explains the exceptions we noted. One starts with the request for help and with the person's feeling about it. It is the feeling behind the request which helps us to see that the request means more than its literal word form.

The response to feeling rather than to the literal content of words is perhaps what most clearly distinguishes helping interviewing from social conversation. It does not mean that one ignores what the person in front of one is saying, but it does mean that one's interest is centered first and foremost on what he is trying to convey to you, and that this is as often conveyed by tones of voice, gestures, hesitancies, and the like as it is by the actual logic of words. Words are often used to protect oneself from saying what one feels. Sometimes what needs picking up and responding to is the very difference between what a person says and how he is saying it. One often needs to say something like, "You are telling me this as if it were good, but you don't sound as if you liked it," or to respond to what literally is a simple statement with, "That seems to trouble you."

In a social conversation the interest is almost entirely on words. A word reminds someone of a story or sets up a new train of thought. What ties one comment to another is the literal content of what is said. The consistency of a helping interview is, on the other hand, that of feeling. An interruption in a helping interview is not so much a change of sense as it is a failure to follow feeling. A child said aggressively to her social worker, "I nearly telephoned you today." The social worker, intent at that moment on creating a "good" relationship with the child, and perhaps a little taken aback by the implied blame in the child's voice, answered, "My, but you must be a big girl to know how to use the telephone." In a social conversation this response would be perfectly allowable. They were discussing telephones, and it did enable the social worker to pay the child a compliment. But from a helping point of view it was an interruption. There was no suggestion that the child was asking for praise. She was expressing anger and a need for the social worker's help.

The importance of listening to feeling and responding to it is particularly significant when we consider what use the helped person is

114

making of what he tells you. What he says about himself is rarely dispassionate appraisal. It is part of the image of himself that he needs to project, not perhaps to the whole world, but to you, at this moment. And, as we have said, the question "Why do you tell me this now?" may be of real importance.

A failure to see this importance and an insistence on the literal content of what is said, instead of on the meaning it has in the relationship, may lead one far astray.

What it does lead to, only too often, is a simple battle of wills. This is what happens when the helped person expresses an apparent wish to do something that the helping person suggests or wants, "if only" certain difficulties could be overcome. Maybe it is to go to a doctor. But there is no transportation. I will drive you, then. But I can't go at the time you are free, and even if you adapt your schedule the doctor doesn't see patients then. If this is somehow overcome, there is the matter of payment, and if this be wangled somehow, then we find that the patient does not trust this particular doctor, or, on thinking it over, is not convinced that he is ill. So the argument proceeds, with the helped person finding more and more reasons why such an action is impossible and the helping person using even more and more ingenuity in overcoming these reasons.

Very early in such an exchange some recognition of the helped person's fear of doctors would have avoided the fruitless struggle. Yet it is surprising how often we fall into this sort of struggle. It is almost as if we have a need to prove the other person illogical or uncooperative and so excuse our failure to help him.

3. Recognize likely feelings, even before they are expressed.

Although each person's feelings are his own and you may, as it were, "guess wrong," there are certain feelings which are so natural and inherent a part of the process that the helper can safely bring them out in the open even when they are not expressed. She may be wrong. If she is, she has usually lost nothing and has in fact done nothing but made a courteous allowance for what the other is likely to feel, as one does when one apologizes for troubling another with a request even though the other is glad to grant it. But often one is right. This happens most often when what one recognizes is in some way the difficulty of taking help, or anger in having to face reality. The neglecting parent, for instance, faced with the protective worker or officer, is much more likely to be able to discuss his situation with someone who expresses some understanding of how unwelcome and threatening his visit must seem than he is with someone who, by her silence or her casual manner, appears not to understand. Tact, in the sense of ignoring unpleasant feelings or situations, is one of the helper's worst enemies. Instead of reducing likely feeling it leaves it as a wall between the helper and the helped. Sometimes the effect of quite a tentative little piece of empathy of this sort can be most dramatic.

A man who had long lived as a lodger with a family took over the parental role for the thirteen-year-old daughter when both parents were killed in an accident. It was, as far as anyone could judge, a purely avuncular relationship with some provision for chaperonage, and when the girl was reported for truancy, the court, seeking the "uncle's" cooperation, accepted him fully as in loco parentis. It was not until a sensitive worker said to him musingly one day, "You know, you must wonder what we all think of you and Jane," that the man broke down and confessed his terror of the whole situation and the blackmail the girl had used, based on some childish familiarity, to force him to allow her more freedom than he thought good for her. He said, "If she gets into trouble, I wouldn't stand a chance in the world." As long as the court had treated him tactfully, trying to convey by their attitude that they saw nothing wrong in the relationship, he could not admit to them his fear of where it might lead.

Possibly in this case the probation officer had sensed the man's underlying fear, but even if she had not, a little "loving imagination" would have suggested that he would naturally be concerned with what the court thought of him and the child.

4. When dealing with an angry or rejecting person, keep your attention on his feeling and do not attempt to defend what he is feeling about.

One of the hardest things to do in all helping, and one of the most essential, is to respond to an angry or rejecting person by concentrating on what he is feeling and not to argue with him. It stems from the understanding that such a person is in need. He expresses his anger to you because, in fact, he needs help with it. But we often deny him this help because the thing he attacks is something dear to us, which we feel a need to protect. It may be our program, or our belief, or a person whom we know to be in trouble and to need sympathy rather than criticism. But the moment a helper tries to defend whatever it is the person she is facing is angry about, she lines herself up against him. She tells him that he is somehow in the wrong to get so angry. If he only understood or had a little more compassion, he would not feel as he does.

This only makes it harder for him to give up his point of view. Even "interpretation" (a favorite word of teachers and child welfare workers) of a child's needs subtly tells the angry person that his anger is unfounded. It also makes clear that one's interest is not in the person to whom one is talking. It is in whatever he is attacking. A mother complained bitterly to a school counselor that her child apparently wantonly failed in school because "he didn't care," although she was sure that he had enough brains to pass. The counselor patiently explained that the child tested dull normal, that he had become discouraged, that if no fuss were made about grades, the chances were that he could do, not brilliantly, but sufficiently well to pass and that what was needed for his good was for everyone to relax. She illustrated the method she had used in her interviews to reassure the child and to help him achieve on tasks the boy believed to be too difficult, and she encouraged the mother to let him develop his undoubted manual skill. The mother accepted the explanation with some skepticism and covert indignation but promised to try. She was back next week saying that taking off the pressure only seemed to make things worse. Now she knew he was lazy and not stupid. He must not have tried in the test. Twice in the week he had scamped his homework, although she knew that it wasn't too hard for him. Did the counselor really believe that she shouldn't see that he at least did the work?

It was at that point that the counselor saw what she had done. She said that it must be hard to feel so badly let down by one's child. The mother at this point began to tell the counselor of her own quitting school despite good grades to marry a man who had no education but was, she agreed, a capable workman. She told of her family's bitter disapproval and insistence that she had lowered herself, of her determination that her child prove a success and confute them, of her fear that he was temperamentally more like her husband's family than hers, and of her attempt to prove that this was not so. Only as she began to consider what all this had meant to her could she say, as she finally did, "It isn't fair to him to make him fight that old battle of mine."

The lesson that one has to learn, and it is a hard one, is that by defending what one feels to be unjustly attacked, one usually only does it harm, but by refusing to defend it, and trying instead to help the attacker, the chances are that the attack will be turned into help. Yet not to defend is tremendously difficult, particularly when one feels the attack to be unjustified or inspired by unworthy motives. Perhaps the most difficult situation of all is when the attacked thing is oneself. But the rule still holds, and if the interest in the other is genuine, not assumed, it works in the great majority of situations.

117

5. Listen, rather than explain or instruct.

Although it is not true to say that helping consists solely of listening, it is probably true to say that a helping interview can often be judged roughly by the proportion of words spoken by the helper and the helped person. Good helping demands the introduction of reality and difference. It requires expressions of empathy and assurance of support. Sometimes the helping person must intervene or channel a stream of thought or feeling. But for the most part these interventions are short and to the point.

The most effective single statement I have seen in practice was made to a neglecting mother who was pouring out her anger against her unfaithful husband and in the process losing sight of what the interview was about, which was the neglect of her daughter. It consisted of four words, interjected into the stream of the mother's complaints, "And meanwhile Barbara suffers," and it resulted in the mother really beginning to face her problem. Much also can be conveyed by what one might call "encouraging noises" or gestures which convey empathy or support.

Sometimes, however, explanation and even instruction are necessary. Sometimes a person actually needs to know how to do something—how to apply for social security, or where to write for a birth certificate. But this is not the kind of explanation and instruction many inexperienced helpers tend to give to those they are helping. All too often what we get instead is a long explanation of why something is so, which is often an indication that the helper is not sure that it should be so, or a reasoned exhortation showing that such and such a course is the desirable one. It is true that occasionally one may find a person who genuinely does not know how he should behave or what to do in a situation, but this is not humankind's most common predicament. Generally he knows quite well, but what he cannot do is to do it. Paul of Tarsus, who had considerable insight into human difficulties, put his finger on the problem when he said that he did not do what he wanted, but did the very thing he hated (Rom. 7:19ff.).

Listening means a total concentration on what the other person is saying and feeling. It is what is so easily lost if we allow other considerations to enter into the interview. Other goals, however worthy, other concerns such as our need to succeed, or be liked, or even to help inevitably dissipate listening. But to listen does not mean to be totally nondirective. Nor does it mean, as it has sometimes been held to mean, acting simply as a mirror and turning back on the helped person all decisions. To reply, as some helpers tend to, almost routinely to any request with "What do *you* think?" is a technique that can most easily be overused.

Sometimes it only has the effect of pushing the helped person away. It says, in effect, that one cannot help. And while clarity can come from the mere act of expressing one's thoughts to another, to rely solely on this process can greatly limit one's ability to help.

A young woman sought advice about enrolling in nursing school. She had worked at one time as a nurse's aid and, as she said, "loved the work." Yet she had left it to become a librarian for reasons which were no longer valid. To all objective questions about a nursing career she could give positive answers. Yet she hesitated to enroll.

The interviewer listened. She shared with the young woman that there was apparently some reason that held her back they had not discussed. The woman said, yes, but she could not place it. Going over what she had said, the interviewer remembered the words "I loved it." Yet the woman had given it up. She asked, "Did you perhaps love it too much?" The woman nodded. "You felt it a kind of self-indulgence?" This brought out all the young woman's feelings about her dedication to helping and her fear that she was in fact satisfying her own needs rather than those of her patients. It ended with the interviewer saying "I love my work, too, and I think it's all right to love it. It helps me do a better job." "Then if it's all right, how soon can I enroll?"

Here the woman could not risk her fear of indulgence until the helper broke through, as it were, and fastened on the one statement in what she had said that seemed to carry meaning.

Nondirective counseling arose from an understanding of the need of the helped person to make his own decisions, but it underestimated the help that he might need in doing so. It does stand as a warning not to take over the helped person's life. To do so is so obviously fruitless that a warning against doing so would hardly seem worth listing were it not for another curious paradox, which is that to take over is very often the result of having been taken over.

6. Hold fast to your function as a helper. Do not take over the helped person's decisions, but do not allow him to control the conditions of help.

The question in a helping relationship is not how much helper and helped control the other, or refrain from doing so. It is what each controls. The helper must not and cannot control the use which the helped person makes of the relationship. At the same time the helped person cannot and must not be allowed to control the helping actions of the helper or the conditions of help itself.

119

Give and take (mutual)

The request of the seeker for help that the helping person "do" something about his problem, make concrete suggestions, tell him what to do is a common phenomenon. It will generally be noticed, too, that when the helping person does this, and requires of the helped person some involvement in it, what the helping person does proves to be inappropriate. How often does one not hear helpers say, "But I thought you wanted me to. . . ." Yes and no. He wanted you to take the responsibility for this decision, but he did not want to have to live with it once it was made.

What is perhaps not always recognized is how hard the person being helped works to control the situation, to get the helping person to do what he wants her to do. He uses the very same psychological tricks that the manipulative helper so often tries to use on him—disarming him, shaming him, challenging him, and appealing to him. But these efforts are not a sign of the helped person's strength or his ability to make decisions for himself. They are exactly the opposite. They are a sign of a refusal to face up to what is needed. One of the characteristics of those people whom we say are suffering from a character disorder and are the hardest of all to help because they have developed infinite ways of disclaiming responsibility is that their first request of any helping person, even a probation officer, is to ask her help in meeting some goal of their own. A boy convicted of drunken driving and manslaughter by automobile, in his first interview with his probation officer, did not ask her for help with his alcoholism, but, "Will you help me get my driving license back?"

We need to reemphasize here that a belief in the client's need to choose does not include his right to use you to further a nonchoice or to escape reality. You are there to be used, but to be used does not mean to indulge. Paradoxical as it may seem, the helping person must be a servant, but she cannot allow herself to be mastered. She must hold fast to what she can properly do, what she is willing to do, and what is realistic and sensible for her to do. Anita Faatz puts it even more strongly. She says that "in every helping process where something does indeed take place, there comes a time when all the strength of the client is gathered into one mighty effort to overcome the strength of the helping person; and if he succeeds, his movement is defeated, and if he does not succeed, he may have won new life."[1]

This is indeed a situation where the desire to help another can prevent one from helping him. It is very easy to be caught in the demands of the person who appeals to us and to start doing things for him instead of helping him do things for himself.

120

A child who was having difficulty with his friends in a Children's Home asked the social worker, first, to talk to the older children to tell them to play with him. When the social worker said that she could not create friends for him, he begged the social worker to be his friend—"Come and play ball with me." It was only when the social worker stuck to her function—that she was here to help the boy find out how to make use of living in a group—that Tom was able to say that what he really needed help with was his anger at boys who didn't seem to care at all about having to be away from home. "I'm afraid I'll become like them." This opened up a discussion which ended in the boy's resolution to make the best of what had happened to him, which was his having to be in the Home.

The usual argument for not holding to a function is that one should meet need where one sees it. It might be that the boy needed a friend to play ball with. But who should this be? Not an all-purpose social worker, but a playmate. It was only in facing the fact that no one could create a friend for him that the boy was able to face what was preventing him from making friends.

The lone helper, the one without a clear function or responsibility, is somewhat at a disadvantage in knowing what role she needs to hold to. She does not have an agency or an organization with clear lines of responsibility to rely on. What she must rely on is her grasp of reality, what she knows that she can do and her willingness to do it. She has to find this strength in herself and in the principles in which she has come to believe.

7. Make clear, as soon as possible, both the conditions of service and the authority and role of everyone concerned.

The need to make clear what authority anyone has was discussed in an earlier chapter. It is the first step in establishing reality. The helped person needs to know what you can do to him. He needs to understand the consequences of his likely struggle with you, and just how far this can go. He needs to know, also, if you have no authority at all. He needs to know how far you are willing to go, what you will do for him and what you will not do, and what responsibilities this will involve him in. In a formal helping situation I have a strong inclination to insist that this understanding be reduced to writing, in some sort of agreement, not because such an agreement is binding in law, or can compel anyone to do what he does not want to do, but as a way of defining a common endeavor, and as something to come back to if the relationship seems to be going astray. It is much easier to say, "This is apparently what we saw that we would do together. How has it changed?" than to point out that the other person is making working together difficult.

In private, personal helping and in more informal situations written agreements would be something of a burden. Nevertheless, written or spoken, detailed or rather general, some such agreement has to be there. Sometimes it will not emerge at first. One may need to explore quite fully what help is being asked before one can begin to think of the role helper and helped will play. Sometimes the situation may be pretty well determined already, by legal requirements or by generally understood more or less formal relationships, such as those of teacher and student, minister and church member, or doctor and patient, but will still need to be made explicit and its implications considered.

Included in such an agreement should be the question of confidentiality. It is not always possible to promise someone absolute confidentiality. A priest may be able to do so, but even a doctor may feel compelled to share information with a relative. Particularly in dealing with children the helper needs to be sure that she really means it before she can promise not to tell anyone, when she may have responsibility of which she cannot divest herself.

A child, about to be returned by a court to her father's custody, told her housemother in confidence that her father continued to molest her sexually on her visits home. The housemother felt herself bound by the promise of confidentiality she had solemnly given the child. Yet she could not see the child returned to the father. Fortunately she was able to help the child tell this herself to the judge. Otherwise she might have been forced to break her word. In this situation the child's fear of the father made this possible. In some way she may have hoped that her confidence would be broken. The same situation can arise, however, when the helped person is planning something dangerous, or illegal, which no one who knows about it can let him do. One may have to tell people that there are some things they cannot tell you in confidence.

A particular kind of condition is that of payment for service. While much service in social agencies is free, and clearly ought to be so, there is no reason why counseling, or consultation, or other kinds of formal helping should not be paid for. Not only are there those who have developed real skill in helping and have undertaken expensive education to increase their skill, who may work independently of any formal agency, but there is often advantage to the helped person if he makes payment. To do so can help him struggle with his feeling of helplessness. Where so much is out of his control, this is something he can control.

122

It may also help him resolve the kind of guilt one can develop just for having been helped.

The freedom that having paid for something brings is particularly obvious in some adoption situations, where being given a child one was not able to bear oneself sometimes ties an adoptive parent in a net of impossible gratitude to the agency which gave him a child. Some less ethical agencies have not been slow to exploit this guilt. To have paid for service can make this unnecessary and, incidentally, cost much less.

8. If possible, set limits, particularly in time.

It is perhaps only necessary to say here that a known period of time both is far less threatening and gives one an often very helpful deadline with which to work, particularly in matters where there is a very important single decision to make, such as the giving up of a child or separation from a spouse. Here the nonchoice is so attractive that if unlimited time is given, things begin to drift. It is also true that in most helping, if there is not significant change in, say, six months, probably something different is needed. Time also permits one to construct certain checkpoints along the way, at which both helper and helped can look at what is happening. The setting of a limit in time has been found very useful in helping an unmarried mother make a decision about giving up or keeping her baby, in working with neglectful parents, and in tackling particular problems that a child may have. In one Children's Home the use of a skilled caseworker was greatly enhanced when it became known that her services would be available on a selective basis for only ten children at any one time, and for six months only, with a checkpoint after three. Children began to use her in a much more purposeful way, saying, "I need to get down to things, because we don't have too much time." Defenses tended to be maintained for less time. The child was able earlier to make up his mind to risk sharing his problem.

In much informal helping, the use of time may not seem appropriate, or indeed necessary, except where the relationship is likely to be of some duration, in tutoring, for example, or in premarital counseling. Yet, if the relationship extends over more than one or two contacts and help is still being asked, the setting of time limits may be wise. It is sometimes good to say, "We've discussed this three times, now. Let's concentrate on the problem for a week (or a month) and see if anything happens. We may find you need some other kind of help."

9. Help the helped person express what he wants and then work with him toward how much of it he can have.

When a person asks for more than you can give, it is important to help him express what he wants and then to help him attain as much of it as possible. The natural tendency is to try to persuade the other person that what you do have is good, even if it is not quite so good as what he is asking for. Or, some helpers will carefully avoid discussion of what they do not have to give, seeing this as fruitless and likely to lead to disappointment. Why discuss the impossible? To take either of these positions is to avoid the kind of reality with which helping has to do. The helped person wants the whole. He cannot have it. But his wanting it is reality just as his not being able to have it is a piece of reality, too.

What will really help him is to face this double reality and to make what adjustments to it he must. If it is you, rather than he, who adjusts one piece of reality (his wants) to the other, he will not gain the experience of meeting the real situation and he will have, in addition, an unmade decision in terms of his ultimate desire. He will inevitably feel that you did not understand, that perhaps you could have stretched the limits if you had wanted to or had known how deeply he really felt. To say, "This is then what you are saying you really want. Now let's see how much of that is possible" is, in any case, much more encouraging than to throw doubt on what he wants.

A child had reacted to foster-home care with a determined effort to get sent home to a hopelessly retarded mother. She came to resent any kindness on the part of foster parents, seeing this as an attempt to keep her away from home. She rejected all efforts to love her. It was only when a foster parent could recognize with her how much she wanted to go home, but how impossible this was, that she was able to say, one day, "Well, if I can't go home, will you be next thing to a mother to me?"

What was done here required of the foster mother a great deal of courage and humility (in the sense that we have used the term). She had to give up pretending that what she, as a foster mother, could give was in any way the equivalent of what a real mother could give. It was not what the child wanted. Yet the child could use what the foster mother did have to give when it was presented honestly as a necessary second-best.

Sometimes, too, we fail to find out what it is that a person is asking when he appears to ask the impossible. A retarded boy told his vocational counselor that he wanted to be an astronomer. Instead of pointing out the skills needed for such a career or trying to talk him into a more reasonable job, the counselor asked him what an astronomer did.

"He looks at stars," the boy replied. The boy was entirely happy with a night watchman's job on a ranch, where he could look at stars to his heart's content.

10. Do not defend a reality that you cannot or do not intend to change.

So often when a person is faced with an unpleasant reality, the helper tries to soften the blow by explaining that there is a good reason why it is so. I have heard many a welfare worker tell her client that his grant is so low "because we must share with everyone equally," or excuse, to a child, his parent not visiting him by explaining that the mother has been very busy lately. Sometimes what may be at stake may be one's own decision—a permission refused, or a grade given.

While the other person may be helped by knowing the grounds on which a decision is made, or an action taken, one needs to be very careful that such an explanation does not become a justification. If one is there to help a person, through empathy and support, to face a piece of reality, to insist, however subtly, that this reality is good is to say to the other person that his feelings about it are wrong, and this makes empathy impossible.

The moment one defends a reality, one raises the question that it can or, at least, ought to be different. One removes it from the status of a reality. One gets into endless arguments about whether it is just, or fair.

This problem often confronts the probation officer, with whom the probationer wants to argue either his innocence or the justice of his sentence. Neither is usually productive. What probationer and probation officer need to face together is the reality of probation, which neither of them can change.[2]

We do, however, have to be careful that the reality we are talking of is something that neither we nor the person we are helping can do nothing about. It may be that the probationer is really innocent, or the grant something the client ought to appeal. It may be that it is not actually a reality. One of the most sensitive bits of helping I have seen was done by a friend of mine, a very direct person, in a Children's Home. She had in the Home a teenage girl, a difficult, rebellious youngster, who began to have morning sickness. She took her to the doctor, and tests showed that the girl was pregnant; but when Mrs. Johns called the girl in and told her the result of the tests, Connie was adamant in her denial that she had ever had intercourse with a boy.

I know what I would have said. I would have said, "Come off it, Connie. You are pregnant, and we need to figure out what to do." The "Virgin Mary complex" is not uncommon in teenage girls. But Mrs. Johns

125

says she caught something in Connie's tone of voice that made her say, "Let's check with the hospital again." The hospital had confused two patients, and Connie's test had been negative. For the first time in her life someone had believed Connie, and from then on she was a different person.

Social workers are often accused of helping people adjust to reality, rather than working to help them change it, or working to do so themselves. Sometimes, I would suggest, one has to do both, but on a different time scale. However much one may feel that conditions are unjust, however much one may want to change them or to help others to do so, for the time being this is reality, and it has to be handled. The important thing is not to become so identified with what is that we deny others the right to protest or act to change it.

11. Allow the person you are helping to fail if he wants to.

To say that the helper should allow the person she is helping to fail perhaps is simply a warning against overprotection, which has been implicit in all that we have said, but the problem needs restating in this form. It has two thrusts.

First, it is a plea not to try to prevent someone from attempting what may seem to you the impossible, which can arise from your lack of faith in what he can achieve if he really wants to as well as a wish to protect him from an experience that may be very poignant for him.

And secondly, it is a reminder that when a person is in the process of failing to do something, it may be because he wants to fail. To help him not fail is then to defeat what he actually wants the most. One of the worst pieces of helping I have ever perpetrated personally had to do with a student in whom I had a great deal of faith and whom I was determined to help become a social worker. But, for some reason, this was not what he wanted to do. When this wish began to show up in poor work, I found myself making allowances for him, grading him a little better than his performance warranted and refusing to allow him either to withdraw or fail. It took him over a year to come to the point at which he could say, "I'm tired of trying to help people" and choose another profession—a year that my refusal to permit him to fail had taken from his life.

12. Formulate the helped person's problem, from time to time, as you see it.

When the helped person has been trying, in one way or another, to get you to understand, clarity can sometimes come if you will say to him,

"It seems to me that you are saying. . . ." You may have misunderstood him, or you may essentially be right. Sometimes, too, this gives the helper the chance to introduce a little difference into the situation by stating the problem in a slightly different light. The person seeking help may reject this difference, or he may find that it helps him to look at it differently himself. *Make sure you are on same*

Such a formulation is always a tentative one. The helper never says, *path* "I know what your problem is," but, "This is my understanding of what you are saying to me. Am I on the right track?" As such it has some of the characteristics of tentative empathy, but it is much more specific.

In the situation we discussed earlier of the young woman who wanted, and yet couldn't quite decide, to go to nursing school, the helper, after listening to one reason after another why the woman could not go to school at this time — lack of money, home obligations, being tired of "learning," all of which the woman herself disposed of as soon as they were challenged — said to her, "I think you are saying that you want to go to school very much, but there's something you can't identify holding you back." This proved very helpful because it cut short a fruitless exploration of objective "reasons" and centered them both on looking for a deeper feeling that the woman could not put into words.

Sometimes it is good to recapitulate agreements: "It seems to me that we have agreed that your problem looks at the moment like this," or "Let me see. You're asking me if I can help you do this, or that."

The whole point here is to keep contact, to test out one's understanding and to try different formulations of it, so that helper and helped do not go off in different directions. *Look at parts of the whole*

13. Partialize the problem.

Suggesting that the helper partialize the problem is sometimes objected to by those who are quite rightly convinced that all of a person's problems are interconnected, that his failure to earn his living, his disagreement with his wife, his fits of dizziness are part of the same underlying pattern. Yet, unless the person is willing to admit total defeat, practically he has to work on one thing at a time. Nor can you really help him with a whole reorganization of his life without working on specific things. The hope is, of course, that by managing to change some small part of the total problem the helped person will find that little bit of extra courage or clarity that will enable him to do something about something else.

Often what one needs to discuss is simply the next step in the proceeding, what you and the helped person can do in today's conference. Other things may have to wait. A human being is capable of tackling only so much at any one time. The grandmother whom we used as an example of starting with the actual request found herself facing a sea of troubles — her granddaughter's rebelliousness; her own feelings about the child's mother, whom she had cut out of her life when she had married unsuitably; her husband's lack of support for her efforts to control the girl (she had whipped her and only made matters worse); her own feelings of inadequacy as a parent and grandparent; her status in the community; and her struggle with her feelings about morality. The caseworker suggested that perhaps all they could do at this time was decide what she would do if the child came home late that night. Yet on considering that one action the grandmother was able to face her guilt for what she had done to her daughter years before and to restore her relationship with daughter, husband, and granddaughter.

Movement often begins with one foot on the ladder. To have come to some decision often means that the next one is not so difficult.

14. End the interview at a point where a decision has been made.

It may not always be possible to end an interview at the right moment. No decision may have been made, or there may be a time set aside for the interview which for some reason may have to be used. But, if there is real movement of any kind in an interview, even if it is of the slightest, there will come a time when the helped person commits himself to something new. It may be the decision to try something he has not quite dared try before, or the decision to risk taking help with his problem, at least in a limited way. Whatever the decision is, it needs consolidating--sleeping on, perhaps, or actually trying out. Although it has been verbalized, it is not yet something with which one is at ease, or familiar. If the helping person at this point tries to capitalize on it, pushes the helped person to go beyond it or to elaborate on it, its original clarity and determination is often weakened or confused. The process is somewhat akin to that of writing a short story. The story must have a beginning, a middle, and an end, but if the writer continues after the punch line, the story loses its point. Many helpers have made difficulties for themselves and for the people they are helping by going on too long in an attempt either to gather more information or to reinforce a decision they believe to have been half made. It is wiser to leave at this point. Most decisions, in any case, are only foreshadowed in the actual interview. They are consolidated outside it. At the point that the helped person says something like, "You know, that might work," it might be wiser to say, "Why don't you think about it, and try it if it seems good," rather than to try to reinforce it at the time.

In a protective interview a young woman who was in deep marital trouble and, in consequence, neglecting her baby, had reached the point of seeing the court worker's visit as helpful rather than threatening. She began to unfold her marital difficulties, and asked the worker if she would talk to her husband. This the worker agreed to do. She would talk with them both. But she would not, at this time, listen to the details of their marital problems. The woman needed to discuss with her husband their need for help, and the part the worker might play in it, before the worker became involved with one party to the dispute.

As a result when she came back she found the couple had begun to identify some of their problems and to start working on them. If she had continued with the woman, she would have involved her in possible solutions, instead of the immediate problem, which was their joint ability to ask for help.

15. Leave something to work on for next time.

To end an interview at the point of a decision is closely related to another problem which helpers sometimes meet. In their eagerness to come to grips with a problem, they discuss all aspects of it in a first interview. This does two things. It commits one to rediscuss next time something on which one has already, more or less, covered the essential points, and it makes little allowance for the kind of growth that occurs between interviews. A second interview in this case is often rambling and repetitive.

This point ties in very closely with a question that we have not answered, and which may well be confusing the reader at this point. We mentioned a few pages back the dangers in a too facile nondirectiveness and a turning back to the client of all decisions, however small. We have at the same time cautioned the helper against the too frequent use of explanation and instruction. We have said that she must not take over, either as a result of being taken over or on her own account. We have insisted that the final decision must always be the helped person's. We have warned against a battle of wills, yet spoken of the need to introduce difference. It may be hard for the helper to know, beset with all these statements, just how active she should be and what she should leave to the person she is helping.

There is, of course, no absolute rule that can be constructed on this subject. Too many factors are involved. The helped person's ability to tackle things for himself, the depth of his need to have us do it for him,

129

the actual possibility of his being able to think or do the thing that is needed all have to be taken into account. Generally, though, unless one is working with a person who is primarily a thinker, I would suggest that both what one consciously allows to the person one is trying to help and what in any case he will take for himself are actions and not ideas. It is the opportunity to act on a decision that has been made during an interview that we actually leave for the next time we meet. It may be a request to think about something we have said, or to try something out, but it involves doing something that will either confirm or deny the movement that seemed in the interview to have been taking place.

16. Test out decisions through requiring action to confirm them.

It is often in action that we discover, and the helped person may discover, that movement is or is not real. In the situation just related, it was the woman's sharing with her husband their need for help and arranging a joint appointment for them both that indicated the genuineness of her own ability to do something about her problem. An adoptive applicant, on the other hand, while asserting his desperate need for a child, shared with the adoptive worker the blueprints for the house he was building. No child's bedroom had been included. Another man, however, who left an office full of doubts of the wisdom of giving up his relief check for a course of vocational rehabilitation arrived next day with a detailed list of the tools that he would need and a self-addressed envelope so that the counselor could let him know at once that they were available. Buses are missed, appointments forgotten, or someone takes some action that commits him to something new—writes a letter, burns his pipes, or resigns his job.

It might be said, in fact, that the whole process of helping is one of trying out new commitments and finding out whether this will indeed help. But there is more to it even than this. It could be said that in trying out the decisions that one arrives at in being helped, directed to certain ends, and with the helper holding him to reality, understanding his difficulty and giving him her support, someone is actually trying out in a protected situation a way of life that later he can live by himself. The helping situation then becomes a kind of laboratory for testing out ways of doing things and, indeed, for finding out whether one can or wants to do them. This is perhaps the most significant knowledge that one gains about people in the process of helping them—the knowledge of how they tackle a problem, what they want to or can do, how steadfast they can be, what are their thresholds of being able to maintain what they have begun. The client, too, learns this about himself.

A belief in this kind of knowledge of people, gained through active participation with them in a process of trying out decisions, does not deny the usefulness of a more formal diagnosis based on the pattern of past behavior. Rather it supplements it and sometimes draws attention to its limitations, which lie chiefly in the fact that a helped and an unhelped person are not necessarily the same. Because this person was not able to handle his problem in the past, alone and without help, does not necessarily mean that he cannot do so in the future if he is offered help. It is such an assumption which makes the negative diagnosis so dangerous, and often so unfair. There is always the possibility that someone, once he is genuinely offered help, can discover strength in himself that no one, much less himself, could possibly know that he had.

In terms of suggestions for practice this possibility means that one often consciously requires of the person being helped that he take certain action before one moves on to the next step. To require this action is not to deny him help if the action cannot be taken, but a way of making clear both to himself and to you how ready he is to go further, or whether the decision that seems to have been arrived at needs further rethinking and perhaps further testing out.

17. In offering advice, leave room for modification.

Closely allied to the principle that decisions should be tested out by requiring that the helped person take some action to confirm them is one that concerns giving advice. Advice has, in much modern counseling, gained a negative connotation. The reason for this is in part the need to move away from a former concept of helping, in which it was believed that what people principally needed was knowledge about how to do things, and which involved little knowledge of the part that feelings play in the giving of help.

To acknowledge, however, that people must make their own final decisions does not mean that advice cannot still be a useful thing. In casual or emotionally neutral situations it is often used. Where it causes difficulty is where it has something of the nature of a command, where it is backed with either formal or informal authority, or where the person giving advice presumes without evidence that she knows much more about the specific situation than the person asking for help.

It is exactly this assumption that is often so wrongly made. The person giving advice, the expert, knows more, it is true, about the general situation. She knows what usually works or how others have solved this problem. She knows less than the asker, however, about the particular situation. She knows rather little about the asker's ability and desire to take certain courses of action, and she is not always aware of particular elements that might make one course of action unwise or another more desirable. This is a fact often forgotten by supervisors in various fields and by experts or consultants. They are the generalists, but the worker, the person on the firing line, the person whose problem is under study, always knows more about the particular.

Detailed advice which allows for no modification in terms of the particular is often either useless or harmful. I can remember a consultant who advised an institution, quite properly as far as expert knowledge is concerned, that the board of a maternity home should include men as well as women. What he did not know was that this particular board saw for itself no function other than making baby clothes. When the home, wishing to take the advice it was given, replaced half its women with men, most of whom came from the business community and did not know how to sew, the men found no work for themselves, and there were not enough seamstresses left on the board to do the job. The consultant's general knowledge needed in this situation to take into account a most individual particularity.

One way of giving advice, and one moreover that both makes allowance for the particular and engages the helping person in action, is what one might call "alternative advice." In this it is assumed that the particular is not known. Advice is given on the premise that if you find A to be true, or what you want to accomplish, then perhaps X is what you should do. But if, in considering carefully the situation as you see it, you believe B to be true, or desirable, then Y is worth trying. This can be expanded to C and Z if needed. The major value of this kind of advice is that it engages the person being helped in trying to fit his particular into the general. It also makes more difficult that resistance to taking advice that we have noted, where the value of the advice is counteracted by following it too literally.

A housemother once was approached by a boy who was in real trouble with his girlfriend. She gave him plentiful advice about what girls wanted from boys, including, in this case, a pretty abject apology, all of which he said gratefully he would follow. But when she asked him a day or two later whether her advice had worked, he shook his head. He said that on further thought he had come to the conclusion that his relationship with this girl was unhealthy, that what she was doing was not objecting to his behavior but seeing to what extent he would abase himself before her. What he really wanted was advice on how to stand up to her and continue to be himself. The housemother's assumption that he must want

Be willing to adjust

to get back in the girl's good graces had prevented him from getting the advice he wanted.

✓ cements it

18. Where important decisions are made, use if possible physical movement or action to symbolize what is happening.

The value of using some form of physical action to symbolize an important decision is something we recognize when we seal an agreement with a handshake, or, as children, with a kiss. We have physically come together, and this fact is remembered long after the actual words have been forgotten. The physical movement carries with it more of a sense of what is actually transpiring than anything that is said. It makes a great deal of difference, for instance, whether an unmarried mother physically gives you her child for adoption or whether you go to the nursery and take the child away. In the first instance she gave you the child; in the second you took it. The actual decisions may have been the same, but the feeling around it, especially after a lapse of time, is entirely different.

The same kind of symbolization can come through the signing of an agreement, or through the very fact that something is written down. It can come through the actual wording of an agreement or an application. It behooves us also to do more to study the effects of the physical arrangements of where we give our help. If we use an office, are we, for instance, separated from the person asking help by a desk, or by a trick of lighting? Are we too close?

This is a subject about which we probably know too little at this time, although some work has been done, in industry and in teaching, on the effects of room arrangement, lighting, and color. For a careful study of the symbolism that confirms or denies decision, it might not be unwise for helpers to ask help from organizations which have studied ritual, such as churches or government, particularly of a monarchical kind. It is a fascinating field and although it is not perhaps essential to helping—good helping has occurred in the most unlikely places and where the symbolism was probably all wrong—this kind of "outward and visible sign" means a lot to people.

19. Start each separate contact where the helped person is at that time.

Suggesting that one start each helping session at whatever point the person being helped happens to be at that time is really a warning that human progress is not consistent. What was done last time may have to be done again. There will be regression as well as going forward, and much may have happened for good or ill since the last time the two of you met.

133

One thing, for instance, that often disturbs a helping person is that the person asking for help may have told you too much last time. He may have come too near his problem, or exposed himself too much. At the time he may have felt that this was safe. He had you to support him. But thinking it over, he is afraid. He may withdraw for a while until he is sure of you again, or try to control you as he has not done before.

While it is often good practice to try to sum up at a new meeting your understanding of what has gone before, this summation has to be offered in a most tentative way. "This was, I think, where we were. Are we still at that point? How does it look to you today?"

To go back again, to reinforce, to put up with the disappointment when someone who has appeared to share so much suddenly shuts up like a clam requires in the helper that trust in the process we discussed in chapter 6. Only as one does not have to be the helper who succeeds in helping this person, only as she can play her part, confident that if she does, the other person will find all the help that he is able to find in his situation, will this actually come true. To be sure of this, though, takes both courage and humility.

20. Introduce difference on the basis of likeness.

We discussed quite fully in an earlier chapter the criteria for introducing difference to a client. These included being sure that the difference to be introduced was necessary to the process of helping the client and did not just stem from one's own opinion, and that one was prepared to help the client with his reaction to it. We also suggested that as much as possible the difference be expressed in the client's own terms.

I once helped a group of people who worked with children whose solution to the problem of boy-girl relationships was to keep the sexes rigidly apart. I wanted them to see that attraction between the sexes was natural and healthy, but that their practices were making it something that had the glamour of "forbidden fruit" and were actually encouraging the children to sneak out at night, which was the problem they were asking me to help them with. I knew that if I began to talk about children's sexual development and needs, or if I quoted modern psychologists, they would see me as a "liberal" who condoned what they saw as dangerous and undesirable behavior. They were members of a strict religious body who went as far as to require children to wear swimsuits in the shower and who rubbed chewing gum in the hair of a little girl they caught primping in front of a mirror. So I began with something that was familiar to them—the Book of Genesis, chapter 1, verses 27 and 31, "Male and female he created them . . . and God saw everything that he had made, and behold, it was very good." After two or three sessions someone in the class approached me. "It's not that I won't do things differently in the future," she said, "but is there any way I can make up to all the children I've denied a healthy upbringing in the past?"

On the other hand a consultant, working with a Children's Home run by Salician brothers and full of a desire to liberate children from what she saw as regimentation, suggested a number of practices that were, although she did not know it, in direct contradiction to the rule of Saint Francis de Sales. Naturally her advice was rejected.

Not productive language

21. Use the question, "Why?" sparingly

Not only is "why" an unproductive question; it is by its very nature accusatory and it is backward rather than forward looking. Once, in making a study of a Children's Home, I asked for lots to be drawn for a panel of adolescents with whom I might confer. One child so chosen was Ruth, who, I was told, could not talk to men and would be useless on such a panel. Yet no child I have ever talked with tried harder to express to me her feelings about the Home. When I reported this, I was met with amazement, as if I had worked a miracle and somehow dissipated this child's fear of my sex. But sex was not the problem at all. What men had always asked Ruth was, "Ruthie, why do you behave as you do?" Either she did not know why she behaved as she did, or she knew perfectly well and was not about to tell anyone. My question had been, "Ruth, do you think that you can stand it here?" This shifted the emphasis from my need to know the source of her behavior to what she wanted to tell me about the Home.

22. Use celebration instead of praise.

Praise is a device used by many would-be helpers. It is thought of as a way of showing appreciation of another and of encouraging him to greater effort. To the extent that it remains this and nothing more, it is a helpful thing. But it is very easy to make something else of it.[3] It can become a way of purchasing a relationship on insufficient grounds. It is often a form of false reassurance: "I'm sure you can do it," when in fact one cannot. Its most serious consequence is, however, when it implies an expectation of another which he feels to be unrealistic. Nothing is more frightening than to be praised above what one knows to be one's capabilities or deserts.

135

To praise another may be also a subtle way of underlining one's superiority to him. The right to apportion praise or blame is the right of a superior.

Celebration, on the other hand, is simply a mark of one's appreciation of what someone else has done or is. A person who celebrates rather than praises says, "I am glad for you because you are glad for yourself." It is important in many helping situations because so many of the people we need to help have had so little occasion in their lives for celebration. Their victories have been few and their defeats frequent.

A ten-year-old I knew once had a phobia about school. About ten o'clock each day the classroom walls would begin to close in on him and he panicked and ran. The Children's Home tried giving him extra work to make up for what he had missed, but I suggested that every hour he spent in school was a victory in his battle against the fear that confronted him day after day in the classroom. We devised a chart and gave him a gold star for every hour he stayed in school. In the meantime we had him see a psychiatrist to try to find out what it was that he was afraid of, which he would not or could not tell us. But when we began to notice his victories rather than his defeats, he began to stay longer in school, until one day he came back with the other children, looking as if he had been dragged backward through a knothole, and panted, "I made it. I made it for a whole day." The housemother baked him a cake with one candle on it to celebrate his first full day at school. From then on he seemed to have conquered his fear, the cause of which we never discovered.

This, incidentally, is one instance where Behavior Modification can be very helpful—in dealing with a specific problem. But although to live under a Behavior Modification system, with points given and taken away for almost anything that one does, can be most oppressive and can deny children, in particular, a lot of spontaneous enjoyment. I have seen perfectly normal children denied a rare chance to spend a weekend at the beach because the cumulative points of their group fell just below an arbitrary standard set by the staff.

One can celebrate many things—not wetting one's bed, or completing a task, or not losing one's temper in a difficult situation. There is always the chance to celebrate something, even the other's mere existence.

Sometimes all helping takes is noticing someone who is not used to being noticed. I have no doubt that the child whom I probably helped most in forty years' work with children in group living arrangements was one to whom I never spoke but whose face I found interesting—that is, strong, watchful, and inquiring—when I saw her in a crowd. I mentioned my feeling about this child's quality to somebody on the staff and found that she was considered a most unsatisfactory and rebellious child in danger of dismissal. The person to whom I spoke asked if she could tell Barbara what I had said. I never saw Barbara again, but three years later, when she graduated with an excellent record, Barbara was asked by someone how she had managed to change so much. She said that the change had begun when she had been told of my interest. "I figured," she said, "that if someone who sees as many children as he does singled me out I had something to live up to." Barbara must have been, of course, almost ready for change, and the real helping was done by the person who recognized her need and relayed my comment, but the thought of how accidental the straw that tipped the balance may have been is a disturbing one. How many times have we not done the helpful thing that would have meant so much, as it did in this case?

23. Know enough about the obvious signs of severe mental illness to know when to refer someone to a doctor or to keep out of a relationship.

A helper needs to know enough about severe mental illness to know when she should refer the person she is helping to a doctor or else not become involved in a relationship with him. People who are admittedly mentally ill can very often be helped with that part of their problem about which they can reason and feel quite rationally. But a person in a severe depression, or who suffers from marked hallucinations or obsessions, or who is plainly living in a world far removed from reality probably needs a kind of help which the ordinary helping person does not have the means to provide. One does not have to be a psychiatrist or to diagnose the illness to get a sense that this may be so. A failure to respond to any difference or reality, an excessive rationalization of highly illogical acts, an apparently fairly total disorganization may be signs about which advice needs to be sought.

It is perhaps particularly important to recognize the signs of one kind of mental illness, paranoia. This is not only because the paranoid is often perfectly rational except in relation to his one obsession, but because it can be extremely dangerous to become part of his fantasy. The paranoid is one who feels so hostile toward the world that to justify his hostility he must believe that he is being persecuted, or that the people he hates are committing terrible crimes. The danger is that he often comes to the conclusion that he has a right, and sometimes a mandate directly from God, to avenge himself or to vindicate his concept of morality, as, for instance, did Jack the Ripper, who only killed prostitutes. Unfortunately, the helping person who holds firm or will not let him have his own way is sometimes included in those against whom he must seek revenge.

One need not, I think, spend too much time suspecting paranoia in the people one is helping. In more than fifty years of helping I have come across only two whose disturbance was deep enough to cause me to take precautions. It might, however, be wise to do so when someone dwells at great length on the injuries done him or when he uses in doing so physically aggressive terms such as "a knife in the back," but we need to remember that mental illness is only an exaggeration of an escape from reality to which all of us are prone. We are all a little paranoid.

24. Don't expect quick results with problems involving long-established habits.

One should not expect a quick fix to problems that stem from long-established habits has particular reference to drinking, or drug taking, or certain forms of sexuality. These have the nature of an illness, even though one might want to dispute the literal correctness of describing them as such. They are often associated with a kind of character that is perhaps in our present state of knowledge less amenable to help than any other. This very character is in itself full of traps for the helper. People with such a character are often very charming, apparently very frank, and full of promises that look like the beginning of movement. Such people can be helped, as Alcoholics Anonymous has shown, and can be helped by the kind of methods described in this book, especially with their related problems, but a great deal of what they do is only tenuously within their power to change.

25. When someone contemplates wrongdoing, ask if it will really solve his problem. - help explore other options

Wrongdoing, crimes, sin are often somewhat desperate and unrealistic attempts to meet a legitimate need. Thus Mrs. Brown's intention to live with the notorious Mr. Timms was the only way she could think of to provide for her daughter. The rapist tries to assert his dominance as a male, which has perhaps been denied him; the embezzler tries to assure either his sense of security or self-worth, which may include having material wealth. The important thing to realize about such acts is that they almost never do satisfy that need. The lecher, perhaps trying to solve his need for closeness, has to go on engaging in more and more exotic sexual experience. The miser goes on accumulating money that he will never need.

Simply to tell a person that what he is contemplating is wrong leaves his need unsatisfied. He either does not accept one's judgment or seeks some other, possibly just as unrealistic way of meeting his need. That is why the most helpful question is often, "Will that really do what you want it to do?"

This question probably should not be asked in extreme situations, or where the need is largely unconscious. Perhaps it is most useful where the action contemplated is revenge, the imposition of a severe punishment, recourse to violence, or desertion.

26. When something has to be done quickly, try relieving pressure first.

Earlier, we criticized models of helping that dealt with symptoms rather than causes, but occasionally we come up against a situation in which a symptom must be addressed immediately because what is likely to happen is irreversible. If someone is threatening suicide, or is, as we say, "at the end of his tether" or "near to explosion" and may assault someone or suffer a stroke, one does not enter into a long-term counseling service with him. That may come later, when the tragedy has been averted. But something has to be done in the here and now.

A useful concept here is that of the "breaking point." We all have the potential to commit some very unwise act, to lose our temper, for instance, or to act crazily in some way. Generally we do not do it, but if we are put under enough pressure, we probably will. How many of us who are parents have not had to grit our teeth and leave the room to prevent ourselves from hitting a child? Most of us could be child abusers but are not, partly because we probably have quite a high breaking point and partly because most of us have not been cooped up twenty-four hours a day, seven days a week, with two or three whining children and no one to talk to. One of the most effective programs in preventing child abuse is "Mother's Morning Out," or some similar program that relieves pressure on a parent. Another is Aid to Families with Dependent Children, which should, although it does not always, help families avoid financial worries.

A medical analogy might be useful at this point. All of us have in our bodies the pneumococci that cause pneumonia, but we do not develop the disease unless our bodies are put under certain strains or our immune systems are damaged. Alcohol and some drugs, for example, may lower our psychological breaking point. But few of us have a breaking point high enough to resist unusual strains. In basic training during World War II, for instance, I was one of four recruits thirty years old or older assigned to a battalion mostly of eighteen-to-twenty-year-olds. The battalion was undergoing an accelerated program. Although, as far as I know, all four of us had been moderately successful in civilian life, none of us finished the course. One man went AWOL. Another developed stomach ulcers. The third became psychotic, and I developed recurrent pneumonia. The reaction in each case was different, but the stimulus was the same.

We may, then, visualize a problem as consisting of three elements. One is the culture or the environment. In a case of child abuse this might involve the belief that the way to solve problems is to use physical force, which is so evident in television, and a child-rearing pattern of using corporal punishment. Another element would be the way in which a particular person reacts to too much pressure. Does he resort to violence, become alcoholic, or lose touch with reality? And the third is the amount of pressure present. These elements could be diagrammed as a column which, as illustrated in the following lefthand figure, exceeds the person's breaking point. In the figure on the right the pressure has been reduced, so there is no abuse. The same result could have been reached if we had been able to reduce the impact of the culture, redirect the person's tendency to use violence, or raise his breaking point, but these are difficult and time-consuming operations, whereas the pressure on him is probably the most treatable.

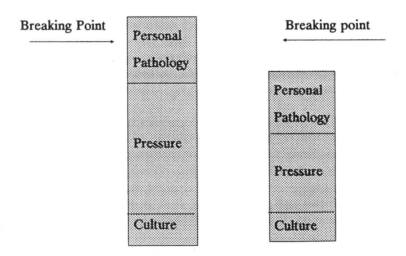

I learned this solution to a critical problem almost by default at the beginning of my social work career. Mrs. Quadri was within ten days of having her eighth child. Shortly after the birth of the sixth, when Mrs. Quadri was at the welfare office, her fifth child, who had a condition known as *ossis fragilis*, or very brittle bones, fell and died from a broken skull. Something similar happened after the birth of the seventh child, this time involving the death of the sixth child. There was no doubt that Mr. Quadri was responsible, but in view of the child's vulnerability the doctors felt that there was not sufficient evidence to bring him to trial. His wife did tell the welfare worker that sometimes he seemed to "lose his mind," and, as he said to me once, there were times when he "didn't know his own strength." He also asked me once if I didn't think five children were enough for a man.

My job was not to prosecute Mr. Quadri but, if possible, to prevent an "accident" from happening to the seventh child. What I did was empathize with Mr. Quadri, who was unemployed on relief and often left in charge of his five small children in a small apartment, and offer foster care for the two youngest children until Mrs. Quadri was back in the home and had regained her strength. Mr. Quadri said that he had found caring for the children very exhausting and agreed to my offer as long as he could see the foster home. Although this was against agency policy, the situation was an emergency, and Mr. Quadri proved to be a solicitous parent in talking with the foster parent. We cared for the children for three weeks but then returned them to an apparently happy six-child family. At that point I would have closed the case, but the agency board, wiser than I, suggested I visit every two weeks for six months. I used to go drink coffee with them and became very fond of the family. Mr. Quadri was a very good father to his living children. Probably my coming gave both him and his wife some support and some sense of being accepted. It was not until several years later that I saw why what I had done had worked.

Mr. Quadri, unemployed and Catholic (so birth control was not an option), probably had a low breaking point, but by relieving pressure on him at a critical time I had managed to reduce his problem to a point below it. When he became employed again, the pressure was further relieved, and on a more permanent basis.

One might say that Mr. Quadri should either have been punished or have received psychiatric help—that the family was still at risk. But I am not sure that either measure would have been helpful. As far as is known, the Quadris have continued to be a family, and have not apparently needed help.

Concluding Notes

The Futility of Blame

That ends my positive suggestions for successful helping. There are obviously some negative things to avoid, such as false reassurance, taking sides in a marital conflict, and blaming someone for his behavior.

Blame is perhaps the most useless and most harmful activity. So and so behaves this way because of his life experience, which was at least partially conditioned by his parents, who behaved this way because of their own upbringing, and so on ad infinitum. One ends up with Adam and Eve, or perhaps the Serpent. Blame also leads nowhere. I read recently in an article on children who appear to court sexual abuse, and in which it was argued that they do so as a result of "counterphobia," or exorcising trauma by repeating it, "We know now whom to blame." I wrote in the margin, "So what?" Would blaming the original offender help him in any way? And supposing the author had found that these children were sexually precocious, would blaming them be of any use?

Sharing One's Own Experience

One question that is frequently asked is to what extent, in helping someone, should one share with him one's own experience? This is not a matter that in my opinion can be answered by saying, "Fully" or "Not at all."

There are obvious dangers in the practice. We have said that the most dangerous helper is the one who has solved her own problem and forgotten what it cost her. There is also a tendency to feel too much like the person one is helping, to be sympathetic rather than empathetic, if one's own experience and the experience of the person one is helping are too much alike.

And yet there is some reassurance when one knows that other people have faced similar problems. This is the dynamic in many support groups such as Al-Anon or Alcoholics Anonymous. One of the best bits of helping I have seen was done by an elderly child care worker who was black, who was confronted with a (white) boy begging for a change-of-sex operation and angry both at life, for giving him a boy's body, and at the Children's Home, for not being willing to grant him his wish. She showed the boy her black wrist. "Do you know," she said, "How many times I've prayed to the Lord to turn it white? But I reckon He must have wanted it black."

142

One might argue that for the boy a sex-change operation was possible, although highly unlikely, whereas the likelihood of the child care worker's becoming white was nonexistent; but under the circumstances the child care worker dealt with reality, conveyed her empathy, did not deny the reality of the boy's feelings, and did not blame him for them, although to many people his desire was unacceptable. She then went on to ask him, since he could not be a girl, what he thought he could do that would be the nearest thing to it, and she found him a job as an aide with babies in a local hospital, where even his uniform was unisex. Maybe he needed psychiatric help, but such help would have taken longer to give. She did what she could for him in the here and now.

The particular situation in which a Christian worker wants to share with the person she is helping her own religious experience will be discussed in chapter 10. All that I will say here is that to be useful, what one shares with another must have meaning to him and must not distract from the business of helping him. In a few cases it may be useful, but it is subject to the same dangers as any self-disclosure.

In this book I have used quite a bit of my own experience. I have done so for two reasons. The first is that it has been through these experiences that I have learned what little I may know about helping. There were no courses and very little writing on the subject when I was in school. The second is that I hope to show that the principles we have discussed really work, and the situations I naturally know about are ones in which I have been involved. If I have given the impression that I am saying, "This is how it ought to be done, because this is how I try to help people," I can only apologize. Some principles certainly exist, but every helper is an individual and has her own style of helping.

CHAPTER 8

Helping in Various Settings

One of the things that has been suggested about the helping process is that it has about it something of the universal. It therefore should be usable in many different settings perhaps not directly associated with help in the ordinary sense of the word. For the most part the examples which have been used in this book have been taken from a one-to-one relationship in which the attempt to help is clearly the purpose of the encounter. These have been varied, it is true — the social worker with her client, the child care worker with a child, the teacher with a student whom she is advising. It has also been made clear that the process does not require that the helped person seek out help on his own initiative. It is as applicable to the work of the probation officer, the judge, and the protective worker as it is to the family counselor. Reality, in these situations, is perhaps of a different nature and includes the authority of the law or of the helper's special function, but the principles are the same.

We might ask then at this point in what other settings the process might operate. Does it apply, and if it does, what modifications are apparent, in situations of a more personal nature, where other and perhaps different relationships exist, such as marriage or child rearing? Does it apply in the business world, in politics, in public administration, in endeavors to bring about change in a community, and to groups as well as to work with individuals?

Reasons for Relating to Others

In order to try to answer these questions, we may need to recognize that people are likely to enter into a relationship with one another for one, or possibly more than one, of four reasons.

1. *To share with another.* In a sharing relationship, the expectancy is that both people will contribute and that the decisions to be made will be, as far as possible, to their mutual benefit. This is the kind of relationship characteristic of marriage, friendship, and business or other partnerships, although both control and helping factors may exist at the same time or indeed replace mutuality, sometimes helpfully, but sometimes in a somewhat disastrous way.

2. *To control the other.* Control has a very wide variety of forms. It includes not only overt forms of domination, but persuasion (except in the form, perhaps, of logic divorced from partisanship), influence, seduction, exhortation, pleading, and demanding. It exists wherever a person brings into the relationship a will that something shall be done, and that the other shall give way to it. It makes no difference, for this discussion, whether the thing to be done is for the other person's good or wholly for one's own, or indeed for a third party's. The other's will must be overcome, whether it be by a salesperson trying to sell a product, by a beggar attempting to beguile a patron, by a mother trying to influence her son, or by a debater arguing a particular point of view.

3. *To compete with him.* In a competitive relationship the two persons may not even meet, but they are a threat to each other. Each wants to get ahead, but each can do so only at the expense of the other. Even where success appears to be due solely to one person's skill or personality, and there is no direct competitiveness with another, he or she is in fact competing with everyone else. There is only so much room at the top.

4. *To help him.* The distinguishing characteristic in a relationship in which one person wants to help another is that the ultimate decision is left with the person being helped. Although the helper may very much wish for certain things to happen, she is for some reason or other prepared to risk that it will not, and that the other will make the final decision

Not a Moral Hierarchy

It is perhaps important to see that there is not, at least as far as motivation is concerned, an easy hierarchy of moral values to be attached to these relationships in themselves. Controlling is not necessarily bad, and helping necessarily good. A baby or a small child may need control. Some criminals must be controlled. The person who wishes to control may do so from the highest motives and may choose this kind of relationship only because he or she does not believe that another will bring about a bearable result. Control is only to be deprecated when it infringes on the right of others to solve their own problems, when it is exercised without a clear mandate to make use of it, when it belittles another, or when the goals to be reached are denied because it has been substituted for help. It is an inferior relationship, it is true, in terms of democratic or even theological ideals, but in a real world it may sometimes be necessary. This true especially if we recognize teaching, preaching, influencing, and even setting an example as subtle forms of control.

The same can be said of competitiveness. Without the spur of competition a great deal of our standard of living would never have been achieved. Without protest and the acquisition of power by groups that formerly did not have it, a number of social reforms would not have taken place. The competition of ideas is essential to progress and indeed justice. The very word "excellence" means doing better than the other person. Governments need a "loyal opposition," and the very system of checks and balances on which our liberty depends is in a sense competitive.

Nevertheless these relationships, which are, in Buber's terms, "I-it" rather than "I-you," are a pity when they exceed the bounds of necessity and become the sole purpose of a relationship. The power to influence may serve legitimate ends, but it becomes harmful if, for example, it is used to influence people to buy things that they cannot afford and do not truly want. Nonviolent protest may be good, but not a protest that ends in bombing a planned parenthood clinic. The use of force may, and often does, produce immediate results, but these are often temporary and leave behind resentment and a desire for ultimate revenge. This is certainly true of a great deal of punishment, both legal and parental. It is also true of more subtle uses of power, such as paternalism or colonialism, to say nothing of male chauvinism or the present demand that one's writing or teaching be "politically correct."

Helping as a Supervisor

We have seen, for instance, that a good supervisor or employer makes use of many helping principles. True, her primary responsibility is to see that the job is done correctly. Hers is a position of authority. But she will get much further if she remembers that she is a generalist and that the worker knows more than she does about the particular problems of the job, and if her advice is of what we have called an "alternative" nature (see suggestion 17 in chapter 7). She will find herself with a better worker if she presents him with the reality that the job must be done well and then offers him empathy and support in doing it.

This helping process is particularly observable in one supervisory function which to many people would seem to have a very strong control factor. Evaluation is often seen as a necessarily judgmental process, involving a superior who judges and an inferior who is judged. But if the organization has developed an adequate set of standards of performance which are related to the job and not to the person doing it, then the supervisor can really be a helping person. Instead of "supervising" — that is, exercising judgment and control — she can help the worker face what objectively needs to be done and offer her support. But in such a situation the wrong question often gets asked.

The first and the most important question is not, "How can I help you meet this standard?"—logical as this may seem. That comes only as a result of a certain answer to a much more fundamental question, "Do you, in fact, want to do it? Is the price that you would have to pay to come up to standard in your work one that you would be willing to pay? If so, I am here to help you, if you want me and can use me. If not you had better start looking for other work. And only you can decide."

It is surprising what strength failing workers of all kinds can muster when they are really helped to face reality in this way. Some, naturally, resign. The price that they would have to pay—the acquisition of self-discipline, the willingness to arrange matters of concern to them outside their work—is too much for them to pay. But most will respond with a genuine effort and a clear understanding that they are being helped, although it may be the supervisor who has to make the final decision about their work. And those who leave usually do so with their heads held high. The decision has been basically theirs.

Transferring Helping Skills

The truth is that a knowledge of helping can often produce results in situations that do not have the giving of help as their primary purpose, and that helping is a bigger component of a number of operations than we generally imagine. That is because it has to do with two essential human tasks, decision making and growth in capability to do things for oneself.

Yet people do not find it easy to transfer their helping skills to a position in which authority is involved. A good helper sometimes, at least until she can see that helping is part of an administrator's job, makes a poor supervisor. For a number of years I taught students who had become quite good helpers as caseworkers but who were now administrators. One would come to me, for instance, saying, "I don't know what to do with Mr. X. I have told him again and again he's got to get his dictation in on time," and I would have to say, "But you know perfectly well that that isn't the way to help someone change. You would never do that to a client. Have you thought of exploring with him his fear of disclosing what he has done, or what dictation means to him? Or is he finding difficulty in being supervised by a woman?"

It is also sometimes difficult to hold fast to one's knowledge of helping when faced with a superior, or an equal, or perhaps most of all with someone whose disapproval can do one harm. The director of a state-financed adoption agency found himself under constant political pressure to make specific placements. Normally, in such situations, he had found himself telling senators that adoption was a complex and difficult process, that one could not start from the needs of those wishing to adopt, that one must start from the need of the baby for a particular kind of home — true material, possibly very helpful if distributed through mass media of some sort, but in the individual situation tending to throw doubt on the senator's knowledge and judgment and even his concern for children.

On one particular day the director, trained to listen to feeling, caught something in a senator's tone that troubled him. Instead of becoming defensive he said, "Senator, I would not have your job for a million dollars. The pressures on you must be enormous." The senator began to tell him what he had to put up with and ended, "You know, I don't believe these people would make good adoptive parents. I just want to get them off my back." The director offered to take the blame if a placement was not made, and the senator left, full of gratitude for the understanding he had been shown. The administrator, in fact, knew that when one is dealing with an angry or rejecting person, one must keep one's interest on his feeling and not come to the defense of what he is feeling about.

Similarly, an administrator new to her job found herself suddenly confronted by a grand jury investigation into the Aid to Families with Dependent Children program, which the grand jury believed to be contributing to illegitimacy. Instead of producing statistics to prove that this was not so or asking whether the grand jury intended that little children should starve, which I have heard asked in similar situations, the administrator acknowledged the grand jury's concern and her own at the amount of illegitimacy in the county. She told them what she had tried to do and invited suggestions. As a result the grand jury became interested in the whole problem and ended by indicting not the welfare department but the whole community for its failure to meet this problem. It suggested that one thing that might be done would be to increase the number of welfare workers.

Helping and the Use of Force

These instances could be looked at in a number of different ways. It could be said, for instance, that the senator and the grand jury were basically well intentioned. They did not attack social work programs with malice or with a settled desire to control them, which might suggest to some that the principles of helping can only be used where one is not up against implacable opposition. Yet initially in each case the opposition appeared to be unyielding. It was the administrator's empathy in each case which made it possible for the opposition to be withdrawn.

It might also be suggested that the administrators were, in each case, simply using a subtle form of control. Despite the risk they took that the other's decision would be inimical, they were simply relying on the likelihood of things going their way. They were using a soft sell. But this suggestion, I believe, discounts the fact that empathy, if it is to carry conviction, must be genuinely felt. The director who faced the senator did not think out a strategy. He was genuinely for a moment feeling for the senator. It is much more that by giving up their own immediate interests these people found that help was possible for those who looked at first unhelpable. In the instant of helping it was the other person who mattered.

Perhaps all we are saying here is that the helping process reflects so accurately the actual nature of humanity that in all human relationships it is generally what will bring people together in cooperation. People are basically more attuned to being helped than to being controlled. On the other hand a person's first reaction to being attacked, or opposed, is to try to control. This is obvious, for instance, in international affairs, where interests are enforced by attempts to control the other and where the acquisition of power inevitably calls up a counterresponse of power. Without wishing here to enunciate a total philosophy of life, I would suggest that there is evidence that controlling another is not the way in which human differences actually get resolved. We turn to power or to control because we do not know how to help.

There are many people, however, who would suggest that the reverse is true – that these two administrators turned to helping methods out of weakness. One risked the senator's and the other the grand jury's negative decision because they were powerless to control them. Realism might suggest that in fact the number of such situations in which help can or should be used is small. These situations might be limited to those in which some good will is possible, or in which we do not have the power to control in any other way. But this assumes not only that control is a really effective method of getting our own way, but that the purpose of life is to get our own way in it. To believe this makes it very important that we are sure that our own way is right.

What is of course very difficult is to see something that we care about very much attacked and not to fight for it. There are situations in which this may have to be done. But it is also true that much more often than we recognize the best way to protect something we care about is not to

149

try to protect it, but to risk it, and to try to help its enemies with their need to attack it.

Helping in an Argument

Very often in an argument, especially if what we are arguing about means a lot to us, we fail to use empathy. When the governor of a state made a political compromise which did not give students all they wanted, they wrote to him putting forth a logical argument why he might want to change his mind. But they ended their letter by accusing him of cowardice and not really caring about people. I cannot imagine any surer way of ensuring that he would not change. We find the same phenomenon when, say, workers in an agency, a church, or a firm find that the administrator vetoes their favorite project. The administrator is reviled as insensitive, when he or she may be acting for the good of the group based on knowledge the workers do not have. I was accused once of insensitivity when I did not authorize expensive cosmetic surgery for a child. I did realize how beneficial the surgery would be, but to allow it would have wrecked a very tight budget and would have deprived a number of other children of the care they needed. It was not an easy decision to make. Nor are decisions taken, sometimes, on the grounds of public relations. They, too, can affect adversely what an agency can do for all children, even though they may be less than desirable for a particular child. Let it be said, however, that wise administrators share their constraints with their staff and if possible with their clients. The more their clients know, the more empathy they are likely to have.

Much the same is true when we are critical of how someone else is doing a job which is not our own. Workers in a child welfare office were much concerned by the decisions of a juvenile judge which seemed to them capricious and which often ignored social considerations. Child welfare workers would strongly recommend certain actions and the judge would do the opposite, sometimes, it seemed, almost in order to spite them.

A new consultant suggested that if the judge were ever to learn to be a judge, he must make his own decisions. She suggested that the office, instead of making recommendations, try to clarify for the judge what were the issues in a case and what might be, from their experience, the likely results of a decision one way or another. In doing this they could express empathy for the difficulty that some of these decisions would entail, the conflicting interests that might have to be balanced, and their willingness to try out whatever the judge might decide would have to be done. The judge made one or two bad decisions for which he had to

150

take sole responsibility, but very soon he learned to trust the child welfare office's experience of what might result from his actions. From being a notorious critic of social work he became in the course of a year or two one of its firmest supporters.

Helping in the Business World

In the world of business there are a number of situations in which the helping process applies. There is, for instance, no more crucial place for the exercise of good helping than in the loan department of a bank. The applicant is asking for help. He has selected one way of solving his problem, that of applying for a loan. This may or may not be realistic in terms of his active will to make productive use of the money. Both his interests and those of the lending institution are concerned. Although the lender must rely to a certain extent on diagnosis, based on past performance, it is also in considering the terms of the loan, its size and period of repayment as well as what it will cost, that lender and borrower come to understand each other and negotiate a sound and useful loan. It is also through this process that the borrower can discover what he really wants to do, and the likelihood that he can keep up his payments will depend to a great extent on his having discovered this. If he borrows unrealistically, or for something that will not give him satisfaction, he is much more likely to find difficulty in repayment.

The helping process may also have much to do with customer satisfaction. Architects are or should be trained in helping their customers express and in fact come to decisions about what they really want in a house. This means the kind of life they lead or hope to lead. If architects impose on their customers their idea of what a house ought to be like — a complaint frequently voiced about some members of this profession — they may find that they are making impossible what their customers really want to do with their lives. Traffic control may be wrong, so that parts of the family obtrude on each other's interests or, conversely, do not come together enough. There may or may not be ways to include provision for an ill parent or grandchildren. The result will be full satisfaction or discontent. Architects, too, may be wise to follow the helping principle of discovering what someone really wants and then helping him come to terms with how much of it he can have, rather than feeling discontent that their hopes have not been taken into account.

Businesspeople who provide a service would also be well advised to consider what the helping process might tell them about false reassurance. All too often they will promise something that they cannot fulfill, but rather than face this reality with the customer right away, they resort to reassurance. The customer in the end is much more dissatisfied. One airline, for instance, apparently makes the practice of trying to cushion the disappointment that a delay may cause by postponing the plane's estimated time of arrival twenty minutes at a time. This may be justified for short-term purposes in that one's tendency is to hang on, hoping against one's better judgment that the airline means what it says, but in long-term reputation it does the line a lot of harm.

These are not, perhaps, strictly helping processes. Businesspeople, despite their protestation that they exist to serve their clients, are usually more concerned with their profit than with change or growth or even satisfying the need of those they serve. The very fact that they work so strenuously to stimulate this need is an indication of this. But to take the position that because the businessperson's ultimate motive is selfish, he or she does not help, or does not need to know about helping, is far too absolute. It ignores the fact that the helper also has needs. The question is rather whether people in business are so intent on profits in the here and now that they permit this concern to override the interests of the client, and this the wise person in business does not do, for in general businesspeople depend in the long run on the goodwill of their clients and on their clients' willingness to trust them. There are many people in business who do, moreover, have a real feel for helping, and many helping people who are at the same time engaged in making a profit. While perhaps most businesses rely more largely on a control relationship — advertising and salesmanship — helping principles are often applicable to much that they do. Even the soft sell is based on the recognition that negatives may have to be faced and dealt with. It is probably true, however, that only a superior product can be promoted by helping principles. An inferior product is not close enough to reality.

Helping in Family Situations

Helping also takes place in less structured situations. In considering first relationships within a family, mutuality, rather than help, is, perhaps, of the first importance. This immediately suggests principles that may contradict those of helping. The very fact of a common interest may suggest that there are times when sympathy rather than empathy may be the more appropriate response. People may need to share their sorrows and their joys. But marriage is in some aspects a mutual helping relationship, in which one partner perhaps offers help at one time and the other at another, or both offer help but in relation to different things. There are clearly situations in which helping does take place, and in such situations

152

the process is an important guide—where, for instance, one partner is troubled and turns to the other, or should but does not.

It is perhaps easier to see the times when helping goes obviously wrong-
-the husband who cannot face reality with his wife about the financial situation, the wife whose support is clearly conditional, the partner who feeds into the other's hypochondria or depression by sympathizing with it. But so much else is involved—their need to live together, the compromises and adjustments they may need to make, even the possible unreality that may have to be manufactured to render the compromise or the adjustment possible at all. Therefore one might say that where relationships are so close and often so total, the basic principles of helping are good to keep in mind and occasionally to use, but one needs to be very sure, first, that helping is what one needs to do.

Helping theory does, however, help us to see some of the limitations of total mutuality. As one sociologist has put it, what is needed in marriage is "cooperative individuality" rather than complete unity.[1]

Helping in the Discipline of Children

With children the principle is different. One may quite often need to help. In fact the whole process of rearing is in a sense a form of help. A mother may need to help a child go to the dentist. As we have said, it would be foolish to tell him that it will not hurt. Instead she needs to be real about it, to permit him not to like it and above all to assure him that she will be with him in the experience.

Even to punish a child can be an attempt to help, and in most cases the how is much more important than the what. Punishment can, of course, be used to enforce demands or to compel submission, and as such is far from helpful. However, the helping factor—"This is it. I know it must hurt. I am here to help you if you want me and can use me"— might have been written in the first place by someone about to administer a mild spanking. It can, in fact, make of a spanking or any other quick punishment what is its only justification—that it is a sharp and immediate reminder that a limit has been transgressed, must be paid for, and will result in a restoration of grace. As such, it differs enormously from the punishment of any kind in which parents continue their displeasure for a length of time, or use some form of the statement, "This hurts me more than it hurts you." Here the attempt is not so much to remind and restore as it is to maintain control and to diminish the child's will. It is the difference between the setting of controls, which can be helpful things if they are not too confining and which may lead to added strength, and the control of another, which in a long-term relationship almost always

153

leads either to conquest or to rebellion. That is why children often like and admire teachers who are strict but fair, and who make their limits clear, but despise those who nag, who plead, or who are "hurt" by children's bad behavior, even though they may be more permissive.

It is a sad but perhaps inevitable fact that child rearing is becoming, in the United States at least, less a matter of controls, within which children make many decisions for themselves within a framework of clear limits that are enforced perhaps too rigorously, and much more a matter of control. Children's play is much more supervised than it used to be. Much more adult "guidance" and "leadership" is given. The times have largely vanished when children disappeared and engaged in their own pursuits for most of the day, appearing perhaps only for meals, as did Tom Sawyer, Penrod, or Elizabeth Nesbitt's children.

Part of the reason for this change may be the objectively far greater hazards of life today, part the living habits of an urban society, but part certainly is due to the kind of beliefs which have stressed "togetherness," manipulation, and persuasion rather than command, and have confused freedom with indulgence. The least free school I ever taught in was one in which there were no punishments but a constant pressure on the children to be productive, to create, and to absorb adult values. While reality for the Victorian child, in terms of adult sanctions, may have been too harsh, and empathy often lacking, reality has too often been ignored of late and subtle control put in its place. Parents have in fact lost their role to represent reality for a child, and this has often been a growth-inhibiting factor.

As the child grows older, parents will find it much more possible, and indeed necessary, to use a helping process. While most of us would, I think, see the failure in communication between many teenage children and their parents as due to too much difference in desires or values, I doubt that this is really the problem. What has happened is that the process of control has broken down as the children become more able to think and act for themselves. A true helping process has never been set up. There are no recognized limits and little empathy and support in meeting them. Negatives toward these limits have not been recognized or allowed since negatives threaten control. The parent has not in fact been different enough, and so is unable to help with the child's new-found difference. A control function cannot, in fact, tolerate difference. Therefore, as many parents can testify, a child may find it more possible to go for help to someone outside the family, to a minister, teacher, or friend, not because of any lack of closeness with his family but for the very opposite reason. With the parent too much is shared. Difference —

difference in ideals, in ways of looking at things, in challenges to established patterns—may be too difficult to express or too unlikely to be found.

Yet I think one has to be careful how one uses helping principles when emotionally involved with the person one is helping. My son once accused me of "acting like a social worker rather than a father." What I had been trying to do was to face him with the reality that the young woman he was engaged to, although a most lovable person, needed more experience—she had led a very sheltered life—before she was ready for marriage. I think I took empathy and support for granted, which is always a mistake. They do have to be expressed. It turned out that what he felt he needed was my unconditional support for him even if he should marry her at once. My wife and I gave them an engagement party. Three weeks later he wrote to say that he and the young woman had decided to "cool it off" a bit, citing as his own opinion the very same factors that I had been concerned about, and which, I believe, he had seen all along. Here what misled me at first was our longtime previous involvement, in which he had felt support was somehow doubtful.

Helping a Group or a Community

Some question, I think, must be raised as to how far the helping process is applicable in trying to help a group. If the group has some common feeling and arrives at conclusions through responding to certain more or less shared goals, it may in fact be helped through this process. The board or staff of an agency may provide a good example. As a consultant to many such groups, I find them, for instance, particularly able to use what we have called "alternative advice" or consultation which involves them in going back to consider their own specialized knowledge of the particular before committing themselves to a course of action. They are quite responsive to the reality of such things as falling enrollment and to the understanding of their goals. They can take considerable difference if there is empathy too and if they are quite clear that the consultant does not wish to control them.

There is a process of helping a group of people with somewhat similar interests discover what they want to do and put it into practice, to create, perhaps, a "neighborhood house" or a social resource, such as a recreation facility or an educational project. Here much of what we have said about helping may hold true. Principles that might have particular significance include listening to feeling rather than content, helping the group express what it wants and then work toward how much of this is possible, partializing the problem, leaving room for modifications when

giving advice, and being interested in the feelings of an angry or rejecting person, but in fact all the principles we have suggested may be important.

And yet a group is not a person. It rather rarely possesses a single
will. Its resistance to taking help cannot be ascribed to ambivalence, for
instance, but is much more likely to be due to differences within itself,
which may have to be explored first until some common will emerges, or
to the fact that the group leader is proceeding from a different set of
values from that of the group as a whole. In fact the term "group leader"
is a somewhat ambiguous one. This ambiguity is obvious when referring
to a city planner, who generally has, in the back of her mind, some specific
goals. She can be something of a coplanner, and in fact must be if she
is to be successful. But a great deal of what she does will involve compromise between the needs of group members and her own vision of
what should be. Yet she can be of real help, particularly in the area of
reality, and can help a group face it with empathy and support.

Help, in fact, can be used in many settings, some of them rather unexpected. One of the most helpful statements ever made to me was on
my first day in the army. The sergeant gathered us new recruits together
for what was supposed to be a pep talk. I had just been drafted, six weeks
after the birth of my first child. I was willing to do my duty, but I certainly hated having to do it. I was not looking forward at all to the patriotic
sentiments to which I was sure we would be subjected and expected to
agree.

The sergeant opened the proceeding by asking who among us was glad
to be there. Not a single hand went up. "Me neither," he remarked. "It's
a dirty, boring, dangerous business. I won't pretend you are going to like
it. But it has to be done, and the better it's done the less time it will take.
I'm here to help you learn how to be efficient at it."

Reality, empathy, and support. The sergeant had used all three, and
I, as well as many of the others I'm sure, faced the weeks of basic training in much better spirits. His comment did not make being there any
more pleasant, but we did not resent it. We "accepted and used" it as
well as we could.

The helping process, then, is something which operates both within
and outside of the formal helping situation wherever the helper's primary
concern is for the person she encounters and she is willing to give up,
even for a moment, her own will, even her will for him, to help him find
something for himself. It is an entirely different process from that we use
to control another, however good for him or for others that control may
be. It is a difficult process, one that involves quite a bit of risk and one

that is probably much underused and certainly much misunderstood. Confusion with such general concepts as that of doing good or of being kind to people, failure to distinguish it from subtle processes of control, equating it with permissiveness and the conviction that in order to help, one must know a lot about the other person have concealed much of its precision and its universality.

To what extent it really expresses something that is basic in humanity and indeed in the universe as a whole is probably a matter of faith, but it is a faith that is based on some experience. The helping process, in facts, works.

CHAPTER 9

Helping and Current Value Systems

In describing help in this book I have made a number of value judgments, some of which are as follows:

- *That* people should be free to choose;
- *That* the individual matters, and that his or her interests cannot be wholly subjected to those of the community;
- *That* a person has neither the right nor the ability to judge others in terms of what they deserve;
- *That* helping people to find their own way is better than controlling them, however subtly;
- *That* feelings and personal relationships matter;
- *That* people should be treated as active parties in the helping relationship and not as passive objects.

Not everyone would or does agree with these values. One could equally well uphold that the ability to get along in life, to avoid stress or trouble, and to acquire adaptive skills is what really matters, that choice is unimportant, that the well-being of the community is much more worth attaining than any individual goal, and that people, on the whole, like a measure of control.[1]

It would not be easy to prove this matter one way or the other, even by the most careful research. The nearest we could come to proving it would be to say that most people want one thing or another, and we know enough about the difficulty of the word "want" to question its validity as a unit of measurement. Outside this we could only say that making certain assumptions about people does or does not lead to certain results.

These results would have to be measured in turn in terms of value judgments that are in themselves unprovable. The only situation in which this kind of research would be valuable to us would be where it could show that belief in one assumption leads to a conclusion that violates a value we hold or that is inconsistent with itself. If we believe, for instance, both that humans operate best in an atmosphere of permissiveness, which would be an assumption about them, and that creativity is good, which would be a value judgment, and if it could be shown that permissiveness

158

leads to a loss of creativity, we would have objective reason to abandon one or the other belief.

All we can say then is that the values I have listed are necessary to the kind of help that this book describes. We then begin arguing in circles. Clearly, unless one holds these values, the kind of help described in this book will not make sense. We will want to do something different — perhaps to condition, or to control, or to discount relationship. We could argue most cogently for our point of view and invoke both our experience and our observation of what people are like and how they behave. We could bring scientific theory to our aid. I read once in a short editorial in a science-fiction magazine that takes seriously the extrapolation of present trends a most convincing application of the theory of evolution to society, with the suggestion that human beings as individuals could be likened to a single cell, such as an amoeba, which was developing, on a vast evolutionary scale, into a colony or society, such as volvox, but would eventually discover, in becoming a specialized part of an organism, access to powers and consciousness hitherto undreamed. Although this is an extreme and imaginative example, many social scientists today appear to be moving in something of the same direction.

There is no point in attempting to refute such conclusions, even if one should want to do so. In the end it comes down to the question of what one believes the universe, and people, and society are all about, whether they have a purpose, and what this purpose might be. In one sense this is a personal matter, and values such as we have suggested can be thought of as wholly individual results of any one person's experience. On the other hand most of our values can be seen to be products of certain common sets of assumptions about the nature of humankind and society which we have learned and grown up with. We may sometimes react against these, but in general we do even this within the framework of certain common value assumptions.

Because these systems of thought have such a strong influence on us, and because they are systems having some inner logical consistency, rather than being mere accretions of disconnected value judgments, it seems important to recognize the effect they have on helping. We may not realize, as we begin to act, that we do so largely in response to one or another of these systems. But to the extent that our values are anything more than idiosyncratic and have any base beyond purely personal preference — to the extent, that is, that our values have any roots — we are apt to be influenced by them.

There are in our culture three such more or less logical systems. There are variations on these, and perversions of them, which may be held by some to be distinct belief systems, but for the purposes of this discussion these three may be sufficient.

Capitalist-Puritan Values

The first such system, and possibly the most powerful among people as a whole, might be called Capitalist-Puritan, or CP. Its basic assumptions might be summarized as follows:

1. Each individual is responsible for his or her own success or failure.
2. Human nature is basically evil but can be overcome by an act of will.
3. The chief goal of human activity is to be successful, which is attained through competitiveness and hard work. Where puritanism is the main emphasis, this goal is correlated with the desire to prove oneself one of the "elect" or otherwise to attain salvation in an afterlife.
4. The primary purpose of society is the maintenance of order in which this acquisition is possible.
5. Unsuccessful, or deviant, people are not deserving of help, although efforts should be made, up to a point, to rehabilitate them or to spur them to greater efforts on their own behalf.
6. The primary incentives to change are to be found in economic or physical rewards and punishments.

The prevalence of these assumptions needs no emphasis at this time. The CP system is the conservative doctrine and is popularly thought of as "American" or even as embodying common sense. As such it is part of the heritage of most of us.

Where the system is overtly puritan rather than capitalist, it is officially God, not humanity, who determines a person's success or failure. Although, philosophically, this might seem to make a big difference, in practice it does not. For one thing, few CPs really believe it, or act as if they do. So closely have God's favor and worldly success become identified that the successful are thought of as "good" and the unsuccessful as "bad" or inferior. Humans take over what was originally God's prerogatives of judgment and chastisement, and those who do not exercise sufficient ambition or will are shamed, exhorted, punished, or left to the workings of the economic system.

Where the CP system of beliefs is associated with certain other religious values, it has strong ethical content. Ethics and economics meet in the matter of work, which has both a material and an ethical value, and in statements applying ethical standards to business enterprise, such as the statement, "Honesty is the best policy," or emphasis on the "service" motive in business.

Where the system is associated with religious or ethical concepts of one's responsibility to one's neighbor, the result may be a real compassion for the unfortunate, such as the orphan or the widow, who have not overtly at least contributed to their own misfortune. The relationship created is normally one of condescension, however, and often demands gratitude or unusual virtue in the person receiving help.

Because the system has a sort of religious base, it is thought of by some as representing the total religious point of view. Herbert Bisno, in his *Philosophy of Social Work,* [2] for instance, took issue with what he considered basic Protestant or Catholic dogma in each of the first six principles of social work philosophy he enunciated. Yet all six of the principles he rejected were not so much religious principles as derivations from a particular theology that have become absorbed into the CP system of belief.

The CP system has been secularized to the point that many people believe in it with no religious consciousness. Others profess religious belief concurrent with it, as it were, or use religious statements to support what is essentially a doctrine of humanity necessary to laissez-faire capitalism. Max Weber, R. B. Perry, R. H. Tawney, and others have traced this development and have given a number of reasons for it, which are not specifically relevant to this discussion. [3]

Humanist-Positivist-Utopian Values

Almost diametrically opposed to this system is one that can be called Humanist-Positivist-Utopian, or HPU. This is the belief system of most social scientists and many liberals, but it is also held to some degree by people who profess CP views and by many religious people, despite some inherent contradiction. Summarized, its basic assumptions can be presented as follows:

1. The primary purpose of society is to fulfill human needs both material and emotional.
2. If these needs were fulfilled, then people would attain a state that is variously described, according to the vocabulary used in the specific HPU system, as that of goodness, maturity, adjustment, or productivity, in which most of their and society's problems would be solved.
3. What hampers them from attaining this state is external circumstances, not in general under their individual control. These circumstances, in various HPU systems, have been ascribed to lack of education, economic factors,

childhood experiences, religious training, and social environment.

4. These circumstances can be compensated for by those possessed of sufficient technical and scientific knowledge.

5. Humans and society are therefore perfectible.

The system is humanist in that those who ascribe to it believe that humans can ultimately solve all their problems, without help from any higher power. It is positivist in that it relies entirely on Cartesian science and has no use for anything that can be classed as spiritual and which cannot be measured by modern research methods. And it is utopian in that HPU-ists believe in inevitable progress both in material things and in human relationships and ethics. It is, perhaps, difficult to see as a unitary theory, because it appears in different forms according to the specific solution to the ills of the world promulgated by its leaders. Thus Dewey believed that education was the key to a better world; Marx, a revision of the economic system; Freud, the early Freud at least, the removal of repressions (a view he later reversed); Woodrow Wilson, a League of Nations; and Lyndon Johnson, an empowerment of minorities and the poor. All had some right on their side. These things are needed. But all had only partial answers, and all believed in the basic tenets of this worldview. Erich Voegelin, in his *New Science of Politics*, calls them "the modern Gnostics," each of whom would bring in the Kingdom without waiting for God to act.[4]

The HPU system constitutes the worldview of most liberals today. It is the heritage of the Enlightenment, and its first prophet was Jean-Jacques Rousseau, who said, "Man is born free, but everywhere he is in chains." Humans are good, society is bad, although why society created by good people should be bad is perhaps hard to say. Its scientific tenor dates back to Comte and Descartes.

Judeo-Christian, or at Least Theistic

A third view, rather rarely formulated, but which is held at least in theory by a number of people, is what I called in the first edition of this book the Judeo-Christian tradition. This is not a perfect term.

The Christian tradition is often associated with the Capitalist-Puritan view, although many might consider CP thought a heresy. Some of my Jewish friends, also, object to the term "Judeo-Christian" because the difference in the Jewish and Christian traditions is not sufficiently recognized in it, and certainly Jewish thought has not been subject to some of the heresies that have marked Christian thinking. Nor would I hold that this worldview is confined entirely to Christians and Jews. Elements of

162

it can be found in native religions, in Islam, and even among those who profess no religion except a sense of being in some way responsible to something outside themselves. It was certainly the view of the little Hopi girl in Robert Coles' *Spiritual Life of Children*.[5] It is behind most of what is taught in Catholic and Protestant churches, except in those churches of the "far right" and the "far left." To Christians it is epitomized in the great commandment to love God and your neighbor as yourself. Despite these limitations, I shall continue to use the term "Judeo-Christian" in the absence of a clearer summary term.

Its basic assumptions can be listed as follows:

1. Humans are created beings, one of whose problems is that they act as if they were not and try to be autonomous.
2. Human beings are fallible, but at the same time sometimes capable of transcending themselves and showing great courage or unselfishness.
3. The difference between "good" and "bad" people is insignificant compared with the standard demanded by their maker, and consequently people have no right to judge each other.
4. People's chief good is in their relationship with one another and with their creator.
5. The purpose of government and society is to ensure justice and opportunity for everyone to live as abundant a life as possible.
6. Love is the ultimate victor over evil, including force.

The position of this ethic vis-à-vis the others is a complicated one. In one sense it lies parallel to them and is a viable alternative, or a middle ground, especially with regard to assumption 2 above, recognition of humanity's simultaneous fallibility and potential. In another, it lies behind them and makes both of them possible.

This position may be much easier to see in relation to CP thought than to HPU thought. The former is a particular and perverted form of the JC doctrine. But in much HPU thought any concept of a creator is denied, as is humanity's dependence on any purpose or direction outside itself. Yet much of the actual value system practiced by humanists has its roots in JC concepts, including nonjudgmentalism, emphasized very strongly in early Christian writers such as Chrysostom in the fourth century,[6] and humans as choosing beings, which is inherent in Jewish and Christian thought since the concept of the Fall. Justice in the sense of equality of opportunity and a fair share of this world's goods is originally a Hebrew concept; so is the ultimate worth and dignity of all people, not just of an elite.

That these values have been adopted by HPU thought, particularly in its humanistic aspect, is undoubtable. But in having been so adopted, they have been cut off from their roots. There is nothing in HPU thought that makes them an utter necessity, to which HPU thought can return if they should be temporarily lost. They are inherited values not essential to a strictly scientific view of the world or of society. JC values can therefore be seen as in some cases an alternative, in some a progenitor, and in some a check or critique of the values of the social scientist.

Beyond the three major sets of assumptions we have outlined there are a number of others that are possible. Existentialism emphasizes humanity's choice and encounter with reality. Except in its more nihilistic form it can, however, reinforce certain aspects of the JC system and certainly does not contradict it. The system of natural law emphasizes humanity's power of reason. There is a Thomistic school of helping theory,[7] just as there is an existentialist one,[8] but these are more variants of other belief systems than fully developed systems of their own.

Values and How They Affect Help

Probably most people are influenced to some extent by all three of these sets of assumptions. All have some value, and it is not so much a matter of saying that one is good and another bad as it is of taking a position nearer or further from one or another extreme. Yet we do need to explore which set of assumptions is more likely to preserve the kind of values we see as important in helping, and which is most compatible with what we can observe in the process of helping as we know it.

Quite obviously the CP position is in general the least likely to lead to help. If people are totally responsible for their own actions, if they can better their condition by an act of will, if they can be induced to change by punishment or reward, then helping becomes a simple matter of us arranging the appropriate rewards and punishments. There is no room for relationship, or concern for another, except in a highly condescending and judgmental way.

It is those who espouse this view who have created the workhouse and the pauper's oath, who demand of children in what used to be called orphanages or of welfare clients that they work harder and behave better than other people, and who are terrified of any welfare measure that would make the receipt of relief in any way bearable or dignified. They assume without question that welfare clients will "naturally" lie, cheat, or steal if given the chance, prefer laziness to work, and feign sickness in

164

order to shirk working. And typically they are much more concerned to punish the few who may do such things than help the many who do not.

Yet this view is not without some positive features. CPs do at least recognize that it is the person in trouble who must bear the final responsibility for his or her own betterment, and this is a valuable corrective, although perhaps too absolute a one, to the tendency in HPU thought to emphasize self-fulfillment even at the cost of responsibility.

In its initial impact on helping theory and practice HPU thought produced a tremendous outpouring of love and understanding. The helped person was freed from the total responsibility he had borne up till then for his own condition. He was no longer a second-class citizen, judged by his fellows. He was valued for his own sake. The particular social science which became the model for helping in the 1930s — analytical psychology — also stressed certain concepts which, if not strictly HPU- -and indeed I believe that they basically belong to JC thought and are not HPU at all — were at least acceptable to those who claimed to be humanists and utopians. These were in general as follows:

1. A sense of people's common vulnerability, a belief (and this is one of Freud's greatest contributions to helping) that there were no longer "sick" and "well" people, but people who were in greater or less difficulty with problems that trouble us all;
2. A habit of looking at problems from the point of view of the helped person rather than from the outside;
3. An emphasis on relationship as the principal means of help;
4. At least in the earlier stages a degree of awe in the face of new knowledge of a somewhat mysterious nature.

But these, which are philosophical rather than scientific statements, were in a sense incidental to rather than part and parcel of HPU-ism's basic assumptions. HPU-ism makes other assumptions which are more questionable. Among these, culled from Herbert Bisno's attempt, in 1952, to discover a common "philosophy" of social work, are that all human suffering is undesirable and should be prevented, or at least alleviated, that all human behavior is the result of a deterministic interrelationship between the biological organism and its environment, and that the scientific method is basic to an understanding of humanity.[9]

Pain and Loss in HPU Thought

Let us look at the first of these assumptions in terms of what we know about helping. Bisno made this statement as a reaction against what he held to be the Christian, but which is actually CP, belief that suffering either is a consequence of sin or is in some way in itself ennobling.

There are of course kinds of apparently purposeless suffering which one would hasten to alleviate wherever they were found. But it is also true that some suffering is a necessary preliminary or an accompaniment to growth. Sometimes one has to come up against despair or pain in order to move forward to a new organization of oneself.[10] If one's emphasis is on the pain or suffering, then one tends to forego the growth that can ensue from a painful struggle. This may be obvious from our former discussion of the importance of not taking away a person's problem, but the tendency to try to relieve pain on any and all occasions is one of the strongest temptations a helping person can meet but must resist.

The desire to avoid pain at the cost of growth can be seen perhaps most clearly in many people's attitudes toward some unmarried mothers. Reacting perhaps from a moralistic stance, doctors and social workers identify so strongly with the pain of giving up a child the mother may love that if she cannot keep her child they make of the whole experience an unreal fantasy in which she never really has a baby at all, so quickly is it whisked away to be placed for adoption. She has little chance to come to terms with what has happened, and so little chance not to repeat the experience. She has little chance to make her decision out of love rather than fear or to abide with it once made. The results are all too often recidivism, an inability to mature, or a deep sense of guilt for having given up her child. The painless way of doing something is sometimes the least productive.

Perhaps this is a semantic problem. Perhaps we need here to make a distinction and even find different words for two very different kinds of pain. One is needless or meaningless suffering, which weakens or leaves scars, to which we might give the name trauma; and the other that temporary pain that would appear to accompany any meaningful change and is indeed the cost of it, which we might call the pain of growth. It should not be forgotten, too, that some people may deliberately choose to suffer in order to reach a greater goal. Mahatma Gandhi would be a good modern example.

Confusion between these two different kinds of pain is particularly apparent when the pain suffered is that of loss. Tennyson once said that it was better to have loved and lost than never to have loved at all. But, in modern psychology, so much emphasis has been placed on the pain of loss that this equation is often reversed. It is better, in many people's minds, not to love in case one has to give up. One finds this argument used in discussing foster homes for children. Some years ago after a painful removal of a child from a home where he was not loved too much but loved too possessively, a normally responsible newspaper suggested that foster children should be moved routinely every few months for fear of such attachments developing.

Yet separation and loss are part of all human experience. We could not in fact do without them. The greatest separation of all occurs almost at the beginning of life, with the act of birth itself. Children progressively separate themselves from their parents, by going to school, to college, and eventually by becoming independent. All these separations are at the time painful, but not necessarily traumatic. The often-made assertion that all separation is traumatic, which has become almost an article of belief in those who work with dependent children, is simply not true. Painful, yes, but not necessarily traumatic. What is traumatic is not the separation itself but the feelings that so often accompany it—the shock, the knowledge of rejection, the anger, and the sense of one's own badness when one suddenly loses a home.

The helping person will then assert that love and concern and relationship are more important than their loss. She will, to return for a moment to the unmarried mother, help the mother to give her child up, if that is what she plans to do, out of love for him and not out of a fear that she might love him. The helper will not, unless the mother forces her to do so, shelter her from the pain of loving and giving up. She may suffer with her in the process—and indeed helping can be both painful and utterly exhausting—but if she really wants to help her, she will not deny her this experience. Nor, if we really have love and concern for others, do we deny them their struggles. To protect someone from reality inevitably means that we have some lack of respect for him.

Humans and the Scientific Method

Bisno's second assertion, that all human behavior is the result of interaction between the biological organism and the environment, commits us to a belief that humans are mechanical beings, however complicated, which is directly contrary to any assumption that they are choosing beings in the active or willing sense. It denies them any part in their own development. They can only be manipulated, or possibly liberated, supposing one was to hold also the general HPU belief in the essential healthiness of the mechanism. This assertion therefore provides us with the basis of

167

a control process, but not one of help, and is one of the reasons why social scientists appear to be turning more and more to control rather than to helping procedures.[11]

The same danger is inherent in the belief that the scientific method is the only valid avenue to an understanding of humanity. As long as the science that was relied on was analytical psychology, the values on which we have commented were stressed—people's common vulnerability, looking at problems from the point of view of the helped person rather than from the outside, a belief in relationship, even an awe in the contemplation of an internal, subconscious world.

But analytical psychology is not the only social science, and it is scientifically one that is considerably suspect, particularly in its inability to produce certain kinds of social results. Professional helpers, particularly those who are concerned chiefly with helping people adapt to their culture, are turning more and more to the external sciences, such as sociology, anthropology, and epidemiology, for the solution of social problems. These sciences have no use for the philosophical emphases that analytical psychology contributed to helping. They look at humanity from the outside, from the viewpoint of society, rather than from that of humanity itself. They care little for relationship and have little sense of awe.

The Illusion of Human Goodness

But the most serious difficulty with a strictly HPU system of belief arises from the assumption that people are naturally good, and that given opportunity they will demonstrate this. A humanist belief that we owe in the first place to Rousseau, it is hardly scientific. It sounds a most hopeful theory and is certainly more productive than its CP opposite, that people are basically evil.

But it does not stand up to examination. Humans are not rational creatures most of the time, and they do not always choose the good. They are often petty, selfish, shortsighted, or defensive, although they can be generous, loving, imaginative, or kind. They are rarely entirely one or the other. To believe in their perfectibility or in their natural goodness leads inevitably to disappointment.

And disappointment, unfortunately, leads to the necessity to take increasing measures to ensure that people do not fail one. This is the lesson, and the paradox, of many humanistic movements, that they begin with an unreasonably optimistic estimate of human nature which cannot possibly be lived up to. Then, when people fail to fulfill these expectations, either more and more exceptions to the general rule are made, or it is assumed that some outside force is intervening that must be combated.

Eventually the exception becomes the rule, and more and more people are protected from their own weakness by a smaller and smaller elite. A belief in the natural goodness of people leads to its own absolute opposite. The process can be seen clearly in the course of events following the Russian Revolution from 1917 to recent times. Lenin and Trotsky believed that once the economic system had been righted, there would be no need for a state—"not even one typewriter," Trotsky said. People would collaborate naturally. Yet the result was one of the most pervasive and intrusive states the world has ever seen.

Much the same sort of thing has happened to the overoptimistic estimate of human nature that was current in the social philosophy of the 1930s. Social work, in America at least, can be shown, during the time since then, to have turned more and more to methods of control. This emphasis has been accelerated by the belief in the absolute nature of the scientific method. It is a demonstrable fact that humans analyzed objectively in terms of such factors as their adaptability and social relationships are bungling, capricious creatures who often do not know their own best interests. It is very easy to pass from this analysis to a belief that they need controlling for their own good.

The Need for the JC Tradition

What, then, is the alternative to CP or HPU thought? It seems to me that we need to accept the enlightenment that HPU thought has brought, but to recognize its limitations and to check some of its secondary values against the JC tradition. This does not mean, let me hasten to say, that one must assent to certain theological doctrines or to be a "believer" to be a helping person. Many of the greatest helpers have been secular humanists—in fact the record of humanists is far better than that of Christians, although perhaps not of Jews, in what they have contributed to helping and in their personal exercise of it.

It may be suggested that some of these humanists shared many of the assumptions of the JC tradition but hesitated to make this explicit because the CP set of assumptions also claims a religious base. This has caused a revulsion against any helping theory couched in religious terms. Many church-related persons have been basically CP in their assumptions.

What does seem clear is that neither the CP nor the HPU assumptions are in themselves enough without the JC tradition. Both offer certain insights—in the case of HPU thought some very valuable ones—without which modern helping would not have developed. But both break down as absolute systems. We need many of their insights but we need something more.

One of the most important insights of the JC tradition is the nature of human beings. Persons are neither the evil beings of Capitalist-Puritan belief, nor as good as many HPU-ists believe. But it is not so much a matter of steering between an over- and an underestimation of their nature as it is of recognizing two different factors in their makeup. The first is their fallibility and the second their ability, in certain circumstances, to work out for themselves something somewhat better than their fallibility would suggest. This is far from saying that they have in themselves a potential which needs only some triggering, or some favorable circumstance, to tap. It means rather that with help, or where they are put to it, or from the depths of despair, they can sometimes transcend their own fallibility. Moreover this ability is found in the most unlikely places. It is often demonstrated by those whom objectively one would be forced to believe are unequipped or incapable. This is the constant surprise one comes up against in helping. Not infrequently it tends to have the air of the miraculous about it.

The JC tradition has some other features that relate to helping. Choosing, in the active and willing sense, is important in this tradition. But again, perhaps we need to make clear that to believe in the necessity of the helped person choosing for himself is not a statement that he knows best what is good for him or that he will always choose the right. To believe that would be sentimentality. That he knows what is best for himself is true only in a special sense: only he knows what he can live with, and only he can put himself into living the kind of life he chooses or that is chosen for him. Unless then he chooses to live this life, he will for the most part only go through the motions of living. He will be living at second hand, which is exactly what the believer in his wholly mechanical or biological nature believes that he does in any case.

Nor are we concerned here with what social workers have called, rather loosely, the right to self-determination. This has to do more with selective choice than with active and willing choice, and if held too absolutely can lead to protecting people from the consequences of their choice, which is the real problem of permissiveness.

As a political and social question, such a right has many obvious limitations, such as the law, the right of others, and perhaps, to some extent, one's own good, although we have to be very careful here to distinguish between some clear and more or less objective disaster with which one cannot cope and what some other person thinks would be good for one. The distinction is not easy and, it would seem, should generally be submitted to law, or political process, rather than be made by the would-be helper.

In helping, the question is all too often asked the wrong way round. It is not that the helping person has in her power the granting or withholding of this right. This is usually determined by society, law, or the culture. The question is rather whether the helper has the right, in the name of help, to limit or try to constrain this right beyond these limits. The use of assumed power, based on some assumed authority of skill, knowledge, or supported responsibility, is a dangerous weapon, however benevolently it is intended to be exercised.

Most of us have a preference for a social and political system in which people are as free as possible to make their own decisions, but none of us imagines that this can be absolutely so. It is therefore very difficult to enunciate a belief in a right to self-determination in any realistic terms, though not so hard, perhaps, to determine how much one, as an individual or a member of a profession, believes oneself authorized to intervene.

The Judeo-Christian tradition also emphasizes relationship, non-judgmentalism, the importance of personal as well as societal problems, and the importance of feelings which some forms of HPU-ism deny. It is also committed to the understanding that pride, or the desire to act as master rather than servant, is the primary sin. It is in this particular that it can be perhaps the greatest moderating force on useful and enlightening scientific discovery. Science, unfortunately, has no built-in protection against pride. While many scientists are humble, it is only too easy for the person who has some knowledge to believe that this very knowledge gives him or her the right to control or dominate others.

CHAPTER 10

Helping and Religious Belief

This chapter is in a way optional. It deals only with Christian beliefs. This is not because I do not respect other religions or think that one cannot be a good helper if one is not a Christian. Judaism has for instance contributed far more than the number of its adherents would suggest to our knowledge of helping. It was the Hebrew people who first came up with the concept of justice which underlies all helping today, the idea that God's provenance is intended for everyone and that no one has the right to take all of it for him- or herself. "What does the Lord require of you but to do justice, love kindness and walk humbly with your God?" (Mic. 6:8). Jews have been overrepresented among the leaders of the helping professions, but because my knowledge of the helping process is limited more or less to the legacy Jews have left Christians in the Scriptures, I do not feel competent to discuss the contribution of modern Judaism to helping theory.[1] Furthermore, since Christianity has been the predominant religion in our country, more serious questions have been raised about its relevance to helping than about that of any other religion.

Is Religion Important to Helping?
In one sense all helping has a religious base. The desire to help another is not, as far as we know, instinctual. All worldwide religions have stressed to some extent responsibility for other persons, kindness or justice to the needy, or self-fulfillment through service.

But this is very far from saying that helping, in the way we have described it, is compatible with a particular theology or belief. Indeed at first sight it may appear not to be so. Certainly many of the insights into helping that we have learned have not come from religious sources, and equally certainly many humanists and agnostics have shown far more ability to understand and practice the process than have those who profess religious faith.

Yet the relationship between religion and the helping process is important for a number of reasons. First, a great deal of helping takes place under some sort of religious auspices. The range of this helping has increased greatly as more and more churches have been interpreting their mission as one of service to the world instead of preoccupation with the state of grace or the afterlife of their individual members. Secondly, much modern helping theory has been developed in opposition — one might almost say reaction — to certain theological ideas and to so-called religious attitudes, which naturally disturbs those who care about religion. And thirdly, some religious people, and religious organizations, are wondering if they have anything in particular, beyond goodwill, to contribute to helping. Some churches believe, for instance, that the right thing to do today is to cease any distinct "religious" effort and to support governmental and community helping programs.

Let us suggest then, four questions, which we will attempt to answer in part:

1. Why do many helping people look still with great suspicion, despite some recent attempts at reconciliation, at religious motives for helping?
2. Is the helping process compatible with religious belief?
3. Does the Christian religion have anything particular, or indeed different, to add to helping theory?
4. How, if at all, does a Christian helper behave differently from a secular one?

Why Do Helpers Suspect Christians?

Association With Capitalist Puritan Assumptions

The first question can be answered to a great extent in terms of the three sets of assumptions that we discussed in chapter 9. To the extent that Christian doctrine has been identified with capitalism; that it assumes, even implicitly, that worldly success and grace have anything to do with each other; that there is any room in it for judgmentalism, or distinction between people on the basis of their supposed goodness or badness; and that it rejects the sinner rather than the sin, the church is operating on CP assumptions and deserves all that the humanists have said about it. Indeed the wave of humanism that swept over the country in the 1920s and 1930s can be considered a most beneficial chastening of Christian theory and practice at that time.

It is this kind of religious identification with CP assumptions that is so strenuously attacked, and rightly, by a humanist such as Bisno in his *Philosophy of Social Work*.[2] He takes exception to such religious beliefs as the value of suffering in creating character, or seeing suffering as the just desert for sin; a philosophical division between the body and the

173

soul; and the identification of certain instinctual drives as "bad" or "immoral." But these are not actually beliefs that would be held by many Christians.

It could also be said that in the 1930s, when much of our present helping theory began to develop, the church, as it was represented in social work, in the activities of church groups, and in its general attitudes, was either CP, paternalistic, or insensitive to need. Indeed HPU thought appeared to offer an alternative. At that time the sense of a new relationship between people, loving and helpful, respectful of the other, transcending caste or culture, which liberal humanists and Freudian psychiatry created, appeared to give new expression to much of what many of us thought religion should be about. In addition, it dispensed with many of the biblical faith's more uncomfortable features, such as problems of sin, judgment, and personal responsibility.

But, as we have seen, HPU thought contained in itself the seeds of its own deterioration. And because, for a time, the church was put to shame, it does not follow that religion must become humanist or deny its essential doctrines if it is to help people. Although in the nineteenth century it was those churches who had no concept of the doctrine of Original Sin, the Unitarians and the Quakers, who had most to give to the social scene,[3] the fault lay not with the doctrine itself—it is the greatest deterrent to pride that can possibly exist—but with the identification between sin and lack of social or material success. It was the divorce between original sin and grace, the puritan habit of ascribing the one to others and claiming the other for oneself, that made original sin such a dangerous helping concept.

There were other problems, too. The tendency to divorce religion from life in this world, to insist on spiritual or otherworldly values rather than on what is happening in the social scene, is another result of the development of the CP set of assumptions. Theology can be perverted to support capitalist assumptions, but, if is to do so, concepts such as concern for people, relationship with a loving Father, repentance, and justice have to be limited to some area of operation—the spiritual—which does not affect everyday life and relationships.

Christians of Grace, Law, and Morality

Another and perhaps an easier way of looking at the problem is to see that there are three very different ways in which Christians have reacted to the Good News of God's forgivingness. Some are enormously grateful for it and can do nothing but try to emulate it in their deal-

174

ings with other people. These I call Christians of Grace. In social work terms they are God's clients, and rather desperate ones at that.

A second group of Christians are also grateful, but in their hearts they are not quite sure that God has really forgiven them and will continue to do so no matter what. They must therefore be very careful to do exactly what God wants. I call these Christians of Law, and they remind me of welfare clients who are glad to receive a grant but know that they must maintain their eligibility if the grant is to continue. Some are very fine people, but they often have little concern for other people. Their own need to assure their salvation is too pressing.

But there is a third group who started perhaps as Christians of Law but who, once they believed themselves forgiven, ceased to be God's clients, as it were, and appointed themselves to His staff to prevent other people from sinning. They feel justified, incidentally, in using most unloving means to do so, often excusing themselves by feeling that they may be assuring the other person's salvation, despite their formal belief in faith rather than observing the Law as the passport to heaven. I call them Christians of Morality. Let me say, however, that being a Christian of Grace, or of Law, or of Morality, has little to do with denominationalism. I have met all three among Sisters of Mercy, Calvinists, Methodists, Mennonites, and members of the Churches of Christ and many other groups. Also most of us are not entirely one or the other.[4]

The Helping Process and Christian Belief

God's Helping Process

It is those who are primarily Christians of Grace who will find not only that their religion and the helping process are compatible, but that there is a very close correspondence between the helping process of God and that of human beings. We should not be surprised. It is unlikely that God would ordain two entirely different processes. And what has God been about since He created humankind but helping us to find "salvation," a word that means health, or well-being, both in this world and the next?

Consider first the description, in chapter 2, of the demands that are made on the person to be helped. These were to recognize that something is wrong with, or lacking in, his situation, which he can do nothing about by himself; the willingness to tell someone else about this problem; according to this other person a limited right to tell him what to do or to do things for him; and the giving up of his present and familiar adjustments in favor of a possibly dangerous but probably more satisfactory life.

These demands have long been familiar in religious thought. Indeed, because they have been familiar in this setting for so much longer than they have in the context of human helping, the church has developed single terms for what is now expressed in helping theory in somewhat clumsy phrases. The recognition that something is wrong and that one can do nothing about it oneself the church calls repentance. This does not mean, let it be said, simply being sorry for what one has done and resolving to do better, but just this very recognition of one's own helplessness and a turning to God for help. The willingness to tell another the church calls confession. The granting to another of control of one's affairs it speaks of as submission; the undertaking to change it calls commitment; and the willingness to give up the known for what, as Paul points out bluntly, is unseen and unknown, it designates as faith.

The atheist or the agnostic, considering this phenomenon, will see this simply as an indication that the process has been known for a long time. When human beings, he or she would say, invented God and sought help from their invention, this was the process they described because this is the way that people actually are helped.

But to Christians such an analogy begins to raise the question whether what they believe and what the helping process requires are not related in a very particular and intimate way—whether in fact the helping process as we struggle to know it is not a faint reflection, but a true one all the same, of a divine relationship.

The human and the divine helping processes are not exactly the same. That would be too much to expect. The process of repentance, confession, submission, and faith is in relation to a divine Person. Submission needs to be much more absolute than it does in the human context. In fact, in the human context it needs to be carefully limited because the person to whom one submits is a person like oneself, and could and might use the relationship to exploit one.

We may feel the same about God. We do, sometimes. Yet it is exactly that quality of God that makes submission possible: that God does not exploit us—that God's service is perfect freedom.

Nevertheless we do resist God, and in doing so we may see more clearly how those we help may and will resist us. How often, for instance, do we not protect ourselves from God by going through all the motions, attending all the services, praising Him exaggeratedly or fulsomely, singing all the hymns, involving ourselves busily in what we imagine to be "His work," and kidding ourselves that this is all He demands?

An understanding of these evasions may help us appreciate more accurately what is meant by "disarming" those who try to help one, or why people demand help on their own terms. Just as it is a fearful thing to fall into the hands of the Living God, so in a lesser way it is fearful to fall into the hands of a helper.

Having seen this correspondence between a human and a divine process, we are then faced with the question of what it implies. Is it just a coincidence, or merely a useful analogy, or does the pattern follow through? Are we here on the edge of a synthesis between our beliefs and our helping activity which might have real significance? Obviously faith might wish it so, and this is the great temptation, to go looking for analogies, just as some people search the Bible for texts to support their theories or prejudices.

Yet it is hard not to be impressed with what happens when we begin to examine the other side of the helping relationship, what the helper puts into it.

Triune Helping

In chapter 5 we developed an analysis of the helping factor into three elements—reality, empathy, and support. We said of them then that they were triune, necessary to each other, needing each to be present in any helping situation, and incomplete without each other.

This statement was developed on a purely pragmatic basis. It states what is necessary to good helping. Yet one might suggest with some confidence that there are characteristics of another triune phenomenon, Father, Son, and Holy Spirit, that correspond very closely to reality, empathy, and support.

God the Father, the Creator, is in Christian thought certainly the author of reality—both the reality of things and that of the moral and natural law, as well as of the laws of causality and consequence. God is also the Wholly Other, the One who is different, who is "God, not man."

Biblical history, as Christians read it, certainly suggests that this reality was not enough. Human beings alone could not, of their own will, face reality and change in relation to it. There was needed an act of empathy, and there is no more characteristic or total act of empathy than that described in the Incarnation—God who became human and yet remained God, "who in every respect has been tempted as we are, yet without sinning." Indeed, the whole theology of "very God and very man," the refusal to consider Jesus as either less than God and not wholly human, or part

177

human, or part God and part human, the insistence that he is a single person "without conversion, composition or confusion,"[5] as the Westminster Confession of Faith asserts, is a struggle with the same kind of problem as that which troubled us a few pages back—how a person can feel another's pain and yet remain separate from it. Both require the concept that in doing two apparently different things at the same time, one does not do either less completely.

Again, the name given to the Spirit, both in the King James Version and the Prayer Book, is the Comforter. Although the word "comfort" has suffered a weakening of meaning since the seventeenth century, its derivation is from *cum* = with and *fortis* = strong. A comforter is therefore one who is "strong with you," and there is no better one-sentence definition of support.

Reality, empathy, and suppor—Father, Son, and Holy Spirit—the analogy may seem blasphemous at first, despite a similar handling of the mystery of the Trinity in Dorothy Sayers's *The Mind of the Maker*,[6] where she applies the doctrine to the creative process.

It is, however, logical that if the person asking for help is analogous to the recipient of grace, then the helping person must, as far as it is possible for a finite, fallible being to do so, model her helping on the actions of God. One almost wishes at this point that one believed, as did Freud, that humanity created God in its own image instead of the other way round, for then one would be dealing only with an additional resource—theology—to help one with insights about one's helping, and not with an imperative that demands of us the near impossible—that imperative, incidentally, that is summed up in the Last Commandment. The authors of the American Revised Standard Edition have clarified the meaning in this commandment of "as" by adding "even"—"Love one another even as [in the same way as] I have loved you."

Supposing then this double analogy to be significant—and there is plenty of room for an honest skepticism still—what are some of its implications? It follows, I think, that help becomes in a new sense the expression of one's religion, not just as the term is often used, one's general but unspecific goodwill toward others, but what one actually believes. It follows too that the helping process is real, that it is not merely a collection of pragmatic principles, that it deserves much closer study than it has received to date, and that where we have got it right, it is much more than a set of useful techniques. It has about it some of the nature of a universal, although we can never, as it were, argue from this point backward. The first requirement of any process is that it can be shown to work. And the analogy suggests that there are other ways in whic the biblical schema is relevant to our work.

Insights for Helping from the Scriptures

In a number of places the Scriptures confirm and illuminate something that is already known in the helping process. One example of this is not so much the fact that people are deciding, choosing creatures, which we probably know anyhow, but the nature of that choice--not a selection of alternatives, as we have seen, but a far more total orientation of one's energies to a goal. Here religion provides us with a much more understandable term in the form of "commitment." We might add, too, that the risk which God took in allowing people free will, rather than creating them as automata, throws some light on the helper's need to treat human beings as capable of choice. The distance between the wisdom of God and the wisdom of even the wisest human being is surely greater than that between us and even the sorriest and most confused person we might want to help.

Again, in struggling to express the quality of the helper's concern (and we might note here that I have adopted the word "concern" from religious rather than secular writers) that has nothing to do with liking or approval and can even be exercised toward those whom one thoroughly dislikes, the concept of agape love and in particular Paul's short but quite exact analysis of it in 1 Corinthians 13 can be of very great use. His insistence that love (concern) is not puffed up, does not insist on its own way, and above all that it never ends is particularly valuable. That statement and Jesus' "Lo, I am with you until the close of the age" (Matt. 28:20) express better than any other what we mean when we say that support must be unconditional. Jesus' life, too, and His death, underlines that empathy always involves suffering, as well as the fact that some suffering is a necessary prelude to growth and accomplishment of one's mission, but not, let me hasten to say, that all suffering is ennobling.

We have emphasized, also, the need to be nonjudgmental. Not only did Jesus, several times, tell us not to judge—the parable of the mote and the beam (or the speck and the log) is perhaps the clearest statement—but Paul explains why we should not judge others. We are all sinners. "All," he writes, "have fallen short of the glory of God," and "there is now no distinction" (Rom. 3:22). It is as if on a vast thermometer indicating goodness and badness from God on down, all human behavior occupies only one degree.

There are other instances in which the Scriptures throw light on helping practice. A perfect example of empathy, which I have used in another

179

curs in Hebrews, when Christ is described as having been ... every respect as we are, yet did not sin. In fact, if I was asked ... o one sentence my advice to a beginning helper, I would say, ... be tempted in all ways as those you want to help are, but don't make the same mistakes."

The Problem of Sin

There are, of course, problems in reconciling helping theory with the Scriptures. One of the biggest is the concept of sin, or, more accurately, sins. To the Christian of Law, or of Morality, and indeed traditionally in at least Protestant churches, sins are thought of almost entirely as deliberate acts forbidden by God.[7] They should be prevented, reproved, and punished. Since these are clearly not helpful methods — people very rarely change from being reproved or punished — and since this concept makes no allowance for environmental factors or for the working of the unconscious mind, sin became a forbidden word in the vocabulary of helping. At the same time many Christians accused secular helpers of being "soft on sin."

There is plenty in the Bible to support this concept of sin, from "man's first disobedience," as Milton put it in the first line of *Paradise Lost,* through the stories of Ham, Onan, David, and Ananias; the Ten Commandments; and a good deal of Deuteronomy, Leviticus, and Numbers. But Jesus rarely if ever reproved a specific sin, and he made one statement that must have surprised his listeners — that to lust after a woman, even if one did not touch her, was to commit adultery. Surely we might think people who lust but do not act on their lust deserve credit rather than being told that they are sinful.

There is, in fact, another more inclusive concept of Sin, which should perhaps be spelled here with a capital letter. Sin is seen as a state of mind which may lead to specific sins but, even if it does not, is in itself sinful. Paul struggles with this in the seventh chapter of Romans. He does not understand himself. It is not he who sins, but Evil working within him.

The ancient church understood this. The Deadly Sins are not murder, theft, or adultery. They are states of mind which cut one off, at least temporarily, from communion with God: pride, anger, lust, gluttony, envy, avarice, and sloth. And when one becomes a helping person, it is perhaps with this concept of Sin that one becomes involved. One leaves the prevention or correction of sinful acts to those whose function it is, or to when, rather than helping someone, one is being a parent, preacher, or teacher. One does not condone or ignore sinful acts, but as a helper is more concerned with Sin as a state of mind.

Sloth and Pride

Two of the Deadly Sins, as St. Gregory listed them, are of particular interest. Sloth, which to most people today means laziness or the unwillingness to earn one's own living, originally meant hopelessness, despair, or depression, and is very close to what we as helpers deal with every day. And pride, according to the church, is the mother of all the other sins. Its original meaning was to forget that one was a created being, and to try to do without God. It was with pride rather than simple disobedience to an arbitrary prohibition that the Serpent tempted Eve, to eat of the tree of the knowledge of good and evil and "be like God" (Gen. 3:5). In modern terms it includes thinking that one knows what is good for other people, assuming the right to control them for their own good, believing that eventually everything about people will be known, being sure that one is right, or as one of Robert Coles's perceptive children said, "being stuck on oneself."[8] And this point leads us to our third question: Does Christian belief have anything in particular to add to helping theory?

Christian Contribution to Helping Theory

In addition to the belief that pride is the mother of all the Deadly Sins, a belief that HPU thought does not recognize and indeed is forced to reject in the name of progress, I would suggest four insights from the Scriptures that throw light on helping theory. No doubt there are many more which I have not identified and which the reader may discover for him- or herself.

Grace

One would be the concept of grace, unmerited favor or the actions of the Holy Spirit, the fact that sometimes, inexplicably, people, as did the Prodigal Son, "come to themselves" and transcend anything that one could rationally expect of them.

The Absolute Worth of God's Children

A second would be the Christian assertion of the absolute worth of every person. Humanists believe in the worth of human beings, but the closer they look at people, the more disillusioned they are bound to get.

Scientifically, humanity is a mess and intrinsically, there is no justification for ascribing worth. The Christian knows this and does not have to be disillusioned. But the Christian also knows that every person is a child of God and so has ultimate worth. To put this another way, the humanist sees people in terms of their behavior, while the Christian sees them in terms of their destiny, which was what caused the theologian Nikolai Berdyaev to say: "The error of humanism certainly did not lie in the fact that it laid too great an emphasis upon man . . . but in the fact that it did not give sufficient emphasis to man, that it did not carry its affirmation of man through to the end, that it could not guarantee the independence of man from the world and included within itself a danger of enslaving man to society and nature. The image of human personality is not only a human image, it is also the image of God."[9]

It Was In Paradise that Humans First Got into Serious Trouble

A third insight, perhaps a minor one, but one I have found useful, is that it was in Paradise itself that humans first got into serious trouble. One does one's best to remove obstacles in people's way and to make the world fairer and less stressful. There is no doubt that it is easier to be good if conditions are favorable, but favorable conditions do not ensure goodness. Human beings have not improved morally as they have expanded their technology. It took the twentieth century after Christ to produce the Holocaust. Adam and Eve's basic sin of pride is still with us. In fact there is probably more of it today than there was, say, in the Middle Ages, and although we in America have seen in the past thirty years an increase in justice, perhaps now in danger of being undone, we have at the same time witnessed an alarming loss of the sense of responsibility and commitment.

Love and Behavior

The fourth is perhaps the most important. The wisdom of the world has always stated, "Behave and you will be loved," but Jesus, when He died for our sins, said, in effect, "You are loved; therefore behave." Paul never suggests that Christians should behave morally in order to please God, but that their behavior should be in response to what God in Jesus has done for them. It is what is known as his "therefore" theology. The whole relationship between love and behavior is reversed. Love comes first, behavior second. It is not an easy lesson to learn. We still, in dealing with our children, tend to use the old formula, and the chief objection to Behavior Modification from a Christian point of view is that despite its positive emphasis it basically teaches the wrong lesson.

What then distinguishes the Christian helper from a secular one? It may be wise, first, to deal with some stereotypes and to say that there are certain things which a helper who is a Christian of Grace will not do or be.

Passing Judgement

She will not, for instance, be more moralistic than a secular one. Rather the opposite. To many a humanist, wrongdoing is something to be noted in another and if possible put right, but the Christian helper is, or should be, conscious of herself as a sinner. She should also be particularly careful in how she deals with the particular issues her branch of the church, and in consequence she herself, sees as particularly heinous sins — maybe in the 1990s, homosexuality and abortion — since they will be for her the hardest to be empathic about. Indeed one of the problems of moralism is its selectivity. Not only is a sin to one person not necessarily a sin to another, and both might be able to find biblical authority for their views, but as Richard Niebuhr has pointed out, what prevented the Evangelical movement from establishing a true source of understanding of the needs of the oppressed and limited it at its best to a kindly paternalism was the fact that poor and rich were guilty of quite different sins.[10] This still might be said of the poor and the middle class today, and even if one were able to convict the recipients of public assistance of both sloth, in the sense of being work-shy, and lust, which I doubt one could do, most of us would hate to be compared with them in respect to envy, gluttony, and pride.

Focus on Evangelism

The Christian helper also will not practice direct evangelism or witness to her own experience as a Christian unless she is involved with members of her own faith or people who are seeking a Christian solution to their problems. This may seem a most unchristian statement. Did not Jesus command us to go and make disciples of all nations, and if one has received a great benefit, should one not share it with others? Should we not witness to Christ?

There are, I think, times when one should. When our church gave a "graduation" dinner for men and women who had completed their prison terms, and for their families, the wife of one of them asked me, "Why are you doing this for us?" I had no hesitation in saying, "Because we are Christians." Her response was, "Oh. I didn't know that Christians cared that much." Her concept of Christianity certainly changed for the better.

Problems in Witnessing to One's Faith

But there are real reasons not to witness, except by deeds, when the people one is helping are not Christians, even though it may look as though they need witnessing the most. One is that it is generally not good helping. People rarely change and grow because they are told that they should.

A second is that most of the people one helps do not as yet trust people. They are still in the first stages of asking for help. It is not reasonable to expect them to trust an unseen Lord about whom they are told by another person. Christians, too, often use a special vocabulary which is foreign to many people. Phrases such as "accepting Jesus" and "being saved," even the biblical "being in Christ," are too abstract for someone who has not had a Christian upbringing or instruction.

To some, too, religious talk conjures up memories of childhood prohibitions: Don't smoke, or play cards, or dance. If you are a girl, don't wear too short a skirt, and never let a boy touch you. Religion is seen as consisting of negatives. I was once approached by a teenage girl who was genuinely repentant for having caused a great deal of trouble. She used four-letter words, was sexually active, and never went near a church. She wanted, she said, to be someone different from what she was, and we spent two rather intense hours defining the kind of person she really wanted to be, at the end of which I said that I thought we were now clear on what she wanted to be but that there was something I didn't know. Did she have the guts to be it? She would have to give up so much of her self-image as a girl who was "with it" and her popularity with many of her peers. She was startled by my question, but, after a minute's thought, she said, very quietly, "I couldn't do it alone. But maybe God and I could do it together." Yet if I had talked to her of God or Jesus before she was ready to do so herself, our interview would have ended there and then. I would have been like all the other people who had preached to her.

The Parable of the Sower

The third reason is that today the chief problem in evangelism is not that people have not heard the Word of God but that their life experience has been such that they have no reason to believe it. If one's only knowledge of having a father is that he beats one or deserts one, how can one believe in a loving Father? One has to experience human love first. A concept that I find useful is derived from the parable of the sower, in which the Word withers on stony ground. But what if the stony ground is tilled, is perhaps fertilized with love? Perhaps our job as helpers is not so much to be the sower, which perhaps only God can be, but to prepare the ground so that when the seed is sown the soil can receive it.

Material and Spiritual Help

Another unfortunate stereotype is that Christian workers deal only with intangible or so-called spiritual help. The idea that counseling and psychotherapy are more important and indeed more effective means of help than giving material aid is not confined to Christians, but Christians have often reinforced it. In the nineteenth century only perhaps the Salvation Army had the sense to see that material aid must at least come first. There is, as we have said, something almost repulsive about the Christian Socialist who was "as liberal with his sympathy as he was chary of meat and coal tickets."[11] Yet Christianity is the only religion whose founder prayed for daily bread, and in Matthew 25, Jesus did not say, "I was in need of counseling and you counseled me," but "I was hungry, thirsty, naked." I like the statement, which is posted in my church, "Bread for myself is material. Bread for my brother is spiritual."

Those Who "Don't Deserve Help"

And finally the Christian helper will not ask if someone deserves to be helped. The early Fathers of the Church had a lot to say on this point. Basil noted that it took great experience to be able to distinguish between those who were really in need and those who asked unnecessarily for alms, and Clement of Alexandria said that by making such judgments one might neglect "some friends of God;" but it took Chrysostom to insist that since we do not deserve God's grace, we have no right to ask people to deserve our help. "Be we as large-hearted as we may," he said, "we shall never be able to contribute such love towards man as we stand in need of at the hand of a God that loveth man."[12]

Jesus, too, never asked if someone deserved to be healed. Nor was He concerned with a question that has troubled Christian helpers throughout the ages and is very much in the forefront today—the effect of help on the character of the person who receives aid. He was much more concerned with the character of the person who gives aid. Ambrose, in the fourth century, perhaps had the only answer: One cannot tell what use someone will make of your help. What matters is that it be given with goodwill.

185

Having said what the Christian helper is not, what is she in a positive sense? Again I can only suggest some of her characteristics. There may be many that I have missed. A number of them are set out in 1 Corinthians 13.

1. Looking for Grace.

First, she will look for evidence of grace in those she helps. She will "rejoice in the good" rather than deplore the bad.

2. Steadfast Reality

She will stand by people to the last, even when they seem hopelessly lost. She will never be disappointed in people, as she will be too much of a realist. When help seems impossible, she will not make the diagnosis that the person she is trying to help is not helpable, but that she does not as yet know how to help him. Even if help seems impossible, she will still care what happens to him.

3. Love Triumphant.

She will have certain principles which she cannot give up, even if they should run counter to the culture and to what the findings of the latest research may show. These principles might include, for instance, that love is the eventual victor, that violence should be avoided at almost any cost, or that wherever possible people should be free to choose. Where research seems to prove the opposite, she should examine the values that lie behind the research. At the same time, however, she should respect honest research and learn from it. Sometimes a piece of research confirms a suspicion that one has, and sometimes it opens the door to a piece of understanding.

4. Watching for Drift

She will watch for drift in her own practice or that of her agency. Unlike most humanists, she knows that all human institutions and practices tend to become perverted in time, even if the original impulse is good. This, indeed, is one of the lessons of the Old Testament. Time and time again the Israelites begin with the highest ideals only to find themselves engaging in meaningless or harmful activity, so that Micah has to remind them of essentials, of what God has demanded of them—to do justice, to love kindness, and to walk humbly with their God. The Children's

Home, for instance, that once fulfilled a most valuable function as an orphanage but that does not change with the times, use new knowledge, or find a new helping role now that there are very few true orphans to care for suffers a drift from being a truly helpful service to one which sacrifices children and their families to institutional pride.

5. Being a Little Tough

The Christian helper will also be a little tough. This may sound surprising. Christians are not supposed to be tough. They exalt Jesus, who told them to turn the other cheek. But in fact the Christian will rely more on helping people face reality than on taking people's problems away from them. She will be less likely to say, "Poor fellow, you never had a chance," and more likely to know that even the chanceless have a choice. Reinhold Niebuhr, in a book published in 1932, said that only the "shrewder insights of religion" could save from sentimentality the liberal Christianity of his time, which was shared by many humanists.[13]

6. True Humility

And finally she will be truly humble. She will know that the more she knows, the more there is yet to know. She will not be puffed up or insist on her own way. She will know that in a good deal of helping it is the process that helps, and she will not claim that it was her skill or her ability to form a relationship that alone made help possible. She will be willing to do the job or the part of the job that falls to her and will be able to give up her client to someone else when that is what he needs. She will be content to be a helper and not have to be a teacher, a role model, or a patron as well. She will know herself a sinner and mean it when she says, "There but for the Grace of God go I."

A word of warning would seem to be pertinent here. Much of the most important work on relationship during the twentieth century has been done by theologians of an existentialist bent, notably Berdyaev, Buber, Tillich, and Maritain. Yet it is very important that we, who are devoted to helping others, do not surrender our own practical judgment to what theologians believe, as so many helping people have surrendered theirs to the external findings of sociology or psychology. We are the doers, the pragmatics. We can care only for what works. Insights, ways of conceptualizing, we can draw from them in plenty, but we cannot allow them to tell us how, in fact, one really helps.

The same is true of our own religious beliefs. We cannot in our discovery of the likeness of the human and the divine processes deduce one entirely from the other. We have, in helping people, to hold rigorously

187

to what experience and research in helping people tells us is useful, even if it should at first appear to conflict with a religious belief. But if this belief is a true one, the conflict should not arise. On the other hand, we can and should, however, use our beliefs to help us discriminate between goals, or to examine the presuppositions on which a piece of research is based.

Final Points

Two more points may need to be made. The illumination that arises from seeing one's beliefs and one's helping practice as analogous is mutual. Each throws light on the other. Just as in my own experience I came much nearer to an understanding of what was meant by support when I considered the implications of God's unconditional love for humanity, so the practice of helping illuminated religious concepts which up to that time had been vague or had gathered to themselves debased or what I call Sunday school meanings.

Thus the Christian helper sees repentance more clearly as a turning to God in one's helplessness rather than as a simple resolve to do better because she knows from helping people that it is this turning to another that works. Forgiveness becomes more clearly a continued concern for sinners despite their sin rather than "cheap grace" that minimizes the fact of sin, because this is the kind of forgiveness people need when they are helped. Even some glimmering may be possible of what it means to love one's enemies when one has felt concern for people one cannot possibly like.

And finally, the insights we have claimed for the Christian helper in no way constitute any superior wisdom or deeper insights. Our Lord the Spirit is not the property of the church or its adherents. Christianity's insights, in this context, are simply and only the logical results of accepting people as creatures responsible to a loving Creator. There is no claim that the Christian will behave in any more democratic, kindly, or generous way, or will be a better helper.

The Christian helper's only claim is that she has certain insights about the way things really are that will temper and regulate her helping and perhaps at times throw light on its processes. This in itself is a big enough claim.

NOTES

Introduction

1. Barbara Wooton, *Social Science and Social Pathology* (London, 1959), p. 281.

2. Robert R. Carkhuff, *Helping and Human Relations: A Primer for Lay and Professional Helpers*, 2 vols. (New York, 1969).

3. Edward R. Loewenstein, "Social Work in a Post-Industrial Society," *Social Work* 33, no. 6 (November 1973): 47.

4. Karl de Schweinitz, *Art of Helping People in Trouble* (Boston and New York, 1924).

Chapter 1

1. This point is made by Kenneth Pray, *Social Work in a Revolutionary Age and Other Papers* (Philadelphia, 1948), p. 230.

2. Martin Buber, *I and Thou*, trans. Roland Gregor Smith (London, 1937).

3. Richard D'Ambrosio, *No Language but a Cry* (New York, 1970).

4. Andt Alaszewski and Bie Nio Ong, *Normalisation in Practice* (London, 1990), p. 1.

5. John of Antioch (Saint Chrysostom), Fourth Homily on Lazarus and Seventeenth Homily on Second Corinthians, respectively.

6. See Dorothy Hutchinson's "A Re-Examination of Some Aspects of Casework Practice in Adoption," *Child Welfare* 25, no. 9 (November 1946): 4-7, 14.

7. The genesis of the parenting theory in relation to the neglecting parent is a complicated one, much involved with difficulty about the problem of self-determination and the growth of "aggressive" or "assertive" casework. I would trace it through articles such as Lionel Lane's "The 'Aggressive' Approach in Preventive Casework with Children's Problems," *Social Casework* 33 (February 1952): 61-66; Annie Lee Davis's *Children Living in Their Own Homes*, U.S. Children's Bureau, Washington, D.C. (1953); and Lorena Scherer's "Protective Casework Service," *Children* 3, no. 1 (January-February 1956): 27-31.

8. See Kermit Wiltse, "The 'Hopeless' Family," *Social Work* 3, no. 4 (October 1958): 19-22.

9. Notably the "Contra Costa Experiment" described in Kermit Wiltse's "Social Casework Services in the Aid to Dependent Children Program," *Social Service Review* 28 (July 1954): 173-85, and programs in Washington, D.C., and the Southwest described in reports of the U.S. Department of Health, Education, and Welfare in the mid-1950s.

10. Edith Abbott, *Public Assistance, American Principles and Policies* (Chicago, 1940), 1:1277.

11. Barbara Wooton, "The Image of the Social Worker," *British Journal of Sociology* 11, no. 4 (December 1960): 376.

12. Joel Fischer, "Is Casework Effective?," *Social Work* 18, no. 1 (January 1973): 5-21.

13. John Powell, *Whose Child Am I?* (New York, 1985).

14. Rurh Ellen Lindenberg, "Hard to Reach: Client or Casework Agency," *Social Work* 3, no. 5 (October 1958): 29.

15. Edward R. Loewenstein, "Social Work in a Post-Industrial Society," *Social Work* 33, no. 6 (November 1973): 40-47.

Chapter 2

1. Gordon W. Blackwell and Raymond Gould, *Future Citizens All* (Chicago, 1952), pp. 26-27.

2. A good description of this kind of situation can be found in Alice Overton's "Serving Families Who 'Don't Want Help,'" *Social Casework* 34 (July 1953): 304-9.

Chapter 3

1. For a more detailed account of this principle, see my article "A Critique of the Principle of Client Self-Determination," *Social Work* 8, no. 3 (July 1963): 66-71.

2. Bertha C. Reynolds, *Re-Thinking Social Case Work* (San Diego, 1938), p. 15.

3. The only contemporary writer who pointed out this anomaly was, to my knowledge, Grace Marcus, who wrote: "How difficult it is for us to accept this harsh truth is revealed by our distortion of it into the facile concept of 'self-determination,' whereby, we can relapse once more into a comforting dependence on free will and, by talking of self-determination as a 'right,' flatter ourselves that a fact which is often intolerably painful to the individual and to society is still within our power to concede or refuse as a social benefit" ("The Status of Social Case Work

Today," in *Readings in Social Casework, 1920-38,* ed. Fern Lowry [New York, 1939], p. 130).

4. Helen Harris Perlman, "Self-Determination: Myth or Reality," *Social Service Review* 39, no. 4 (December 1965): 410-21.

5. Anita Faatz, *The Nature of Choice in Casework Process* (Chapel Hill, N.C., 1953), p. 128.

6. An excellent article on this subject is David Soyer's "The Right to Fail," *Social Work* 8, no. 3 (July 1963): 72-78.

7. Kenneth Pray, "A Restatement of the Generic Principles of Social Casework Practice," in *Social Work in a Revolutionary Age and Other Papers* (Philadelphia, 1949), p. 250.

8. An interesting handling of this subject is Paul Halmos's *Faith of the Counselors* (London, 1966).

9. Faatz, *The Nature of Choice,* p. 53.

10. Ibid.

Chapter 4

1.William Glasser, *Reality Therapy: A New Approach to Psychiatry* (New York, 1966).

2. For an attack on the word "client," see Barbara Wooton, *Social Science and Social Pathology* (London, 1959), p. 289. Recently, British social workers have criticized the word as implying dependence on the social worker. See David W. Harrison, "Reflective Practice in Social Care," *Social Service Review* 66 (September 1987): 343-404.

3. Kermit Wiltse, "The 'Hopeless' Family," *Social Work* 3, no. 4 (October 1958): 19-22.

4. The best example of this that I know is Annie Lee Davis's comment in *Children Living in Their Own Homes,* U.S. Children's Bureau (Washington, D.C., 1953). She states that to bring to neglecting mothers one's demands that she change is not an imposition, since in "an atmosphere that is warm, understanding and nonblaming" they "begin to feel that they too can become better parents, and most parents want to be better parents. It is part of the total culture of the country" (p. 34).

5. For a fuller explanation of the family clarification process see my article "What Else Can Residential Care Do? And Do Well?," *Residential Treatment for Children and Youth* 4, no. 4 (Summer 1987): 25-38.

Chapter 5

1. Evidence of Octavia Hill before the Royal Commission on the Aged Poor, 1895, excerpted in Gertrude Lubbock, *Some Poor Relief Questions* (London, 1895), p. 275.

2. Edward Dennison, from *Letters and Writings of the Late Edward Dennison M.P. for Newark,* ed. Sir Baldwin Leighton (London, 1872), p. 145.

3. *Annual Report of the Society for the Prevention of Pauperism*, 1818, quoted by Edward Devine, *People and Relief* (New York, 1904). It is interesting how the report lumps the improvident, the unfortunate, and the depraved together as if misfortune were a sin.

4. The title of an article in a social work journal which I can no longer identify. Date, ca. 1932.

5. Wlliam Glasser, *Reality Therapy: A New Approach to Psychiatry* (New York, 1966).

6. These sentences were first formulated, with one difference, in my article "The Nature of the Helping Process," *Christian Scholar* 52 (Summer 1960): 119-27. The reformulation from "that it hurts" to "that it must hurt" was made at the suggestion of a class of welfare workers in Maine and is obviously more correct.

7. David Soyer, "The Right to Fail," *Social Work* 8, no. 3 (July 1963): 72-78.

Chapter 6

1. Erich Fromm, *The Art of Loving* (London, 1956), pp. 57-63.

2. This process is outlined in detail in Ruth Gilpin's *Theory and Practice as a Single Reality* (Chapel Hill, N.C., 1963).

3. Ruth Ramsey, "Concern, Like and Dislike in the Supervisory Process," unpublished paper included in vol. 3 of *Studies in Social Work Practice,* University of North Carolina (1965).

4. Mrs. Ramsey and I were unable to find the word "concern" used in social work or related literature. She traced its possible origin as a "helping" word to Erich Fromm and Paul Tillich, both of whom use the word in this sense.

5. Fromm, *The Art of Loving,* p. 47.

Chapter 7

1. Anita Faatz, *The Nature of Choice in Casework Process (Chapel Hill,* N.C., 1953), p. 105.

2. There are two good articles on probation that make this point: Everett Wilson's "The Nature of Probation," *Social Service Review* 20, no. 3 (September 1946): 376-402, and William Lofquist's "The Framework and Experience of Juvenile Probation," *Social Casework* 48, no. 1 (January 1967): 17-21.

3. For an excellent treatment of this, see Jessie Taft, "The 'Catch' in Praise," *Child Study* 7, no. 5 (February 1930): 133-35, 150.

Chapter 8

1. Robert O. Blood, *Marriage* (New York, 1962), p. 347.

Chapter 9

1. The classic study of this desire is Erich Fromm's *Escape from Freedom* (New York, 1941).

2. Herbert Bisno, *The Philosophy of Social Work* (Washington, D.C., 1953), pp. 5-24.

3. Max Weber, *The Protestant Ethic and the Rise of Capitalism* (London, 1930); R. B. Perry, *Puritanism and Democracy* (New York, 1944); R. H. Tawney, *Religion and the Rise of Capitalism* (London, 1926). See also a nontheological rejoinder to Weber, nearer to my thought here, H. M. Robertson's *The Rise of Economic Individualism* (Cambridge, England, 1933).

4. Erich Voegelin, *The New Science of Politics* (Chicago, 1952), p. 129.

5. Robert Coles, *The Spiritual Life of Children* (Boston, 1990), pp. 25-27.

6. See, for instance, his Fourteenth Homily on the Book of Romans.

7. See, for example, Mary J. McCormick, *Diagnostic Casework in the Thomistic Pattern* (New York, 1954).

8. See, for instance, John J. Stretch, "Existentialism: A Proposed Philosophical Orientation for Social Work," *Social Work* 12 (October 1967): 97-102.

9. Bisno, *The Philosophy of Social Work*, pp. 5, 6, and 72.

10. See, for instance, Marian R. Gennaria, *Pain: A Factor in Growth and Development* (New York, 1943).

11. This trend has been apparent for a number of years. I first noted it in an article called "The Political Theory Implicit in Social Casework Theory," *American Political Science Review* 47 (December 1953): 1076-90, in which, however, I believe I was too sanguine about the ability of a particular theory of social casework to resist the trend. The actual change is pinpointed in my "Self-Determination and the Changing Role of the Social Worker," in *Values in Social Work: A Re-examination*, Monograph IX, in the series sponsored by the Regional Institute Program of the National Association of Social Workers (1967), pp. 84-97.

Chapter 10

1. For good discussions of Jewish religious thought as it affects helping and social welfare, see Herbert H. Aptekar, *The Dynamics of Casework and Counselling* (Boston, 1955), and Alfred J. Kutzik, *Social Work and Jewish Values* (Washington, D.C., 1959).

2. Herbert Bisno, *The Philosophy of Social Work* (Washington, D.C., 1953).

3. A. F. Young and E. T. Ashton, *British Social Work in the Nineteenth Century* (New York, 1956), p. 36.

4. I have enlarged on this concept in a pamphlet, "The Client's Religion and Your Own Faith in the Helping Process," Group Child Care Consultant Services, monograph 7, Chapel Hill, N.C., 1982.

5. Westminster Confession of Faith, chap. 7, art. 2. The Belgic Confession describes the nature as "not divided or intermixed" (art. 7).

6. Dorothy L. Sayers, *The Mind of the Maker* (London, 1942).

7. The Larger Catechism of the Presbyterian Church defines sin as "any want of conformity unto, or transgression of, any law of God, given as a rule to the reasonable creature."

8. Robert Coles, *The Spiritual Life of Children* (Boston, 1990), p. 15.

9. Nikolai Berdyaev, *Slavery and Freedom*, trans. R. M. French (New York, 1944), p. 44.

10. Richard Niebuhr, *The Social Sources of Denominationalism* (New York, 1929), p. 67.

11. Edward Dennison, from *Letters and Writings of the Late Edward Dennison M.P. for Newark*, ed. Sir Baldwin Leighton (London, 1872), p. 145.

12. John of Antioch (Saint Chrysostom), Fourteenth Homily on the Book of Romans.

13. Reinhold Niebuhr, *The Contribution of Religion to Social Work* (New York, 1932), pp. 67-68.